WHEN
RELIGION
BECOMES
EVIL

~

WHEN
RELIGION
BECOMES
EVIL

~

CHARLES KIMBALL

HarperSanFrancisco
A Division of HarperCollins*Publishers*

WHEN RELIGION BECOMES EVIL. Copyright © 2002 by Charles Kimball. All rights reserved. Printed in the United States of America. No part of this book may be used or reproduced in any manner whatsoever without written permission except in the case of brief quotations embodied in critical articles and reviews. For information address HarperCollins Publishers, Inc., 10 East 53rd Street, New York, NY 10022.

HarperCollins books may be purchased for educational, business, or sales promotional use. For information please write: Special Markets Department, HarperCollins Publishers, Inc., 10 East 53rd Street, New York, NY 10022.

HarperCollins Web site: http://www.harpercollins.com
HarperCollins®, ■®, and HarperSanFrancisco™ are
trademarks of HarperCollins Publishers, Inc.

FIRST EDITION
Designed by Joseph Rutt

Library of Congress Cataloging-in-Publication Data
Kimball, Charles
When religion becomes evil / by Charles Kimball.
p. cm.
Includes bibliographical references.
ISBN 0–06–050653–9 (cloth)
1. Good and evil—Comparative studies.   2. Religions.
I. Title.
BJ1406 .K56 2002
291.2'118—dc21   2002068903
03 04 05 06 RRD(H) 10 9 8 7 6 5 4 3

For
Kyle Yates, Hugo Culpepper, and Wilfred Cantwell Smith
Mentors and friends who no longer "see through a glass dimly"

CONTENTS

ACKNOWLEDGMENTS

Quotations from the Qur'an are based, with revisions by the author, on *The Meaning of the Glorious Koran*, text and explanatory translation by Muhammad M. Pickthall (Mecca: Muslim World League, 1977).

Short portions of chapters four, six and seven are revised versions of analyses I first published in "Roots of Rancor: Examining Islamic Militancy" (*The Christian Century*, October 24–31, 2001), *Religion, Politics and Oil: The Volatile Mix in the Middle East* (Abingdon Press, 1992), and *Striving Together: A Way Forward in Christian-Muslim Relations* (Orbis Books, 1991). I am grateful to *The Christian Century*, Abingdon Press and Orbis Books, respectively, for permission to incorporate several paragraphs into this present book.

Many of the ideas that follow have been tested and refined through numerous lectures, panels, and sermons. In addition to the congenial and supportive environment I enjoy at Wake Forest University, three universities provided opportunities to develop portions of this book during the first half of 2002. I wish to thank Ohio Wesleyan University for the invitation to deliver the Merrick

Lecture, Transylvania University for the invitation to deliver the Marshall Lecture, and Furman University for the invitation to present lectures in its annual Pastor's School.

The perspectives I offer draw upon experiences and insights gained over the past three decades. There are many people who have contributed substantially to my understanding and deserve recognition. My clear indebtedness to some is reflected in the text and notes. Many others who sharpened and challenged my thinking—ranging from graduate school friends, professors, and colleagues to individuals who shared a taxi or a cup of coffee and conversation in Cairo, Jerusalem, Beirut, Geneva, or New York—will not be so readily apparent. Several people have offered valuable suggestions and correctives in the process of refining portions of several chapters. I am grateful to Steve Boyd, Chris Chapman, Jill Crainshaw, Jay Ford, Mary Foskett, Scott Hudgins, Bill Leonard, Blake Michael, and Lyn Price. Mark Tolliver also provided critical insights as well as invaluable research assistance. I am especially indebted to Jeff Rogers, a gifted scholar and longtime friend who was a constant source of support and critical reflection throughout this project.

No author could hope for more helpful professionals than those with whom I've worked at Harper San Francisco, most notably Roger Freet, Terri Leonard, Julia Roller, and Priscilla Stuckey. I am particularly grateful to Steve Hanselman, who guided my work on this book from start to finish. He helped both to frame larger issues and to fine-tune points with editorial suggestions.

Writing a book is often a solitary enterprise. For me, it is also a family project. With love and gratitude I thank Sarah and Elliot, our college- and high school–age children, who both affirmed their dad and endured him with good cheer. Highest praise remains for my spouse, Nancy. She has been my best friend, confidant, sounding board, and loving critic on a life journey neither of us could have predicted thirty years ago when we were married as seniors in college.

Finally, allow me a brief word about Kyle Yates, Hugo Culpepper, and Wilfred Cantwell Smith. While I have been blessed by the personal support of many gifted teachers along the way, these three took me under their respective wings during my undergraduate, seminary, and doctoral programs. They all continually affirmed my scholarly inquiry and ministerial endeavors over the years. All three lived rich and full lives; all three passed away during the past two years. I dedicate this book with love and appreciation to these three mentors and friends.

INTRODUCTION

R eligion is arguably the most powerful and pervasive force on earth. Throughout history religious ideas and commitments have inspired individuals and communities of faith to transcend narrow self-interest in pursuit of higher values and truths. The record of history shows that noble acts of love, self-sacrifice, and service to others are frequently rooted in deeply held religious worldviews. At the same time, history clearly shows that religion has often been linked directly to the worst examples of human behavior. It is somewhat trite, but nevertheless sadly true, to say that more wars have been waged, more people killed, and these days more evil perpetrated in the name of religion than by any other institutional force in human history.

Questions about why people do bad things—sometimes unspeakably evil things—in the name of religion are not new, of course. Theologians and philosophers have long wrestled with questions about the sources and manifestations of individual and corporate evil. Satisfactory answers to such perennial questions are neither straightforward nor easy. But the questions have taken on a singular urgency at the dawn of this new millennium.

The dangers posed by people and groups inspired by or operating under the guise of religion have never been clearer. The tragic events of September 11, 2001, underscore the point. We may never know with certainty what was in the hearts and minds of the nineteen men who hijacked the four planes that changed the world that day. But this much is clear: several key leaders among the hijackers and the *al-qaida* ("the base") network supporting them were inspired and motivated by a particular understanding of Islam. The five-page, handwritten letter left by ringleader Muhammad Atta revealed a religious worldview seeking to justify the behavior. The meticulous planning and preparation were set in a wider framework as he and his cohorts prepared "to meet God."[1] Similarly, Osama bin Laden's widely publicized Jihad Manual and his various taped messages following the attacks on the World Trade Center and the Pentagon were laced with religious language and imagery designed to motivate his followers.

Muslim leaders who clearly wanted no association with the despicable acts of violence publicly reiterated that Islam is a religion of peace. They denounced the terrorists' behavior and supporting interpretations of Islam as false and illegitimate. President Bush echoed a similar message repeatedly during the days and weeks after the attacks: "We have no quarrel with Islam, which is a good and peaceful religion."[2]

Other images of Islam further confused the picture. Osama bin Laden and his network had strong supporters not only among Muslims in Afghanistan, but also in Pakistan, Indonesia, Egypt, Saudi Arabia, and elsewhere. A number of columnists and highly visible Christian leaders in the United States also seized the media spotlight in order to proclaim their particular message about "true" Islam. Some spoke about Islam, the world's second largest religious tradition, as somehow inherently violent and menacing. To bolster the argument, writers and popular preachers frequently highlighted selected passages from the Qur'an to "prove" a particular point.[3]

As a longtime student of Islam, the Middle East, and the interaction of religion and politics, I was drawn deeply into the swirl of activities following the attacks and the subsequent "war on terrorism." Judging from the hundreds of questions I fielded during many national and international media interviews and dozens of speaking engagements—in university, corporate, and church-related settings—most people remained confused about Islam and the forces at work in many predominantly Muslim countries. Who were these hijackers? What is the meaning of *jihad?* Why do people call Islam a religion of peace? How many other "sleepers" might there be in the United States? Canada? Europe? Who and where are the estimated thousands of *al-qaida* operatives? How can we make sense of the Islamic connections in the midst of volatile political, economic, military, social, and cultural dynamics?

The media focus was as intense as it has been on anything in recent memory. But this event was unlike the Iranian hostage crisis two decades earlier or the Gulf War of 1991. This time the conflict was not "over there." The television images were not those of locked embassy gates in Tehran or chanting demonstrators or night bombing raids on Baghdad. The devastating pictures from New York and just outside Washington, D.C., were all too close and real. Americans felt vulnerable to powerful forces they did not really understand and could not easily control.

Indiscriminate violence against innocent people occurs with numbing frequency. But the events of September 11 were not the result of a disgruntled postal worker or a serial killer or angry and confused adolescents in high school. The attacks were carefully planned and skillfully executed by seemingly intelligent people whose level of commitment to their cause included suicidal self-sacrifice. They intentionally blended in with mainstream society as part of a larger plan. They cleverly used the rules in place—those dealing with the detection of airplane hijackers—to accomplish their mission with three of the four commercial airliners.

The world most U.S. citizens—and Canadians and Australians and many in Western Europe—thought they knew changed on September 11, 2001. We had crossed the Rubicon and there was no turning back. Daily life for the foreseeable future would be different.

Activities as mundane as opening one's mail, boarding a commercial airplane, or even attending a major sporting event were no longer so simple or routine.

The challenges posed by religious diversity combined with the inescapable fact of global interdependence are now as clear as the September sky over New York that fateful day. Political and economic instability and changing cultural values are readily evident both in our society and in the world community. Combine these ingredients with narrow religious worldviews and the violent patterns of behavior too often manifest in human history, and you have a highly volatile mix. And, we now know with certainty that there are many potential weapons of mass destruction and that it doesn't take many people to wreak havoc on a global scale.

Religious ideologies and commitments are indisputably central factors in the escalation of violence and evil around the world. The evidence is readily available in the headlines of our daily newspapers: "Hindus and Muslims on the Brink of War in Kashmir"; "Serbian Christians Stand Trial for Atrocities Against Bosnian Muslims"; "Palestinians Killed by Jewish Settlers in the Occupied Territories"; "Muslim Militant Kills Twenty with Suicide Bomb at Jerusalem Pizza Parlor"; "Murder Trial Begins for Fundamentalist Christian Minister in Abortion Doctor Case." And the list goes on.

Where does the problem reside? Some suggest that religion itself is the problem, arguing that religious worldviews are anachronistic. Religion, in this view, is irrelevant at best. It may be inherently divisive and destructive. Don't conflicting truth claims inevitably lead to conflict? Many people embrace this perspective in our age of disbelief. It has obvious implications not only for human self-understanding, but also for corporate life in the public square. Whatever one's personal outlook, it is crucial that we recognize the centrality of religion and try to think clearly and discuss thoughtfully the various ways religious faith and commitments interact with our society and our world. To say that religion is the problem may capture part of the truth, but it is ultimately an unhelpful response to a host of urgent and troublesome issues—from wrestling with ethical questions about the beginning or end of life, stem cell research, and therapeutic cloning to finding appropriate expressions of religion at the often-difficult boundary between religion and public life.

At the other end of the spectrum, devout adherents of particular traditions offer unambiguous answers. They understand their particular vision of Christianity or Islam or even Buddhism as the "true" way; everything else, by definition, is false. Popular Christian versions of this orientation are as close as your television remote control. Tune in religious broadcasting for an hour—anytime, day or night—and you will get the point. Answers to all one's personal, financial, and physical problems are neatly packaged and readily available. Viewers are encouraged to express their appreciation for the particular ministry on the air by sending in a "love offering." It is highly probable that a rigid theology of exclusivism will be woven into the rhetoric of whatever program you happen to tune in. Different religions and virtually every conceivable form of evil and suffering will be linked simplistically with satanic forces.

Surely, a more nuanced response is needed. A clearer understanding of the nature and reality of human religiosity helps us embrace the tasks ahead more cogently. Is religion itself the problem? No . . . and yes. Within the religious traditions that have stood the test of time, one finds the life-affirming faith that has sustained and provided meaning for millions over the centuries. At the same time, we can identify the corrupting influences that lead toward evil and violence in all religious traditions. The first chapter of this book explores the nature and importance of religion in the ideal as well as a less-than-ideal lived reality.

My approach includes scholarly, experiential, and personal dimensions. On one level, my method is that of a comparative historian of religion. A comparative approach has many benefits. It helps us see the structures, patterns, and tendencies that various religious traditions share. It helps us see what is attractive, what provides meaning and hope for people in different times and places. It also exposes shared tendencies and common pitfalls. In daily discourse, most people tend to think and talk about their own religion in terms of its ideals. At the same time, often unconsciously, they often characterize other religious systems in terms of poorly understood teachings and the visibly flawed behavior of adherents. A comparative approach exposes such disjunctures and enables us to see religion as a broader, human, phenomenon.

In the central portion of this book I examine five major warning signs of human corruption of religion. When one finds one or more of these dynamics at work, history suggests that serious trouble lurks just ahead. The inclination toward these corruptions is strong in the major religions. At the same time, I suggest that helpful correctives are found within the religious traditions themselves.

The focus for this study centers on Christianity and Islam for two distinct reasons. First, these are the two largest religious communities in the world, with some 1.8 billion and 1.3 billion adherents, respectively.[4] Together, Christians and Muslims make up almost one-half of the world's population. Both religious traditions are global in scope. And both engage with political structures more readily than do other major religions. Contemporary developments in Israel also figure prominently into this volatile mix. Thus, the interactions between and among the various descendants of Abraham represent many of the most dangerous flashpoints on the planet.

Second, a strong missionary impulse is central for both Christianity and Islam. Basing their position on a solid foundation of monotheism, Muslims and Christians frequently have advocated a narrow exclusivism. Ironically, these central tenets often feed attitudes and actions that are diametrically opposed to the heart of the religion being espoused. Christians and Muslims are certainly not alone in this regard. Similar dynamics among Jews, Hindus, Buddhists, and others will be highlighted also.

The examples included in the book are selective, not exhaustive.

At various points, I offer explanatory notes and bibliographical references for those who wish to go further or deeper. Although it should be clear, it is worth stating emphatically at the outset what I am not saying. I am not calling the different movements, groups, and individuals discussed here evil. Instead, I am pointing to warning signs that alert us to the potential for evil behavior. When one or more of the warning signs discussed here are in place, it is all too easy for sincere people and well-intentioned religious groups to harbor destructive attitudes and justify deplorable actions based on what is deemed essential to their life of faith. Being sincere doesn't exempt people or groups from critical scrutiny.

Some examples illustrating the warning signs are unambiguous and straightforward; some are rooted in more subtle attitudes and actions that, when examined, have far-reaching ramifications. Getting at the dangerous dynamics requires critical analysis of issues that lie at the very heart of religion, such as the nature of religious truth, the authority of sacred texts, and the pursuit of the missionary impulse. There is room for considerable disagreement and debate on these and other matters discussed throughout the book. Although many of us have been taught it is not polite to discuss religion and politics in public, we must quickly unlearn that lesson. Our collective failure to challenge presuppositions, think anew, and openly debate central religious concerns affecting society is a recipe for disaster. We'd better take a few steps back and consider how we got where we are before simply pushing forward. As a wise friend once put it, "When you are standing on the edge of a cliff, progress is not defined as one step forward!"

Understanding the factors that can and do lead people of faith and goodwill—wittingly or unwittingly—into destructive and evil patterns of behavior must be a high priority on the world's agenda. Distinguishing between corrupt forms of religious expression and authentic, life-affirming forms is essential if we hope to reduce the global threat. At one level, the concern here is pragmatic. We simply must find better ways to share the planet with people whose worldviews and ultimate commitments differ from ours. The challenge pertains across the lines of the religious traditions, but it relates also to the great diversity within the traditions themselves.

The urgency here cannot be overstated. Several recent influential books have helped to focus discussion on the powerful and dangerous dynamics of globalism in a world in which local communal and sectarian roots remain very deep. These include Thomas Friedman's award-winning book, *The Lexus and the Olive Tree;* Benjamin Barber's important book, *Jihad vs. McWorld: How Globalism and Tribalism Are Reshaping the World;* and the provocative book by Robert Kaplan and Samuel Huntington, *The Clash of Civilizations and the Remaking of World Order.*

The issues are local as well as global. Our society increasingly mirrors the larger world community. For more than ten years, religion scholar Diana Eck has been studying and documenting the changing religious landscape in the United States. Working with some eighty graduate students at Harvard University in "The Pluralism Project," Eck has arrived at stunning results. At the beginning of the new millennium, the United States is the most religiously diverse nation in the world. There is simply no doubt: Main Street has changed. Islam is now or soon will pass Judaism as the second largest religion in the United States. There are more Muslims in America than there are Presbyterians and Episcopalians combined. Los Angeles is the most complex Buddhist city in the world.[5]

I hope this book can help us coexist at a pragmatic level. But I believe something more is needed. If we are to live long into the new millennium, our diverse, interdependent society and world demand new paradigms, new ways of understanding particularity and pluralism. Many traditional ways of viewing the world and relating to others are, at the very least, inadequate. They are becoming increasingly dangerous. I am convinced that it is possible to be a person of faith with integrity—a Christian, a Hindu, a Jew, a Muslim, a Buddhist—and at the same time recognize that one's own experience of

God does not exhaust all the possibilities. A constructive outlook of religious pluralism can take us beyond simple tolerance of others; it can provide a framework for celebrating diversity and embracing it as a source of strength. Rather than being necessarily divisive, religious traditions can provide models for tolerance. The last portion of this book discusses these issues directly, inviting us to explore new ways of thinking about ourselves and of engaging with others as we move forward into an uncertain future.

In the pages that follow, readers will observe that I wear more than one hat. I am a scholar and a religious professional. My doctorate is in the history of religion (comparative religion) with specialization in Islam, the Middle East, and Jewish-Christian-Muslim relations. I am also an ordained Baptist minister. Much of my study and work during the past twenty-five years has taken place at the intersection of religion and politics. Far from being impartial or dispassionate, I am deeply and personally connected with the subject matter presented in the pages that follow. A brief overview outlining my background will help both to clarify my orientation and to set the context for this book.

My paternal grandfather was one of nine children in a Jewish family that emigrated from the Poland-Russia border in the 1880s. It is a long and colorful story. Like many Jewish immigrants, through hard work and education many family members improved their status over a generation. My grandfather and one of his brothers were instrumental in this process. Beginning on the street corners of Boston, they turned their song, dance, and comedy routine into a highly successful career in vaudeville. The brothers shared their economic success generously with the extended family. At the height of his career, Grandpa met and married a Presbyterian chorus girl in the vaudeville show. He remained Jewish; she remained Presbyterian. Their four children—my father and his three brothers—all became Christians.

My grandfather was the most wonderful person I knew. My brother, sisters, and I were raised with a very positive understanding of Judaism. We were imbued with the notion that it was good to be Jewish. Growing up in Oklahoma, I discovered at an early age that many people did not share this view of Judaism. Although the Jewish population in Tulsa was relatively small, I vividly recall hearing and reacting strongly to derogatory comments uttered casually about Jews. As in most American communities in the 1950s, Protestants and Roman Catholics were clearly divided. Protestants commonly voiced exclusive claims to truth. Many of my Baptist or Church of Christ friends, for instance, were convinced that the Methodists, Presbyterians, and Episcopalians were in grave danger of missing the true gospel of Christ. Catholics were not even on the map in their view. They spoke about "Christians" and "Catholics" as though these were entirely different categories. I was ten years old when these issues played out on the national scene as the Catholicism of John F. Kennedy raised serious concern among Protestants during the 1960 presidential campaign.

While debates between and among Christians of different denominational backgrounds never struck me as of ultimate consequence, I was troubled deeply by people who made disparaging comments about Jews. As a child, I interpreted these as direct ridicule of my grandfather and the extended family. It was clear that such comments were rooted in ignorance and prejudice (I didn't know the term *anti-Semitism* at the time), for they contradicted my experience of and relationships within my family.

During high school and college, I became deeply involved in church and church-related organizations. At the same time, I began an academic study of religion through an undergraduate minor at Oklahoma State. I was both puzzled and intrigued by the relationship between Christian truth claims and the truth claims of others. Three years at the Southern Baptist Theological Seminary in Louisville, Kentucky, provided rich opportunities to pursue the study of world religions and the theological questions related to Christian faith in a religiously plural world. I was fortunate to have excellent faculty mentors throughout college and seminary. At each step along the journey, people challenged, encouraged, and nurtured the focus of my study and theological reflection.

In 1975 I began doctoral study at Harvard. In addition to enjoying the vast resources of the university, doctoral students in comparative religion at that time had the unique opportunity to live in the Center for the Study of World Religions. This setting fostered daily interactions with other doctoral students of various religious backgrounds, Harvard faculty, and visiting scholars from all over the world. It was a stimulating and congenial context in which to explore issues of particularity and pluralism. As a part of my studies, my wife, Nancy, and I spent the 1977–78 academic year studying in Cairo and traveling in Egypt, Jordan, Syria, and Israel/Palestine. It was a fascinating time to be in the Middle East. We were living in Cairo when Anwar Sadat stunned the world with his surprise trip to Jerusalem in October 1977. We learned a great deal living and traveling in the Middle East, as reactions to Sadat's initiative reverberated throughout the region and the U.S.-brokered peace process between Egypt and Israel began in earnest.

Two years later another dramatic international event captured the attention of the world media: student militants seized the U.S. embassy compound in Tehran and held fifty-three Americans hostage. From the outset of what would become a 444-day ordeal, the Iranian government indicated its willingness to meet with representatives of the religious community rather than U.S. government officials. Through an unusual series of events, I was one of seven people invited to Iran in December 1979. Since I was one of two clergy in the group who had studied the Qur'an and the Islamic religious tradition, Iranian religious and political leaders received me warmly.

On two other occasions (in 1980 and 1981), my colleague, John Walsh, and I were invited back to Iran to help facilitate communication where little was taking place. These efforts attracted considerable attention in the international media since we were among the only Americans involved in personal meetings with Ayatollah

Khomeini and other leading ayatollahs, then-President Bani Sadr, Ali Akbar Hashemi ar-Rafsanjani, the speaker of the parliament, the foreign minister, and many other political and religious leaders. On each trip we spent several hours meeting with the student militants occupying the U.S. embassy compound. Between December 1979 and the middle of 1981, I took a leave of absence from dissertation work in order to concentrate on issues surrounding the hostage conflict. In addition to the intense experiences during two of those eighteen months, I wrote a number of background and op-ed articles for major publications, appeared frequently on national and local television and radio programs, and traveled throughout the country lecturing in colleges, universities, seminaries, conferences, churches, and synagogues.

In 1982 I began work as the director of interfaith programs for the Fellowship of Reconciliation, an international organization committed to nonviolent conflict resolution. Two years later I assumed responsibilities as director for the Middle East office at the National Council of Churches (NCC). I served in that position for seven years. My work with and on behalf of the major denominations (Methodists, Presbyterians, Lutherans, Episcopalians, Disciples, various Baptist and Orthodox churches) required extensive international and domestic travel. It involved working in war zones and refugee camps as well as meeting with heads of state, diplomats, religious leaders, activists, academics, and journalists on a regular basis. The churches' work in the Middle East included mission and service programs (carried out cooperatively with the indigenous populations) as well as education and public policy initiatives in the United States. During the past twenty-five years I have traveled to various parts of the Middle East more than thirty-five times.

From 1990 to the present I have been working in a university setting. My research, teaching, and writing continue to focus on the study of world religions and their interactions. I understand my work in the university, with churches and other religious groups, and in the wider community as part of a larger vocation. My ideas and activities have been challenged and refined by personal, academic, and experiential factors during the past three decades. Like everyone else, I am subjective. I try always to understand and be responsive to the various ways I am subjective as a person of faith, a student of religion, and one who is committed to fostering understanding and cooperation among people who share this fragile planet.

In 1959 Wilfred Cantwell Smith, a monumental figure in Islamic studies and the comparative study of religion, summarized the trends in scholarly circles and looked forward to the next phases:

> The traditional form of Western scholarship in the study of other [religious traditions] was that of an impersonal presentation of an "it." The first great innovation in recent times has been the personalization of the faiths observed, so that one finds a discussion of a "they." Presently the observer becomes personally involved, to that the situation is one of a "we" talking about a "they." The next step is a dialogue where "we" talk to "you." If there is listening and mutuality, this may become that "we" talk *with* "you." The culmination of the process is when "we all" are talking *with* each other about "us."[6]

We live in a dangerous world in which many people talk of a "we" and a "they." Religion is at the heart of what matters most to the vast majority who inhabit this planet. It is my hope that this book will stimulate discussion and facilitate the processes whereby we are all talking more constructively *with* each other about "us."

~ *One* ~

IS RELIGION THE PROBLEM?

Religion is a central feature of human life. We all see many indications of it every day, and we all know it when we see it. But religion is surprisingly difficult to define adequately. To illustrate the complex, multidimensional nature of religion, I sometimes present students in my Introduction to Religion course with the following assignment on the first day of class: "Take the next few minutes and write a brief definition for religion." What happens next is predictable. After excitedly removing paper from a backpack or notebook and placing pen in hand, the confident facial expressions begin to give way to awkward puzzlement. Some smile nervously; many avoid eye contact. Clearly, these bright students know what religion is. Many seem to be embarrassed by their inability to articulate a cogent definition.

THE PROBLEM OF DEFINITIONS AND THE LIMITS OF OUR PERSPECTIVES

The problem of defining religion is a good point of departure for this book as well. The word *religion* evokes a wide variety of images, ideas, practices, beliefs, and experiences—some positive and some negative. Putting these disparate elements into a coherent frame of reference is no small task. It takes some effort. It forces us to step back and reflect on our presuppositions. Most people, for instance, assume that religion involves human thinking about or engagement with God, gods, or some less personal understanding of ultimate reality. They might well envision individual or communal responses to the transcendent, such as prayer, worship services, rituals, moral codes, and so on. Some people naturally think immediately of the life and teachings of Jesus or the Buddha when they think of religion; others might picture the pope or Billy Graham or Mother Teresa in their mind's eye. To complicate the picture further, personal experiences factor in as well. An individual may think of her confirmation or his bar mitzvah. If she or he has had some negative personal history with "organized" religion, then that, too, will surely figure prominently into the presuppositions.

The word *religion* also conjures up images of destructive or even cruel behavior. Assumptions about religion now include violent actions rooted in intolerance or abuse of power. During the year following the attacks on New York and the Pentagon, Americans were inundated with media images of Islamic suicide bombers, Hindu fanatics attacking Muslims (and vice versa) in Northern India, and Christian clergy being arrested and escorted to jail on charges of criminal sexual misconduct.

Many of our current associations with religion are changing, in part because our vantage point is significantly different from that of the generations before us. Although the world has always been religiously diverse, we have a much more conscious awareness of religious pluralism today. Unlike a nineteenth-century Christian living in Europe or the United States, who may only have heard or read about people called Jews, Muslims, and Buddhists, a twenty-first-century Western Christian experiences their presence through social interaction and television images that pour in daily. Put another way, Rudyard Kipling's famous line "East is East and West is West and never the twain shall meet" may have made sense in the nineteenth century but not today. North and South have joined East and West in a system of globalization Kipling could not have imagined.

Whether or not we have wrestled consciously with issues of particularity and pluralism, at some level we are aware that religion is a complex component of human life. We know that religion encompasses much more than our own particular tradition or personal experience. Like the students in Religion 101, most of us have many ideas and images about religion. Some come from experience; some come from personal observation or media images; some ideas have been passed on culturally in subtle and not-so-subtle ways. Putting the diverse elements into a broader framework for understanding, however, turns out to be more challenging than most people expect. Many of us don't make a concerted effort until we feel the need to do so. Frequently, we operate instead with a kind of "detailed ignorance" about religion.

The field of economics provides a good analogy for our understanding of religion and its role in the world. Many of us know a fair bit about economic realities. We invest enough time and energy, hopefully, to avoid making poor economic decisions about homes, investments, and retirement plans. Few of us have PhDs in economics, however. Few of us are able to make sense of the daily onslaught of economic numbers and at the same time place those in a larger, global, economic context. When something destabilizing occurs, it may force us to look again at how we have allocated our retirement funds or whether it is wise to buy a new house or car in a volatile market. Uncertainty exposes the gaps in our understanding, and so we tend to pay more attention, to ask more questions, to think more broadly about the economic realm and how it affects us personally. We may not become experts, but many of us will certainly make a concerted effort to learn enough about the details and the bigger picture so we don't make costly decisions unwittingly.

World events at the outset of the new millennium provide an impetus to take a step back and think more broadly about religion and the turbulent forces connected with religion in our world.

Regardless of one's personal views about religion, the comparative study of religion offers an effective way to tackle the problem of detailed ignorance.

Help from the Comparative Study
of Religion

A common method for understanding world religions involves a fair-minded, descriptive approach. Gathering data and organizing the facts about a particular religion is a reasonable place to start. We witnessed this in the aftermath of the September 11 attacks. Journalists, religious and political leaders, and many non-Muslim citizens were anxious to understand what was going on and why. Although Islam is a global religion and Muslim activists and countries have appeared often in the news for several decades, many people discovered how little they actually knew about the world's second largest religion. Any hope of making sense of the multiple and often conflicting images required some kind of basic introduction to Islam. Prominent television personalities like Oprah Winfrey, Peter Jennings, and Christianne Amanpour conducted miniseminars for their respective networks. Print journalists—from major daily newspapers and large national weekly publications—joined in the process. Churches, synagogues, and mosques organized educational programs. Universities and civic organizations featured expert panels and presentations.[1] Many such educational efforts were both necessary and appropriate. Through these initiatives, people could take the first deliberate steps of an important journey beyond the local and familiar, to the global and less familiar.

It is daunting to present basic information about a world religion in a fair and understandable way in a very short time. Anyone who does so should try to describe another tradition in ways that most adherents of that tradition would recognize and affirm. This is not to say that people cannot or should not make value judgments. We all do this all the time. But the first step should be to present information accurately and fairly. Today, unlike many years ago, there is no shortage of data; a great deal of information is readily accessible. Moreover, it is increasingly the case that the audience at public presentations will be religiously diverse. Having Muslims, Jews, Christians, and religious skeptics in the audience for a presentation called "Understanding Islam," for instance, keeps the teacher or public speaker honest and careful about the ways she or he interprets the material. Accurate information should be the basis for whatever value judgments people ultimately make.

Yet, however much one refines a presentation on Islam, an hour or two is hardly enough time to do justice to the breadth and depth and richness of a religious tradition and civilization that helped shape the world over fourteen centuries. The basics of Islam are relatively straightforward. Islam is a radical monotheism. There is no God but God. God is the Creator and the Sustainer of life. God is intimately connected with human lives from moment to moment. The Qur'an affirms that all human beings will be held accountable to God on the Last Day. If one embraces this view, the central concern then becomes: What does God require of me? What must I do to be found worthy on the Day of Judgment? Moving beyond this point requires some understanding of revelation, of the exemplary life of Muhammad, the prophet of Islam, and of requirements for the life of faith in community, beginning with the Five Pillars of Islam, the obligatory ritual-devotional duties.[2]

Like all religious traditions, Islam became more and more complex as it developed into a civilizational system with social, political, economic, military, and religious dimensions. Different legal schools and sectarian groups emerged in various parts of the Muslim world, which within one hundred years of the death of Muhammad extended from Spain to India. Sufis, the mystics of Islam, took their place as another major and multifaceted stream within the larger system. The Sufis draw attention to the interior meaning of religion, and in particular of Islam. We haven't even begun to consider issues like the roles and treatment of women in Islam, the meaning of *jihad*, contemporary aspirations for an Islamic state, Islamic views on religious diversity, and so on.

If Christians turn the picture around, the challenging assignment comes into sharper focus. Imagine a Muslim in Bangladesh, a woman who had studied Christianity and lived among Christians for years, charged with the task of teaching a group of interested people the basics about Christianity. What would she include? Exclude? Why? Obviously, she would need to mention Jesus and his teachings. At the heart of this religious tradition is the early church community, which proclaimed that his death was not the end. Some comments about the sacred texts affirmed by Christians (the Hebrew Bible and the New Testament) would need to be included. Perhaps a selective overview of the growth and spread of Christianity over two thousand years would help the interested Bangladeshi Muslims understand how this branch of the Abrahamic tradition has come to be the largest religion in the world today.

The limitations of such a brief overview are immediately obvious. Many decisions have to be made about how much material to cover and in what depth, since every religious tradition includes a bewildering array of data. Assuming the teacher is well versed, how far would she be able to go explaining the quest for the historical Jesus? Would she include information on the canonization of the New Testament or early church debates about the Trinity or the nature of the Incarnation? How about the emergence of the monastic tradition or the major schisms that led to the many sectarian divisions among followers of Christ? Would the history of the papacy be helpful for her audience? The Crusades? Information about the Quakers or Russian Orthodox Church? The roles and treatment of women? Would she venture an explanation for the decades of hostilities between Protestants and Catholics in Northern Ireland or the atrocities committed against Bosnian Muslim women and children by Serbian Christians during the 1990s? Could she explain various Christians' views on religious diversity? Should she?

These questions reveal the limits of a descriptive approach. A religion cannot be adequately comprehended as a self-contained, abstract collection of teachings and practices. Discovering the facts about a religion is a good place to start, but much more is needed. Understanding religion requires reflecting on how adherents of the religion understand and interpret its elements, for religion does not exist in a vacuum; it exists in the hearts, minds, and behavior of human beings. It is a very human enterprise, a lived reality.[3] To say that Muslims embrace the Qur'an as the Word of God is true, yet the various ways Muslims appropriate the sacred text is the more complex and pertinent matter, as we will discover in the chapters to come.

As a field of study, comparative religion (sometimes called the history of religion) includes but goes beyond focused inquiry on a particular religious tradition. Some scholars, for instance, concentrate on the historical interaction among traditions. The lines separating Hindus and Buddhists or Jews, Christians, and Muslims frequently, on close inspection, turn out to be poorly defined and very flexible. Religions often share sacred stories, sacred space, and sacred people. We can trace patterns of cosmic dualism, for instance, through several traditions originating in the ancient Near East. The Zoroastrians defined the cosmic struggle between good and evil in terms of Ahura Mazda and Ahriman (God and Devil figures), angels and demons, heaven and hell. These became important features of ancient Judaism, Christianity, Manichaeism, and Islam.[4] Every religious tradition—from major world religions to indigenous tribal religions in Africa and North America—has its sacred story (or stories) about the creation of the world, and many incorporate similar features or motifs. In some cases we can see clear linkages between traditions; in many instances the striking similarities cannot be explained easily either by geographical proximity or the movement of peoples.

Events associated with biblical characters and stories in Israel/Palestine, Jordan, and surrounding areas make this region of the world the "Holy Land" for Jews, Christians, and Muslims. Jerusalem, the political capital and religious center that Jews believe was established by King David three thousand years ago, is viewed in qualitatively different terms than other cities at the eastern end of the Mediterranean Sea. Within the confines of the old city of Jerusalem, religious Jews continue to revere the Temple Mount, the site of the Temple that was destroyed by the Babylonians in 587 B.C.E. and again by the Roman army in 70 C.E. Christian tradition incorporates the sacred stories of the Hebrew Bible, and in addition for Christians Jerusalem is particularly sacred as the setting for the Passion narratives, the Gospel accounts of the final week of Jesus' life, the Crucifixion, and the Resurrection on Easter Sunday morning.

Muslims also recognize biblical figures and stories as part of God's revelation through prophets and messengers. Jerusalem is the third most sacred city in Islam, in large part because of Muhammad's association with it.[5] Muslims believe that Muhammad was transported miraculously to Jerusalem, where he prayed with the prophets of old at *masjid al-aqsa* (the al-Aqsa Mosque). A few hundred feet away, it is believed, Muhammad ascended into heaven for a vision of paradise.[6] The site marking this event is the Dome of the Rock (the gold-domed building that is the signature of Jerusalem today). The outcropping of rock over which the dome is constructed is believed by Jews to be Mount Moriah, the site where Abraham was preparing to sacrifice his son. There is much more to say about the interplay of sacred space and stories among the various descendants of Abraham. The more one knows, the less sharply one can draw lines and define the different religions as separate and discrete. These three major religions not only are interdependent; they also begin with the foundational affirmation of the same God.

A comparative approach also reveals a number of common characteristics shared by most religious communities. Despite distinctive worldviews and conflicting truth claims, religious traditions function in similar ways and even share some foundational teachings. All religious traditions, for example, distinguish between the sacred and the profane. As illustrated above, defining events or sacred stories set particular people, places, times, and objects apart from the mundane. Hindus and Buddhists, practitioners of Shinto, and Native American traditions have their parallel sacred stories, people, objects, mountains, rivers, and the like.

The religious life in the community is always structured around these components. The calendar in every religion, for example, tends to follow an annual cycle during which the defining sacred events (for example, Christmas, Passover, Hajj, Diwali, Buddha's enlightenment) are retold, celebrated, and often reenacted through rituals. Calendar rituals—be they weekly worship services or annual celebrations—follow predictable patterns and have similar goals in virtually all religious communities.

Every tradition marks key stages in the human life cycle (birth, coming of age and initiation into the community, marriage, and death) with similar kinds of rituals. These rituals change the status of the individual as he or she moves through life. In life-cycle rituals across religions, the structures and stages are different but equally definable.

All religious traditions also provide social organization for their adherents. Religious life is fashioned in relation to the social organization, with moral codes and ethical principles that define appropriate and inappropriate behavior.

Religions also offer an analysis of the human predicament, and they outline a path toward the desired goal. The understandings about the human condition are defined differently and the goals are not the same, but the functional patterns across religious traditions are comparable. Interestingly, most religious traditions look forward to some kind of future hope in a new age. Many groups within the major religions revere a savior figure, one who will help usher in the new age, either here on earth or in a heavenly realm.

The comparative study of religion helps us see such interconnections between religions, including similarities in how religions are used by adherents and even similarities in doctrines. The examples above briefly illustrate the comparative approach employed in this book. At one level, it is necessary to identify and describe basic facts about a religion in a way that is both recognizable to people within that tradition and intelligible to others. But we must go further, seeking to discern what the data mean to some adherents, particularly those whose harmful actions are directly related to how they understand their tradition. It is then possible to draw broader conclusions. We will return to several of the themes mentioned above in later chapters as we examine common ways religions are often corrupted and become vehicles for violent and destructive behavior.

Identifying common characteristics among religions is not the same as saying all religions are the same. Clearly, they are not. In fact, one religion is not the same from one century to the next or from one continent to the next or from one town to the next or, for that matter, from one worshiping community to another one across the street. To illustrate the diversity among Christian communities, a church history professor I once had presented the following challenge to our class. If we would prefer not to do a research paper, we could instead invent our own heresy. It had to be a full-blown doctrinal position on a significant component of Christian teaching. The catch? It had to be a new heresy. We couldn't use one that had been propagated previously by some leader and community in church history. Those of us who liked a good challenge spent a couple of weeks meeting and talking about possible doctrines we might construct. In the end, we grasped the points our professor was trying to make: almost any interpretation we might draw out of the biblical materials had already been proffered by others; and it's not easy to define the term *heresy*.

If diversity exists within one religious community, it exists as well within each member of that community. We all are in a process of change. If we are thinking, observing, listening, reading, or otherwise processing information daily, we are continually changing in small and sometimes substantial ways, including with regard to our own religion. Who among us is completely static? Who can say our views remain exactly the same no matter what data is fed into our brain? Religious understanding is an ongoing and very human process.

If all religions are not the same, neither is it the case that all religious worldviews are equally valid. Those that have stood the test of time have clearly worked for most of the people who embraced them. This historical fact must be taken seriously, but it does not mean that all roads lead up the same mountain. Events in our world today suggest that value judgments are sorely needed. I believe there are criteria that we can use to make informed and responsible decisions about what is acceptable under the rubric of religion and what is not. Freedom *of* religion is a good thing. So is freedom *from* the religion others may wish to impose on those who differ.

A comparative approach to religion can help us clarify the ways human beings are interconnected and interdependent. Understanding that religions as well are mutually dependent has moral implications for our time. In 1966, two decades after the Holocaust, the renowned Jewish scholar Abraham Heschel spoke of our interdependence in religion. In a speech entitled "No Religion Is an Island," he said,

> The religions of the world are no more self-sufficient, no more independent, and no more isolated than individuals or nations. Energies, experiences, and ideas that come to life outside the boundaries of a particular religion or all religions continue to challenge and to affect every religion. . . . No religion is an island. We are all involved with one another. Spiritual betrayal on the part of one of us affects the faith of all of us.[7]

Heschel's words ring truer today than ever before. In view of the long history of conflict between and among religious people and communities, it is important to ask whether or not human beings are up to the challenge. Are religious people capable of building on the best in their respective traditions? Or are we doomed to live on religious islands or doomed to build contemporary versions of crusader castles until we find more effective ways to destroy one another in the name of God?

Is Religion the Problem?

For people on the receiving end of violence motivated or justified by religion, the consequences have always been deadly serious. Today, almost anyone anywhere could be a victim of destructive behavior originating half a world away. The horrible toll of religious bigotry or destructive theological certainty no longer has predictable or defined geographical limits. How could the people going to work in the World Trade Center or the Pentagon possibly have imagined the convergence of forces and events that would end their lives that morning?

The potential for mass destruction is not new, of course. But we are in a new situation. The possibility that religious zealots will instigate or be the catalyst for unspeakable devastation is not far-fetched. History leaves no doubt that some religiously motivated leaders or communities can, and are even willing to, unleash violence and terror in the name of their god or convictions. Contemporary debates about globalism versus tribalism or the clash of civilizations raise important questions about the future of human civilization. Religiously based conflict figures prominently into such debates. Clearly, the status quo is untenable in the long run, if not the short term. All of this begs the question, "Is religion the problem?"

Why Those Who Say Yes Are Right—
in Part

Responses to this question come from several directions, from religious and nonreligious people alike. The way one answers the question "Is religion the problem?" depends largely on how one understands religion. For many today, the answer to this question is a resounding *yes!*

Many religious people see religion as the problem. By *religion,* they invariably mean other people's false religion. A substantial number of Christians, for example, embrace some form of exclusivism that says, "My understanding and experience of Jesus is the only way to God. Any other form of human religious understanding or behavior is nothing more than a vain attempt by sinful people on a fast track to hell." Stating it succinctly, they may say, "Christianity is not a religion; it's a relationship." Religion—that is, non-Christian religion—is viewed as a human construct and therefore flawed, while Christianity is more authentic, therefore not a "religion." Karl Barth, the highly influential twentieth-century German theologian, constructed his multivolume *Church Dogmatics* on this very distinction.

However convincing this may sound to some Christians, it doesn't square with reality. The lived reality of Christianity throughout history just is not appreciably different from what one finds in other major religions. A strong case can be made, in fact, that the history of Christianity contains considerably more violence and destruction than that of most other major religions. Arrogant confidence in one's own tradition coupled with condescending dismissal of others ironically reinforces, by example, the argument that religion *is* the problem. It is all too human to compare the ideal version of one's own religion with the visibly flawed lived reality of other religions—a tendency found in all traditions. We have seen that the comparative study of religion helps to level the field and encourage honest inquiry. Church history also exposes repeatedly the gap between the ideal as exemplified in the teachings of Jesus and the way Christians have lived and actually behaved.

Mahatma Gandhi's experience of Christianity stands as a powerful recent illustration and indictment. Gandhi encountered Christianity when he lived under British colonial rule in India, as a "colored" person in the apartheid system of South Africa, and as a student in England. Gandhi loved the Gospel stories, particularly the teachings of Jesus. He found Jesus' words to be compelling and true. Although he was befriended and supported by some open-minded

Christian clergy, he found the larger picture in India and South Africa rather bleak. While Gandhi considered himself a follower of Jesus, he believed many Christians and "Christian civilization" contradicted Jesus' teachings. For Gandhi, actions spoke louder than words. Gandhi sought to live out the ideal of Jesus' teachings, which he found consistent with the heart of his own Hindu tradition.[8] Martin Luther King Jr. also tried to live out the words and vision of Jesus. King found strength in the exemplary life of Gandhi as he, too, faced the oppressive "Christian" forces supporting racial segregation and opposing civil rights.

The rigid exclusivism embodied in the view that "Christianity is the only truth," as we will see in the next chapter, is the foundation for a tribalism that will not serve us in the twenty-first century. Parallel positions can be found in Islam and, to a lesser extent, in other major religious traditions. But even these rigid positions include many variations, and though their narrowness may lead more easily toward violence, that is not a necessary outcome.

Many others perceive religion as the problem in a totally different way. They argue that traditional religious worldviews have run their course, for science has made a mockery of religion. Religion, in this view, is an anachronistic way of viewing our world and the cosmos—specifically, a dangerous anachronism. This perspective has merit and widespread support. Several examples within this book could be used to strengthen the case. The rise of modern scientific inquiry challenged religious presuppositions, since questions about the natural order, for which people had looked to religion for answers, could be more confidently solved by directly observing and experimenting in the physical world. The famous case of Galileo reveals the uneasy relationship between traditional theological thinking and scientific inquiry. In 1633 church officials found Galileo guilty of heresy for asserting the Copernican theory that the earth moved around the sun. Galileo was harassed and placed under virtual house arrest for seven years until he finally recanted. Church officials have long known that the essence of Galileo's argument was correct and that their own doctrine was based on faulty assumptions. Even so, it took the Catholic Church more than three and a half centuries to issue a formal apology for the Galileo affair.[9]

Religious worldviews and inflexible doctrines among Christian groups have often presented serious problems in the face of scientific inquiries and hypotheses. The infamous 1925 Scopes trial in Tennessee continues to be known through the play *Inherit the Wind.* That trial pitted evolutionary biology against a literalist approach to the creation accounts in Genesis. The debate continues today—frequently in local school boards—with some proponents of the "Christian" position advocating what they call creation science. If religion required intellectual assent to the proposition that the planet is less than ten thousand years old and the creation story (or one of the creation stories) in Genesis was literally the way the earth was created, then I, too, would have major reservations. When my students read the Izanagi and Izanami creation story from Japan or sacred stories from Native American tribal people, they immediately discern the use of symbolism to convey powerful messages about the overall sacredness and the place of humans in creation. When Jews and Christians read Genesis 1–3, they find rich and powerful teachings about meaning, purpose, and human responsibility in creation.[10] It is also obvious that this is not a scientific textbook. Is the universe a kind of three-layer cake? Do serpents talk? Is there really a tree in the Garden of Eden the fruit of which will confer eternal life? A religious orientation that lands you in William Jennings Bryan's corner at the Scopes trial is dangerously anachronistic. Religion that requires adherents to disconnect their brain *is* often a big part of the problem.

WHY THOSE WHO SAY NO ARE RIGHT— IN PART

Huston Smith, author of *The World's Religions,* the book that has introduced several generations of college students to comparative religion, in his most recent book, *Why Religion Matters,* addresses those who would define religion so narrowly and then dismiss it.[11] In his view, the primary crisis we face at the beginning of the new millennium is spiritual. Using the metaphor of a tunnel, Smith argues that scientism and materialism have conspired to block many from seeing the big picture. Scientism is the belief that the scientific method is the only or at least the most reliable way of getting at the truth and that material entities are the most fundamental elements of existence. The dominance of this view is reinforced by secularized higher education and is propagated uncritically by popular media. In addition, he suggests that the legal system in the United States is leaning strongly toward interpreting the religion clause in the First Amendment in ways that severely restrict any religious activity with respect to the state. In Smith's tunnel, scientism is the foundation or floor. Higher education, the law, and the media represent the sides and the top of the tunnel, respectively. The result: a narrow, inward-looking orientation that effectively blocks the metaphysical from view.

Smith is clearly not opposed to science. On the contrary, he celebrates scientific inquiry and achievements. Scientism, not science, is the dogmatic culprit he seeks to expose. And he does so convincingly. Smith tries to lead us out of the dehumanizing tunnel, a place devoid of transcendence. Religion matters, he says, because it opens us to a universe filled with purpose and beauty. Is religion the problem? Huston Smith says no. Smith is one among many exploring the interplay between science and religion.[12] Religion and science, many of them say, often address different questions. Religious inquiry, because it is not limited to material sources, may draw on a wider range of epistemological sources, or ways of knowing, to address matters of ultimate meaning in human existence.

> The religious sense recognizes instinctively that the ultimate questions human beings ask—What is the meaning of existence? Why are there pain and death? Why, in the end, is life

worth living? What does reality consist of and what is its object?—are the defining essence of our humanity. [These questions] are the determining substance of what makes human beings human. . . . The conviction that the questions *have* answers never wavers, however, and this keeps us from giving up on them. Though final answers are unattainable, we can advance toward them as we advance toward horizons that recede with our every step. In our faltering steps toward the horizon, we need all the help we can get, so we school ourselves in the myriad of seekers who have pondered the ultimate questions before us.[13]

Those who would dismiss religion simply as an anachronistic way of viewing the world often tend to think of religion in narrow terms. Viewed from this perspective, religion *is* often a major problem. A broader, deeper, more inclusive understanding of religion is necessary for religious and nonreligious people alike.

Joseph Campbell articulated similar points repeatedly in his legendary six-part television series with journalist Bill Moyers, *The Power of Myth*.[14] For Campbell, the messages communicated through the mythological traditions of the world—from tribal cultures to the great world religions—are all about being alive, the thrilling mystery of existence. They teach us how to live a meaningful and moral life as an individual and in community. The sacred stories that have nourished and sustained human beings combine historical information with symbolic imagery. Those who simply dismiss sacred stories as untrue miss the point. Demanding historical veracity as a prerequisite for truth is another kind of tunnel vision. To do so is to mistake poetry for prose.

Joseph Campbell loved exploring the religious and mythological imagination. He spent his life studying, writing about, and teaching what he called the "song of the universe." Raised a Catholic, he was strongly drawn toward a classical Hindu understanding of the ultimate unity of being. He, too, clearly believed that religion was not the problem. Nevertheless, he was visibly upset and horrified by the behavior of "religious" people in Lebanon during the years he and Moyers were filming *The Power of Myth*. He angrily denounced those who were slaughtering one another because they couldn't see beyond their particular metaphors and "names" for the same God.

Many religious people take a middle position on the question of whether religion is the problem by suggesting that not religion but people are the problem. This is curiously analogous to the line often quoted by opponents of gun control: "Guns don't kill people; people kill people." Viewing people, not religion, as the problem has considerable merit since, in the final analysis, it is attitudes and actions of people that are at issue. As we have noted earlier, however, religions are not free-floating, abstract entities. They come to life as traditions embraced and lived out by people. But just as people shape the direction of their tradition, so also traditions exert power over people; the influence does not flow in one direction only because the relationship is a dynamic one. To borrow from the gun control debate, proponents of gun control respond to the people-are-the-problem position by saying, "It's not so simple. When guns are easily available, crimes of passion and deadly accidents are far more likely." Religious structures and doctrines can be used almost like weapons. We will see examples of people becoming enslaved to ideas or going to great lengths to protect their religious institutions against perceived threats. If religious institutions and teachings lack flexibility, opportunities for growth, and systems of checks and balances, they can indeed be a major part of the problem. Like other institutional structures, some religions cease to serve the purposes for which they were intended. Is religion like a loaded gun? In the hands of Osama bin Laden, one could make a good case for saying yes; in the hands of Mohandas Gandhi, the analogy is obscene.

Is religion the problem? No. And yes. The answer turns in part on how one understands the nature of religion. At the heart of the religious orientation and quest, human beings find meaning and hope. In their origins and their core teachings, religions may be noble, but how they develop almost invariably falls short of the ideal. Adherents too often make their religious leaders, doctrines, and the need to defend institutional structures the vehicle and justification for unacceptable behavior. Whatever one's personal views about the nature and value of religion, it is a powerful and present reality. Thoughtful people of faith must try to learn more about the perils and promises contained within the global, human phenomenon we call religion.

Taking Religion Seriously— Globally and Locally

We have said that religion is arguably the most powerful and pervasive force in human society. This is both a historical fact and a dynamic reality shaping our present and future world community. As such, we all must take religion seriously. Thomas Friedman's award-winning book, *The Lexus and the Olive Tree,* provides a useful framework for understanding both the complexity of our increasingly interdependent world community and the central role of religion and culture. He argues that a new system—globalization—has now replaced the Cold War system that dominated the world during the decades prior to the demise of the Soviet Union in 1989. We can only understand globalization, Friedman argues, when we understand that the sharp lines once separating politics, culture, technology, finance, national security, and ecology are now disappearing. It is hard to discuss one area or dimension without referring to the others. The title of his book reflects two major poles that attract and sustain human beings. The Lexus symbolizes all the burgeoning global markets, financial institutions, and computer technologies with which we pursue higher living standards today. The olive tree, on the other hand, "represents everything that roots us, anchors us, identifies us and locates us in this world." Religion, in my view, is the largest and deepest root, anchoring and sustaining the life of the tree.[15]

Thomas Friedman knows a lot about olive trees—literally and symbolically. His earlier, Pulitzer Prize–winning book, *From Beirut to Jerusalem,* builds on his many years as bureau chief for the *New York Times* based in those war-torn cities. He knows well that the major conflicts he has covered—the ongoing Israeli-Palestinian-Arab conflict and the fifteen-year, multisided war in Lebanon—were and are not simply religious wars. But religion figures prominently into the mix of convoluted political, economic, social, and historical dynamics. Those who hold simplistically that these tragic conflicts are never-ending fights among the descendants of Abraham[16] misinterpret events as much as social scientists who think everything can be explained in terms of social or political or economic factors. We need to see the interplay of all factors, as Friedman advocates. To analyze accurately and move toward conflict resolution we must take religion seriously as a major component in the mix.

Another prolific and award-winning author, Stephen Carter, made a related plea to take religion seriously in his book, *The Culture of Disbelief: How American Law and Politics Trivialize Religious Devotion.* The book continues to generate attention a decade after it was first published.[17] A Yale law professor and an active Episcopalian, Carter presents a variety of ways guardians of the public square politely affirm an individual's right to believe as he or she wishes while continually treating religion as trivial and unimportant for serious people, something not to be mentioned in thoughtful public dialogue. Like Huston Smith, Carter demonstrates that being a person of both reason and religion is not an oxymoron.

Much of Carter's book deals with familiar issues between religion and politics. Supporters and detractors have rallied around and railed against portions of his arguments, yet his main point holds up well: religious voices must be taken seriously in the shaping of public policy. In the midst of social and political debate, we must once again find appropriate ways to hear the religious convictions of a Martin Luther King Jr., as when he wrote from a Birmingham jail or delivered the immortal "I Have a Dream" speech in the nation's capital. Carter concludes by arguing that religious voices must be included in the political debates about euthanasia, abortion, and capital punishment. He suggests, and I concur, that reflections on the boundaries of life involve an irreducibly religious dimension. Shouldn't explicitly religious voices be among those debating such issues in the public square?

Several highly visible incidents in the first years of the George W. Bush presidency illustrate these issues well. As a candidate for the presidency in 2000, Bush was once asked, "Who has been the most important influence in your life?" Without hesitation, he replied, "Jesus Christ." The response generated snide remarks and dismissive responses from various quarters, underscoring Carter's case. In 2001, when the issues of therapeutic cloning and the harvesting of stem cells took center stage in the United States, President Bush drew the line on the basis of what he perceived as morally acceptable. He was quite sure human beings ought not to "play God." While he couldn't preclude what private researchers might do somewhere in the world, he could not endorse government funding for the controversial research or harvesting stem cells from the remains of future abortions. There was no doubt that President Bush brought his religious faith into his decision-making process. He wasn't preachy, but his religious convictions were evident. We might hope that he will help enlarge the table as the debates about therapeutic cloning and abortion and capital punishment continue. In the rich tapestry that now constitutes the United States, it is imperative that the thoughtful voices of Hindus, Buddhists, Jews, Muslims, Sikhs, Taoists, Native Americans, and others be ever more audible in the public square.

Much to his credit, President Bush spoke about and modeled an inclusive approach to religion in the immediate aftermath of the September 11 attacks. Known as an active and practicing Protestant Christian, Bush worked hard to prevent a hostile national backlash against Islam and Muslims. He spoke repeatedly of Islam as a "good and peaceful religion." He conversed with Muslim leaders and visited the Islamic Center in Washington, D.C. The president publicly decried the sporadic attacks and hate crimes directed at Arabs or Muslims. Some of his strongest supporters on the religious right were visibly disturbed by his positive comments about Islam, a matter to which we will return.

President Bush appeared determined to keep the "war on terrorism" from descending into a conflict between Christianity and Islam. With the notable exception of an early gaffe (when he called the "war on terrorism" a great "crusade"), the president avoided direct appeals to his understanding of Christianity at a time when Osama bin Laden seemed determined to define the conflict in Christian-Muslim terms, as a struggle between the forces of "true" Islam and the infidels (including Muslim leaders and nations aligned with the United States). Even so, Bush employed powerful religious imagery as he spoke about the confrontation between "good and evil." People and nations had to make a choice. There was no neutral ground. You had to align with the forces of good and help root out the forces of evil or be counted as adversaries in the "war on terrorism." The clear implication was that those on the side of "good" could and would come from all religions and all nations.

THE PROPENSITY TOWARD EVIL

When President Bush juxtaposed good and evil, he articulated a familiar frame of reference by tapping into the deep tradition of cosmic dualism. The reality of evil is at least as old as human awareness. In the biblical narrative, as soon as God completes the work of creation and sees that it is "good," humans fall prey to the temptation to partake of a forbidden tree in the Garden of Eden, "the tree of the knowledge of good and evil." Just after the man and woman are expelled from the garden, readers are brought face-to-face with a violent manifestation of evil: Cain murders his brother Abel.

We resonate with the concept of evil because we know it is an ever-present reality. The desire for coherent explanations concerning the origin and nature of evil is global. Every religious tradition must render one or more explanations for the persistent reality of evil and injustice. The answers vary widely, but they appear in every tradition.[18] Nonreligious people also seek to understand the propensity toward evil, in part to minimize suffering and avoid potential disaster. Even those whose offer no particular explanation for evil, injustice, pain, and suffering—people who simply shrug and say, "stuff happens"—are generally not so casual when "stuff" happens to them or their loved ones.

We know evil to be both an individual and a corporate reality. Social and psychological factors are always involved. Individual temptation toward destructively self-serving behavior comes in many forms. Many of the heroic figures in the Bible, for instance, cannot always overcome the powerful allure of violent and destructive behavior at a personal level. Moses lashes out and kills an Egyptian. King David's adulterous lust for a married woman compels him to send her husband, a soldier faithful to his king, to certain death in battle. The apostle Paul openly confesses his struggle to overcome selfish and sinful behavior in order to do what he knows is right: "I can will what is right, but I cannot do it. For I do not do the good I want, but the evil I do not want is what I do" (Romans 7:18b–19).

We are familiar as well with the mob mentality. Group dynamics can fragment individual consciences, and otherwise decent people sometimes do horrific things. Although Pontius Pilate could find nothing wrong with Jesus, according to Luke's gospel, when the mob cried out, "Crucify him," Pilate acquiesced. Well-known examples of evil group behavior, such as the My Lai massacre during the Vietnam War and lynch mobs in the United States, remind us of the horrific consequences of corporate evil. Religious communities can be swept up in a zealous fervor and develop a mob mentality in support of a particular charismatic teacher or a doctrine deemed sacrosanct. The psychology of group behavior is real and powerful. Such blind religious zealotry is similar to unfettered nationalism. Sometimes the two become explosively intertwined.

Individual and corporate manifestations of evil and destructive behavior will be obvious in many examples below. But our concern is neither with the source of evil as a problem for theological or philosophical reflection nor with the social or psychological understanding of evil behavior. Rather, we are concerned with understanding the present and future reality of religiously motivated behavior that is harmful or malevolent. We are concerned with identifying those recurring attitudes and actions that lead to violence and suffering in the world. Whether or not one is personally religious, it is imperative that we all try to understand and address those patterns of behavior in religion that threaten the future for everyone.

So the focus of this study is pragmatic. The more effective we are at identifying dangerous patterns of corrupted religion, the more likely people of goodwill can avert disaster inspired or justified by religion. Whether or not one believes that religion itself is the problem, the diverse religious traditions will continue to be a powerful fact of life in our increasingly interdependent world community. Whatever philosophical or theological explanation one may hold for the evil things that happen, approaching the future passively is unacceptable. In the aftermath of September 11, it is incumbent on all of us to educate ourselves about religious attitudes and behaviors that lead to widespread suffering.

A propensity toward evil within religious communities always provides warning signs. Certain obvious attitudes and actions can serve as harbingers of impending harmful or malevolent behavior. In what follows I present five clear signals of danger, providing examples of each, in the belief that early detection is the critical first step in forestalling disaster.

As human institutions, all religions are subject to corruption. The major religions that have stood the test of time have done so through an ongoing process of growth and reform, a process that continually connects people of faith—Jews, Hindus, Muslims, Buddhists, Christians, and others—with the life-sustaining truths at the heart of their religion. The religions differ in many ways, of course, but they converge in teaching both an orientation toward God or the transcendent and compassionate, constructive relationships with others in this world. Jesus captured the essence of this in response to a question about the greatest commandment:

> You shall love the Lord your God with all your heart, and with all your soul, and with all your mind. This is the greatest and first commandment. And a second is like it: You shall love your neighbor as yourself. On these two commandments hang all the law and prophets. (Matthew 22:37–40)

At the heart of all authentic, healthy, life-sustaining religions, one always finds this clear requirement. Whatever religious people may say about their love of God or the mandates of their religion, when their behavior toward others is violent and destructive, when it causes suffering among their neighbors, you can be sure the religion has been corrupted and reform is desperately needed. When religion becomes evil, these corruptions are always present. Conversely, when religion remains true to its authentic sources, it is actively dismantling these corruptions, a process that is urgently needed now. Unlike generations that have gone before us, the consequences today of corrupted religion are both dire and global.

The challenges before us are formidable and deadly serious. They do not, however, constitute insurmountable obstacles. The ability to resist evil resides with individuals, and individuals make up religious groups. Human responsibility—for people within religious communities and those with no religious affiliation—is the vital component in any effort to alter destructive attitudes and actions.

While there are no easy answers or simple solutions, there are reasons for hope. Although religion has often been a large part of the problem, I will argue in the final portion of the book that this need not be the case. When significant changes in communication and cooperation across religious lines occur, I believe we can move into an era in which the invaluable resources of religious traditions themselves will shape a more hopeful and healthy future for all of us who share this fragile planet.

~ *Two* ~
ABSOLUTE TRUTH CLAIMS

Any inquiry into the corruption of a religion must begin with the claims to truth it makes. Invariably, religious truth claims are based on the authoritative teachings of "inspired" or sagelike charismatic leaders or on interpretations of sacred texts, often connected to such gifted leaders. They permeate the religious traditions in both obvious and subtle ways. In every religion, truth claims constitute the foundation on which the entire structure rests. However, when particular interpretations of these claims become propositions requiring uniform assent and are treated as rigid doctrines, the likelihood of corruption in that tradition rises exponentially. Such tendencies are the first harbingers of the evil that may follow.

Understanding that every religious tradition has elements that tend toward such rigidity and exposing the dangers and fallacies of maintaining such rigidity are vital steps in bringing to light healthy alternatives. Authentic religious truth claims are never as inflexible and exclusive as zealous adherents insist. Corrupt religious truth claims always lack the liberating awareness that humans are limited as they search for and articulate religious truth. These points were underscored thirty years ago during my first semester at the Southern Baptist Theological Seminary in Louisville, Kentucky.

I enrolled in a theology course, the Doctrine of the Atonement, taught by Dale Moody, a well-known conservative theologian. What could be more basic or central to Christianity than Jesus' death and resurrection? Throughout the course we studied biblical materials and read extensively from the writings of leading Christian thinkers—from early church leaders Iranaeus, Origen, and Augustine to Anselm, Aquinas, Luther, and Calvin, as well as several major contemporary theologians. By the end of the semester I had an A in the course and far more questions than concrete answers about the central truth of the world's largest religion. Why was Jesus' self-sacrifice necessary? Why do the four Gospels differ significantly in the recounting of this sacred story? What exactly happened on Good Friday, during the next two days, and on Easter Sunday morning? What was accomplished and how? Does everyone benefit or only the ones God has chosen? Does Jesus' sacrifice have significance for anyone who doesn't know anything about him or it, such as small children or people living in remote corners of the world? If so, how? If not, why not? I learned invaluable lessons that semester: the most basic truths in religion include many presuppositions and require considerable interpretation; and sincere people can and often do appropriate truth claims in substantially different ways.

For two thousand years, Christians have proclaimed the gospel—Jesus is the incarnate Son of God who died for the sins of the world—to people all over the world. Similarly, Muslims came out of Arabia in the seventh century with a basic declaration of faith, the *shahadah:* There is no God but God and Muhammad is the messenger of God. As with the Christian gospel, the *shahadah* is not as simple and straightforward as it initially appears. The thirteen words are pregnant with meaning and possible interpretations. They embody major implications about God, the nature of the human predicament, appropriate ways to live in this world, and guidance toward the ultimate goal of human existence.

The Muslim affirmation of faith, the first of the Five Pillars of

Islam, rolls off the tongue: *La ilaha illa 'llah wa Muhammadur rasulu 'llah.* If one declares this creed with heartfelt conviction, he or she is a Muslim. But what does it mean to bear witness to these truths? What does it imply about God or the meaning and purpose of human existence? The first portion rejects polytheism or any kind of cosmic dualism in favor of a radical monotheism. The most heinous sin in Islam is *shirk* ("associating something with God"). God is one; God is alone; there is no God but God. This theological truth claim has deep implications about loyalties and priorities in the temporal realm. Ultimately, no earthly power or human being should claim one's allegiance in any way comparable to God. Going yet deeper, many Muslims suggest that people must be careful in their pursuit of such things as wealth, fame, power, sex, self, or national aggrandizement. These trappings can easily rise to the level of *shirk* and ensnare people. In the end, God stands alone as the object of one's piety, honor, loyalty, and worship.[1]

The second half of the creed relates both to God and to the function of Muhammad. God, who is understood by Muslims as the Creator, Sustainer, and ultimate Judge at the end of time, has not left human beings alone. God communicates to humankind through many prophets and messengers, the last, or "seal," of whom is Muhammad. In Islamic understanding, the Qur'an is the divine revelation and the ultimate authority revealed by God, which helps humans know about God as well as how to live in accordance with what God desires. The Qur'an says that the messenger of God is a "beautiful model" (33:21). Thus, the sayings and actions of the messenger, called the *hadith*, become a second source for the *shari'ah* (the "path," "guidance," or Islamic law). The legal and ritual-devotional duties make up a structure that provides guidance and discipline for people who, in their pride and sinfulness, tend to forget that God created and sustains them and will hold them accountable on the Day of Judgment.

This initial explication of the Islamic statement of faith immediately brings up serious questions. Are Christians guilty of *shirk* if they associate a human being, Jesus, with God? Are Christians who affirm the doctrine of the Trinity really polytheists? How do you resolve the tension between total allegiance to God and civic responsibility within a less-than-perfect, Muslim-led country? How is a Muslim to live in a land governed by non-Muslims? These and a host of other questions implicit in the creed are addressed in the recognized Islamic sources of authority. Nonetheless, Muslims have often differed in their interpretations of the guidance provided in the Qur'an, the *hadith* (authoritative sayings and actions of Muhammad), and the opinions of legal scholars.

Disagreements about how to interpret religious truth claims lead to division and fragmentation within Islam, just as in all major traditions. Christianity, which began in modest surroundings two thousand years ago in Palestine, now includes thousands of officially recognized churches and denominations worldwide.[2] In the unfolding story of Christian church history, divergent views and practices frequently have been perceived by others as distortions of fundamental truths. The problem is magnified across religions. Adhering strictly to particular interpretations of truth claims allows people to feel justified in holding all kinds of attitudes and behaviors, including beliefs and actions that contradict well-known teachings of their religion.

When zealous and devout adherents elevate the teachings and beliefs of their tradition to the level of *absolute* truth claims, they open a door to the possibility that their religion will become evil. As we will observe in the chapters that follow, people armed with absolute truth claims are closely linked to violent extremism, charismatic leaders, and various justifications for acts otherwise understood to be unacceptable.

Contemporary examples of fundamentalist Christians attacking, sometimes murdering, doctors and others who work at abortion clinics illustrate the point. On March 10, 1993, Michael Griffin shot and killed Dr. David Gunn outside an abortion clinic in Pensacola, Florida. Five days later, the Reverend Paul Hill appeared on the

Donahue television program seeking to justify Griffin's act. Hill subsequently became a leading figure among extremists in the antiabortion movement. He wrote and spoke out frequently in support of violence against people who perform abortions. Fourteen months after Dr. Gunn's murder, Paul Hill decided he, too, must act: he murdered Dr. John Britton and his traveling companion, James Barrett, as they arrived at the same clinic in Pensacola on the morning of July 29, 1994.

Hill and many others are part of a national organization of Christians called the Army of God. The group communicates, shares resources, organizes meetings, and networks with other like-minded groups through an electronic Web site. The absolute truth claims uniting members of this loose-knit organization are unambiguous: abortion is legalized murder; abortion is an abomination to God; true Christians must engage in direct action to stop what they see as a slaughter of innocents. Their literature includes a lengthy manual for action, many position papers, and commentaries on selected news stories from around the world. The materials are replete with verses from the Bible strung together in an effort to suggest that their truth claims are synonymous with God's view:[3]

> They sacrificed their sons and daughters to the demons. (Psalm 106:37)

> O that my head were a spring of water, and my eyes a fountain of tears, so that I might weep day and night for the slain of my poor people! (Jeremiah 9:1)

> Am I now seeking human approval, or God's approval? Or am I trying to please people? If I were still pleasing people, I would not be a servant of Christ. (Galatians 1:10)

> In your struggle against sin, you have not yet resisted to the point of shedding your blood. (Hebrews 12:4)

There is no doubt about the depth of commitment and certainty of Michael Griffin, Paul Hill, and others who justify their actions. But these passages have nothing to do with abortion. In fact, the Bible says nothing specific about this highly emotional and controversial issue. One might argue that the sixth of the Ten Commandments—"You shall not murder" (Exodus 20:13)—is a basis for opposing abortion. The vigorous debates about when life begins and what constitutes human life immediately arise. Even so, among the millions who strongly oppose abortion on religious grounds, only a small, extremist fringe embraces fully the absolute truth claims described above. Most vocal opponents of abortion accept the practice in cases of rape, incest, or a threat to the life of the mother. Not the extremists. It is sadly ironic that soldiers in the Army of God intentionally break the commandment not to murder in order to stop people they consider guilty of murder.

While truth claims are the essential ingredients of religion, they are also the points at which divergent interpretations arise. When particular understandings become rigidly fixed and uncritically appropriated as absolute truths, well-meaning people can and often do paint themselves into a corner from which they must assume a defensive or even offensive posture. With potentially destructive consequences, people presume to know God, abuse sacred texts, and propagate their particular versions of absolute truth.

KNOWLEDGE OF GOD

Across the globe and through the centuries human beings in all cultures have tried to comprehend and articulate our place in the cosmos. God or some understanding of the transcendent is at the heart of the quest. Two major factors present formidable obstacles. First, there are many possible ways of knowing: experience, observation, reason, intuition, revelation, and so forth. Even people who think they draw only on divine revelation as their source for religious truth in fact are using other epistemological sources at the same time. Second, whatever is apprehended or known, no matter how profoundly true it may be, can be communicated to others only by way of symbols. This is obvious when we think of art, music, poetry, sign language, or body language. But it is often overlooked when we are communicating through prose, whether oral or written. Religious truth claims are most frequently stated in the language of prose. However, languages are essentially big, complicated symbol systems. And even if you know the symbols well, words and phrases move at many levels and require nuance and explication.

We can easily see the need for and limitations regarding symbolic language when we pose a simple question: What do we mean when we say "God"? Ask yourself that question. The exercise is instructive. I pose the question to students in Religion 101 each semester when we explore various ways people in different traditions conceptualize divinity. I sometimes read from a simple yet provocative collection compiled by Deidre Sullivan or play an excerpt from one of Robert Fulghum's reflections on the divine.[4] Students invariably smile knowingly and ponder seriously when they hear many of their own conceptualizations echoed in the words of Luther, Lincoln, Tolstoy, or Einstein as well as children, telephone operators, attorneys, construction workers, and poets. In small group discussions they discover their conceptualizations are many and varied. They recognize their personal views have changed over time and in many instances are still developing. We need language and symbols, but these are pointers at best.

Is God a larger-than-life grandfatherly figure sitting in the clouds on a big throne with angels nearby playing lovely music on harps? That image remains popular with many Jewish and Christian children, who, at a particular stage of cognitive development, tend to conceptualize things in very concrete terms. But biblical writers show how important it is to move beyond simple anthropomorphic language to more abstract concepts. In the third chapter of Genesis, God is described in very humanlike terms—crunching leaves while walking in the garden and calling out to Adam and Eve, who are hiding behind a tree. Isaiah's vision of the heavenly throne is awesome for the soon-to-be prophet. The book of Job ends with a stern reminder that human beings—even the most righteous man on earth—cannot begin to comprehend God.

The Abrahamic religions traditionally describe God as omnipotent, omniscient, and omnipresent. The implications connected with such attributes are both numerous and challenging. If God knows everything and God can do anything, what is God's relationship with evil and injustice? Theologians wrestle with the questions under the rubric of *theodicy,* or the "justice of God." If God is omnipotent, why didn't God prevent the airplanes from striking the World Trade Center towers? Or, as some religious leaders suggested, did God actively participate in the events of September 11? Osama bin Laden and Jerry Falwell seemed to agree on this point: bin Laden interpreted the destruction of the towers and the crash into the Pentagon as a sign of God's support for his struggle against evil; Falwell suggested these horrifying events were God's way of telling us of his displeasure with abortionists, pagans, feminists, the ACLU, People for the American Way, and gays and lesbians.[5] Is God somehow connected to everything that happens? In what sense, if any, are human beings free and responsible? Is God intimately involved in every detail of human life, as the Qur'an suggests with the striking image "God is closer to you than your jugular vein" (50:16)? Did God create the world and then somehow step back from the process, as many early American deists believed? Or, as many Hindus and mystics in various religions suggest, is God (or gods) best understood in terms of limited human attempts to point toward the Reality that animates the cosmos?

Islamic understanding, as noted earlier, begins with a radical monotheism. Yet Muslims show considerable flexibility in their approaches to the knowledge of God. Despite human limitations, they believe we can know a great deal about God. The Qur'an reveals God's nature through God's actions and attributes in the ninety-nine names of God: All-Powerful, All-Merciful, All-Seeing, the Most Exhalted, the Holy, the Just, the Guardian of Peace, the Resurrector, and so on.[6] Alongside and intertwined with the majority Sunni (orthodox) teachings, the Sufis (mystics) have pursued experiential paths to God through music, dance, and methodical recitation of the divine name. Karen Armstrong's superb study, *A History of God,* describes the dynamic, often volatile, interplay within and among Muslims, Christians, and Jews as these children of Abraham articulated their experiences and perceptions of God over four millennia. More recently, Jack Miles's Pulitzer Prize–winning book, *God: A Biography,* provides a wonderfully insightful and provocative exploration of the images of God shown in the Hebrew Bible. Both books invite readers to respond more thoughtfully and humbly to the question "What do we mean when we say 'God'?"[7]

When particular conceptualizations lead to rigid doctrine and cocksure certainty about God, the likelihood of major problems increases rapidly. We have seen this played out with unsettling frequency as various, often self-appointed, religious leaders boldly speak for God. In the aftermath of the September 11 tragedies several prominent, media-savvy Christian clergy felt compelled to expose publicly the evil nature of Islam. Jerry Falwell, Pat Robertson, and Franklin Graham, the son of Billy Graham, were among the most visible. Not content simply to proclaim the truth of their understanding of Christianity, at different times and in slightly different ways, each of these men attacked Islam as a false religion and declared that Allah was a false god. These assaults were terribly divisive, particularly at a time when President Bush and other political leaders were joining voices with many Jewish, Christian, and Muslim religious leaders to strengthen all people of goodwill in collective efforts against violent extremists who claim to be inspired by their religion. In addition, Falwell, Robertson, and Graham revealed their ignorance.

Allah is simply the Arabic word for God. People who speak Arabic—including the more than fifteen million Christians who live in the Middle East today—pray to *Allah;* people who speak French pray to *Dieu;* people who speak German pray to *Gott.* I've joined in many Christian worship services in Egypt, Lebanon, Syria, Jordan, and Israel/Palestine over several decades. We always pray to Allah. But this is more than a matter of language. Taking to the airwaves to claim that Muslims are worshiping a false god is irresponsible. It reveals both how woefully uninformed prominent leaders can be and how easy it is to become enslaved to inflexible truth claims about God. In either case, it is unconscionable to use bully pulpits to fuel ignorance and bigotry.

Islamic self-understanding couldn't be clearer: Allah is the God Jews and Christians worship. God, according to the Qur'an and the subsequent teachings of Muhammad, has spoken to humankind through many prophets and messengers, including biblical figures like Noah, Abraham, Moses, David, and John the Baptist. Jesus is one of the most important and prominent figures in the Qur'an; he is mentioned ninety-three times by name in the sacred scripture of Islam. There is simply no ambiguity here. Jews, Christians, and Muslims are talking about the same deity.

Derogatory proclamations about Islam from prominent Christian leaders in the United States are part of a long history.[8] In a later chapter we will explore ways such exclusivist truth claims and theological certainty have resulted in horrifying actions against Jews. In the six decades since the Holocaust, many Christians have learned a great deal about our history and the consequences of anti-Semitism. But many Christians cling with arrogant certainty to rigid doctrines about God's nonrelationship to Jews, Muslims, and others. One of the more bizarre examples occurred in 1980 when Bailey Smith, then president of the largest Protestant denomination in the United States, the Southern Baptist Convention, made national news by announcing that God does not hear the prayers of the Jews. Besieged by reporters and understandably annoyed Jewish as well as Christian leaders, Smith later defended his position as a hard fact taught by the scriptures. He explained that it was not that God doesn't want to hear the prayers of the Jews; it is simply that he can't. In Smith's view, prayers not uttered in the name of Jesus simply cannot get through to God.

Bailey Smith—and, sadly, millions of others—backed into a corner from which he presumed to declare what God can and cannot do. How did God hear the prayers of Abraham, Moses, and David? Did the heavenly switchboard operator only assume the role of blocking all messages without the tag line "in Jesus' name" after the Resurrection? If so, how does Smith make sense of Paul's lengthy discourse that stresses God's continuing relationship with the people of Israel (Romans 9–11)? The tenth chapter of the Book of Acts also undermines such inflexible truth claims. The story of Cornelius not only makes clear that God hears prayers, in this case, the prayers of a Gentile; it also illustrates how theological education remains an ongoing task. The story presents a fascinating portrait of Peter, the most prominent of Jesus' disciples and the leader of the early church. Peter discovers at a late stage in his life and ministry that his understandings of God are far too narrow. If ongoing theological education is helpful for Peter, surely Bailey Smith, Jerry Falwell, Pat Robertson, and Franklin Graham could benefit as well.

Religious truth claims about God or the transcendent necessarily rely on language. When the language stiffens into unyielding doctrines, people frequently take on the role of defending God. One has only to look at the recent history in Lebanon, the former Yugoslavia, Israel/Palestine, Nigeria, or Indonesia to see how easily zealous individuals and religious communities can justify obviously evil behavior directed at fellow children of Abraham. Of course, the civil strife in all these lands is not simply about religion; historical, political, social, and economic dynamics also figure substantially in the convoluted conflicts. On close inspection, however, we often find narrow truth claims about God that judge others guilty of propagating dangerous falsehoods or consider them something less than fully human. When adherents lose sight of the symbolic nature of language about God, religion is easily corrupted. Rigid truth claims, particularly in times of conflict, are the basis for demonizing and dehumanizing those who differ. In some instances, defending truth claims about a particular sacred text provides justification for behavior that contradicts central truths of the religion the text informs. An example from the Nichiren school of Japanese Buddhism illustrates the perils involved.

THE ABUSE OF SACRED TEXTS

Nichiren, founder of a major school that continues to bear his name, was deeply distressed by the proliferation of texts, teachings, and practices among Buddhists in tumultuous thirteenth-century Japan. He was absolutely certain that the Lotus Sutra was the only valid sacred text. Nichiren viewed people like Shinran, Honen, and others in their Pure Land schools as nothing less than slanderers of the Dharma, or True Law. In his writings, Nichiren argues that prohibiting the slander of the Law is the best way to ensure stability within the nation and peace in the world at large. While he does not explicitly define what "prohibiting" means, he openly declares that anyone who kills those who slander the Dharma will not suffer the normal karmic consequences. Nichiren quotes the Buddha as saying that one who kills any person will fall into the realm of hell, hungry ghosts, or animals, except in the case of a slanderer of the Dharma.[9]

Clinging with tenacity to a sacred text and absolving people who would kill those whose teachings differ is far from the norm in Buddhism. This kind of attachment to a text contradicts essential Buddhist understandings about the problematic, grasping nature of the human condition.[10] Killing without karmic consequences is antithetical to universal Buddhist teachings on nonviolence as well. Despite such contradictions, Nichiren Buddhism not only took root and thrived for centuries; it lives on today as the foundation for the influential new religion Soka Gakkai.

Sacred texts provide a rich source of wisdom and guidance in the vicissitudes of life. Like all things powerful, sacred texts can be misused through a kind of sanctification of the whole and through selective reading and interpretation. Sacred texts are the most easily abused component of religion. Daily newspapers and broadcasts are filled with examples of religious and political leaders citing selected verses or phrases from the Bible or Qur'an in support of policies that affect the lives of millions. Sacred texts provide an accessible and authoritative tool for promoting an agenda or cause. Shakespeare's poignant observation is apropos: "Even the devil can cite scripture for his purpose." Regrettably, substantial numbers of people are susceptible to simplistic theological rhetoric based on prooftexts. Manipulative exploitation of revered texts can lead to violent zealotry.

Islamic suicide bombing is an extreme example of the phenomenon. This increasingly common tactic took root and flourished during the multisided civil war that began in Lebanon in 1976. Car and truck bombs became a horrific feature of the urban warfare in Lebanon. The practice moved to another level in 1983 when a teenage Muslim boy detonated a truck full of explosives in front of the U.S. marine barracks in Beirut. The building was destroyed and 239 Americans died in the attack. Within days, the U.S. forces in Lebanon had packed up, boarded amphibious vessels, and departed.[11] I traveled to Beirut a few weeks after this devastating attack as part of a small ecumenical delegation of Christian leaders invited to meet with President Amin Gemayal and various religious and political leaders. There are no adequate words to convey the sobering sadness and anger I experienced when Lebanese leaders took us to the site of the collapsed building. In the course of the four-day visit, I met with Shi'ite Muslim leaders from the Amal ("Hope") movement, Hizbollah ("Party of God"), and various Sunni groups. At their invitation, my colleagues and I were escorted through the slums and war-torn areas where their various communities lived. I saw and experienced the breeding ground for suicide bombers. Whether or not people agreed with the action directed at the marines, one message came through clearly: the suicide truck bomber succeeded in striking the Achilles' heel of the United States; terrorism worked.

Having been directly involved in the Iranian hostage crisis as well as the conflicts in Lebanon and Israel/Palestine, I saw twenty years ago that Muslim extremists were developing more effective ways to combat the vastly better equipped forces they perceived as the enemy. The Hizbollah refined the practice of suicide bombings in their fight against Israel's military occupation. In 1982 the Shi'ites in southern Lebanon welcomed the Israeli army, but the ongoing war and occupation eventually turned most Shi'ites into Israel's bitterest foe. After more than a decade and over seven hundred casualties, it was the Hizbollah fighters and suicide bombers that ultimately drove Israeli forces out of Lebanon. *The Sword of Islam,* an unvarnished BBC documentary focusing on the growth of militant Islamic groups in Lebanon, includes an interview with a visibly upset and confused Israeli Prime Minister Yitzhak Rabin: "These terrorists are willing to kill themselves to strike our soldiers. They believe they are going directly to heaven. We've never seen anything like this from the Palestinians." Nearly two decades later those words haunt Israelis, who have experienced the rapid growth of this phenomenon among Muslim extremists in Palestine.[12]

Osama bin Laden's *al-qaida* network used this tactic in various settings: U.S. embassy bombings in Kenya and Tanzania in 1998, the attack on the USS *Cole* off the coast of Yemen in 2000, and the assaults on the World Trade Center and the Pentagon in 2001. The foundation for this exceedingly powerful and destructive phenomenon is found in a highly selective reading and interpretation of the Qur'an. Absolute truth claims are established and propagated in order to recruit volunteers for suicide missions. More than three hundred individual Muslims didn't just wake up one day during the past two decades and decide to kill themselves. They were individually recruited and convinced that they could do something great for God and their people. In the process, they would go immediately to paradise and would guarantee a place in the heavenly abode for their families as well.

The Qur'an includes many references to a great Day of Judgment at the end of time. While the particulars of Islamic eschatology are as varied as one finds in other religions, traditional views portray a scene in which individuals are given a book (of their own deeds) and soon thereafter dispatched to heaven or hell. God's mercy enters into the picture in different ways, but in a very real sense, we judge ourselves by our actions on earth.[13] All of this connects ultimately to the Islamic understanding of revelation and the guidance God has provided through prophets, messengers, and the Qur'an. There is a provision, however, for those who die "striving in the way of God." The Qur'an makes clear that these faithful go immediately to paradise: "Say not of those who die in the path of God that they are dead. Nay rather they live" (2:154). Muslims have always interpreted these and related texts (such as Qur'an 3:169–71) as a promise for martyrs. Rather than wait in an intermediate state between one's death and the Day of Judgment, martyrs go directly to the seventh heaven, the highest realm, where the prophets also reside. But who determines what constitutes martyrdom? Unlike the majority Sunni Muslims, the Shi'ites have an organized, hierarchical structure for clergy. Recognized leaders in particular settings can and do render such decisions. Extremist leaders in Hizbollah did just that. Several such leaders declared that attacks against Israelis that resulted in death constituted martyrdom. These extremists in Lebanon and Palestine also cited one of the controversial passages in the Qur'an to justify the attacks on Jews:

Fight in the cause of God those who fight you, but do not begin hostilities; for God does not love such injustice. And kill them wherever you find them, and drive them out from the places where they drove you out; for persecution is worse than slaughter; but fight them not at the sacred mosque, unless they [first] fight you there; but if they fight you, slay them. Such is the reward of infidels. (2:190–91)

Osama bin Laden widens the interpretation to include Christians and even Muslims who do not support his cause. The passage is sharp and certainly needs clarification. Most Muslims understand this and similar texts in the context of their historical time: fighting back was a valid response to those who were attacking Muslims in the time of Muhammad. Muslims and others who have studied the Qur'an also quickly point out that such verses must be understood in relationship to dozens of passages that affirm Jews and Christians as People of the Book, who, like Muslims, are promised a place in heaven.[14]

The profile of a typical recruit for suicide bombings has been predictable: a young man with little education from a poor or modest family background. Videotapes of recruiting, training, and final preparation consistently show the future *shahid* (martyr) repeating simple affirmations about God's promise of paradise for him and his family. A recruit's pledge to become a martyr is irrevocable. Interviews with imprisoned would-be martyrs whose bombs failed to detonate reveal their belief that hell awaits those who break such a solemn promise.[15]

Only a highly selective reading of the Qur'an can produce this kind of narrow interpretation. Such a stance ignores completely the multiple and unambiguous admonitions in the *hadith* against any form of suicide. It also overlooks strict Islamic prohibitions against killing women, children, and noncombatants, even during times of war. For these reasons, many Muslim leaders in the aftermath of September 11 denounced the violent extremists as terribly misguided and uninformed about fundamental teachings in Islam. Education within Islam and providing alternatives for the dispossessed are essential antidotes to the absolute truth claims that undergird violent extremism in the name of Allah.

Truth claims based on selective reading of sacred texts lead to various corruptions in religion that do not result immediately in violence. But narrow, absolute truth claims can and often do have destructive consequences. Many Christians claim the Bible is the verbally inspired Word of God, literally true in every way. Millions embrace such a view, apparently without much reflection. They defer instead to authority figures who define "the" Christian position on various issues ranging from human sexuality to the physical age of the planet. If you are not persuaded that religious truth claims based on prooftexts as interpreted by authority figures can have harmful consequences, think about the history of anti-Semitism or the justification of slavery or discrimination against women or attitudes and behavior toward homosexual persons.[16]

Christians who say they take the Bible literally are either ignorant or self-deluded. No one takes the Bible literally. Serpent-handling Pentecostal Christians in Appalachia may come closer than anyone else. They put their life on the line each week when they try to follow literally the words of Jesus as recorded in Mark 16. Christian leaders who berate those who don't take the Bible literally find other ways to interpret the last chapter of Mark. Similarly, I'm not aware of people who advocate self-mutilation in obedience to Jesus' words in Mark 9:43–48 or the execution of disobedient children, as called for in Deuteronomy 21:18–21. The validity of a literalist approach is further undermined by the act of translation. The Bible was written in Hebrew and Greek. The presence of nearly two dozen contemporary English translations points to the challenge of communicating the meaning and intent of the original text.[17] While the King James translation of 1611 is still favored by some people, no one in the English-speaking world today speaks or spells that way. Muslims, on the other hand, have always recognized the problem. They insist that the Qur'an must be read and recited in Arabic. Any translation is, by definition, an interpretation.

Peter Gomes, the minister at Harvard's Memorial Church since 1974, succinctly identifies the fallacy and danger of taking a literalist approach to the Bible:

> Literalism is dangerous for two reasons. First, it indulges the reader in the fanciful notion that by virtue of natural intelligence the text is apprehensible and therefore sensible. Despite

genuflections to the notion of original or authorial intent, meaning is determined by what the reader takes out of the text, and this meaning the reader attributes to the author. Thus, what the reader thinks is there becomes not merely the reader's opinion, but the will of God, with all the moral consequences and authority that that implies. . . . The second danger of literalism is that the power of private judgment may well obscure the meaning of a text by paying attention only to what it says. . . . Allegories, typologies, and symbolic interpretations are to be avoided in favor of the pure and uncorrupted word. Literalism does not want the text held hostage to these devices, but literalism itself is hostage to the eighteenth-century illusion that truth and meaning are the same thing, and that they are fixed and discernible by the application of the faculties of reason and common sense.[18]

Fundamentalists often build absolute truth claims on a kind of logic that does not hold up under scrutiny. The example of Pat Robertson, Jerry Falwell, and Franklin Graham insisting that Allah is not the same God is again instructive. Their rationale is based on selected passages in the Gospel of John where Jesus is portrayed as speaking of his unique relationship with God.[19] The argument, which each of these three proffered publicly, begins with the interpretation that the God of the Bible is one and the same as Jesus. Therefore, Muslims who talk about Allah in a way that does not include this same understanding of Jesus cannot be talking about the same God.

There are two major flaws with such a rationale. First, to be consistent, these same people would have to say that Jews are not talking about the same God as Christians. Bailey Smith was willing to go some distance down that path, but Robertson, Falwell, and Graham demur. Second, this argument assumes a kind of human logic: if *a* is true, *b* must be false. Where is that same logic when these Christians talk about the Trinity or the incarnation of Christ? How can God logically be three and one at the same time? How can Jesus be understood as fully human and fully divine simultaneously? At this point, Robertson and company, like most Christians since these questions were addressed in the great ecumenical councils of the fourth and fifth centuries, speak of the "mystery" of the Trinity and the "mystery" of the incarnation. If at the heart of Christian theology one affirms that human logic is inadequate to explain the mystery of God, how can one casually declare that one-fifth of the world's population is mistaken about Allah being the God of the Bible because this claim is logically inconsistent with an interpretation of a passage about God in the richly theological Gospel of John? How can Jews be talking about the same God as Christians if they do not equate Jesus with God? A little clear thinking, honesty, and humility can go a long way toward tempering such bold truth claims by authority figures with easy access to the mass media.

But clear thinking and honesty about one's sacred texts are not easy. Most people are not encouraged to ask critical questions within their own tradition. Viewed from another perspective, the issue becomes clear and the importance of critical inquiry is easy to see. Suppose someone approached you in an airport with a Qur'an in hand. Concerned that you know the truth and not continue on a sure path to hell, this person informs you that the book he is holding is the literal Word of God. It holds all the answers to life's questions. It provides God's guidance. If you embrace and follow its teachings, you can have eternal life in heaven. Assuming you were willing to talk to the sincere, obviously committed evangelist, what would be your response? Would you say, "What wonderful news!"? Would you accept the bold truth claims uncritically? Or would you ask some basic questions: How do you know it is the Word of God? Where did it come from? Why should I take your word for it? My experience teaching intelligent undergraduates at top universities over many years reinforces the view that most Christians don't grow up learning to ask such basic questions about their own sacred texts. The same is true for most Muslims. Jews, on the other hand, have had a long tradition of reflecting on and speculatively interpreting their sacred texts. While Jews are not exempt from the trap of rigidly defined absolute truth claims about sacred texts, a long history of learned and critical inquiry diminishes the dangerous inclination. Robert Alter, a distinguished professor of Hebrew and comparative literature, clearly shows in *The Art of Biblical Narrative* how in the Jewish tradition meaning is not a property of a text but something that must always be wrestled with and continuously sought and redefined.

> Indeed, an essential aim of the innovative techniques of fiction worked out by the ancient Hebrew writers was to produce a certain indeterminacy of meaning, especially in regard to motive, moral character, and psychology. . . . Meaning, perhaps for the first time in narrative literature, was conceived as a *process,* requiring continual revision—both in the ordinary sense and in the etymological sense of seeing-again—continual suspension of judgment, weighing of multiple possibilities, brooding over gaps in information provided. As a step in the process of meaning in the Joseph story, it is exactly right that the filial betrayal of Genesis 37 and the daughter-in-law's deception of Genesis 38 should be aligned with one another through the indirection of analogy, the parallels tersely suggested but never spelled out with a thematically unambiguous closure, as they are in Midrash.[20]

The Christian Bible contains sixty-six books (more if your Bible incorporates the Apocrypha) written over a period of nearly a thousand years. It includes poetry and prose, parables, prayers, speeches, prophetic utterances, letters addressed to specific people and circumstances, apocalyptic literature, legal documents, and so on. However one might understand these sacred texts as inspired, interpretation is required at many levels. Fortunately, many accessible, contemporary resources are available for Jews and Christians who take the Bible too seriously to approach the text with a simplistic literalism.[21]

The misuse and abuse of sacred texts comes in many forms. This must not, however, obscure the compelling fact that sacred texts have been a constant source of strength, inspiration, and guidance for people in many cultures for more than three millennia. In ways unimaginable one hundred years ago, Christians in the West now have ready access to translations of texts cherished by hundreds of millions of Hindus, Buddhists, Taoists, Muslims, and others. Scores of venerable texts are as close as a visit to the religion section in a large bookstore or a few clicks on Internet links. And many people are finding refreshing nourishment as they sample from the deep wells that have sustained others for centuries.[22] Approached from another perspective, sacred texts are an increasingly important focus in the comparative study of religion. Wilfred Cantwell Smith's final major work, for example, explores scripture as a category that may "enhance our understanding of what it means ultimately to be human—what it has meant and could or should mean."[23] While liberating to some, a comparative approach is highly threatening to those whose theology implies a monopoly on truth. The challenge is particularly poignant for Christians and Muslims whose self-understanding includes a missionary requirement to carry their message to the rest of the world.

The Special Challenge for Missionary Religions

It is no accident that the world's two largest and most widespread religions include a missionary imperative. Unlike faithful Hindus, Jews, Taoists, and practitioners of Shinto, Christians and Muslims are expected to carry the Good News and the Islamic call to faith, respectively, to the far corners of the world. Although they disagree on the precise nature of God's revelation and the paths to the ultimate goal, adherents in both traditions agree that their faith incorporates a missionary mandate. Far too often in both traditions, however, a narrow understanding of mission has combined with cultural imperialism and military power in ways that destroyed any witness to God's love and mercy.

Examples of missionary-related abuses abound. The history of the spread of Christianity and Islam in Europe, Asia, Africa, and the Americas (for Christianity) is a checkered one at best. Pick a continent and study the behavior of those who came in the name of these religions. Raw power and conquest sometimes dominated the process. Conversion by force is often intertwined with moving stories of people whose faith and courage changed them and their communities in many positive ways. Certainly missionaries made life-changing contributions, making possible greater opportunities in health care, education, and the economy, but celebrating the positive doesn't tell the whole story. When missionary zeal is informed by absolute truth claims defining who is "saved" and what is acceptable, the propagation of religion frequently includes sinister dimensions.

The California mission system (1769–1834) as founded and developed by Father Junípero Serra exemplifies the problem. Serra's piety, courage, and commitment to evangelize Native Americans have been affirmed by his critics as well as by those who advocated for his beatification in 1988 (a formal step toward canonization as a saint in the Roman Catholic tradition). A professor of theology, Serra left Spain for the mission field of the new world in 1749. By the time of his death in 1782, he had walked some twenty-four thousand miles through Mexico and California and established twenty-one Franciscan missions. However noble his intentions, his methods and close cooperation with Spanish government and military officials were cruelly devastating to the indigenous people. The mission was, in fact, part of a larger strategy of colonization and conquest. Serra and his fellow missionaries traveled to new territories with Spanish military contingents and apparently understood themselves as agents of both God and the civil government.[24]

Serra and others like him viewed the native population as savage heathens who had to be disciplined as children. Their version of discipline would warrant state intervention and charges of child abuse in California today. The Franciscans were convinced that cultural conversion was a prerequisite to conversion to Christianity. With righteous determination, "they went about the task of dismantling what they regarded as the backward traditional lifeways, social structures, mores, and values of Indian peoples." Missionaries destroyed towns, separated families, instituted slavery and economic exploitation, applied religious coercion ruthlessly, and carried out various types of corporal punishment. George Tinker, a Native American seminary professor and pastor to Lutherans and Episcopalians in Denver, closely examines Serra and three other highly respected historical missionary leaders and concludes that they were naive and possibly unwitting partners in genocide. Without question, the California mission is part of a larger pattern beginning with the subjugation of Aztecs and other native peoples in Mexico. Franciscans, Augustinians, and Dominicans carried the enterprise north into Texas, New Mexico, Arizona, and California.[25]

The uncritical mixing of religious, political, military, and economic realms in the missionary conquests of the Southwest offends contemporary sensitivities and contradicts the cherished principle of the separation of church and state. It is far closer to the military, political, and religious expansion of Islam in the seventh and eighth centuries. These and missionary movements in Asia and Africa reflect another era and outdated worldviews. In different ways at different times, Christian and Muslim missions rested on absolute truth claims—stated or assumed—that theirs was a superior culture and religion. In fairness to early Islamic expansion—across North Africa and into Spain, through the Fertile Crescent and across Mesopotamia and Persia into India—there is little evidence of widespread conversion at the point of a sword. Despite provisions for "protected peoples" within Islamdom, limited economic opportunities and strong social pressures proved to be compelling for many subject people over time. Like the conquering Muslims, many people were moved deeply by the message of Islam and interpreted the dramatic worldly success of this civilizational system as a sign of God's favor.

The point here is not to chastise missionaries for their inability to see beyond the contexts in which they operated. Our concern relates to the present and the future. At what points are people whose faith tradition includes a missionary imperative blind today? Can missionary efforts be pursued in healthy, constructive, and noncoercive ways? These questions loom large in a world where the world's most powerful political and military power, the United States, is predominantly Christian. They are not rhetorical in a world where substantial numbers of Muslims with enormous fiscal resources believe Islam has been subjugated for centuries and should now reassert its role as the preeminent religious and civilizational system in the world.

Missionary activities informed by absolute truth claims that define sharply who is "in" and who is "out" continue to shape the landscape. The Southern Baptist Convention, for example, specifically targets Jews, Hindus, and Muslims in the United States during their most holy days each year. Tens of thousands of zealous believers seek to convert Jews during Yom Kippur, Hindus during Diwali, and Muslims during the month of Ramadan. Mormons, Christian Scientists, and others are also considered legitimate targets in this version of spiritual warfare. The orchestrated campaign falls somewhere on the spectrum between irritating and deeply offensive. Most people I know are less than thrilled when Bible salesmen or Jehovah's Witnesses appear on their doorstep or telemarketers call during dinner. One can easily imagine how most Christians would respond to an intrusive missionary house call from a sincere devotee of Louis Farrakhan's Nation of Islam on Easter Sunday or Christmas Day. Well-meaning Southern Baptists might benefit from the wisdom of Jesus as articulated in the Golden Rule: "In everything, do to others as you would have them do to you; for this is the law and the prophets" (Matthew 7:12).

In many Muslim countries, a far more oppressive system is in place, with severe restrictions placed on citizens. It is illegal, for instance, for non-Muslims to proselytize Muslims. In Saudi Arabia, the guardian of Islam's two most holy sites, Mecca and Medina, people of other faiths are not even allowed to worship in any public way. There are heartrending stories of Muslims in Egypt and elsewhere whose conversion to Christianity resulted in a death sentence or at the very least complete abandonment by their family. All of this belies the central Islamic teaching that God created human beings as free and responsible agents. Muslims who believe they safeguard Islam through such stringent legal and social policies appear to ignore one of the most quoted and revered messages in the Qur'an: "There can be no compulsion in matters of religion" (2:256). This central tenet affirms that each person is responsible for himself or herself. Authentic faith cannot be coerced through aggressive missionary tactics or protected by prohibiting free inquiry or punishing anyone who deviates from the norm.

The way forward is not blocked. Christians and Muslims need not and should not abandon their core commitment to sharing their respective versions of God's good news with humankind. As intimated above, they should remember that converting others is not their responsibility. First and foremost, mission is a matter of bearing witness. Guidance on how best to bear witness is found at the heart of both traditions. The New Testament and the Qur'an both emphasize that the love of God is manifest in the ways people relate to others. Both traditions teach that human beings will be accountable on the Day of Judgment. The sacred texts include strikingly similar passages about the criteria for judgment. Jesus' teaching indicates that many will be surprised on the Day of Judgment when the Son of Man separates people as a shepherd separates sheep from goats. The separation is based on how people responded to others who were hungry, thirsty, strangers, naked, sick, or in prison (Matthew 25:31–46).

Similarly, vivid judgment scenes in the Qur'an make clear that each person's life will be fully revealed and that wealth and power on earth will provide no benefit. Those who "were not careful to feed the poor . . . [have] no advocate this day" (Qur'an 69:13–35). Social and ethical injunctions throughout the text emphasize the importance of compassion toward the most needy and marginalized—widows, orphans, and the poor. While belief systems are important, the focus in the end is more on orthopraxy than on orthodoxy.

Many of the problems with missionary activities are tied to issues of power. One can often find healthy models for mission in settings where Christians and Muslims are minority communities. The ecumenical work between U.S. churches and the churches in the Middle East during the 1980s often centered on meeting the kinds of human need Jesus talked about in Matthew 25. In my experience working as a liaison between and among these churches, I discovered that Christians in the West could learn a great deal about mission from Christians in Lebanon, Palestine, and Egypt. People in these churches seek to meet human needs in the midst of war even as hostilities are sometimes directed at them, and their presence and witness are far more powerful than the street corner evangelism propagated by many Western Christians to this day. For many years, with the help of U.S. churches, the Middle East Council of Churches provided food, shelter, medicine, clothing, and other services to all people who were victimized by the horrific, multisided civil war in Lebanon. It was the only organization trusted by the various Christians, Muslims, and Druze who were fighting one another. The Christians with whom I worked in Lebanon took seriously the call to love God and love your neighbor as yourself. Many visibly tried to live out the Golden Rule.[26]

Muslims engaged in prison ministries in the United States provide another compelling model for responsible mission. Christian clergy and chaplains in various denominations openly acknowledge that their Muslim colleagues have been far more successful in drug and prison rehabilitation programs. Reaching out to people in dire need and providing a nurturing community for the path back to responsible life in society is a powerful form of missionary activity. Unfortunately, most non-Muslims in the United States see only glimpses of this dimension of Islam through popular books and movies, such as the story of Malcolm X. A better understanding of the positive manifestations of Islamic mission can help offset the media propensity to focus on what is most violent and sensational. It can also help non-Muslims appreciate one reason Islam is rapidly emerging as the second largest religion in the United States.

A Human View of Truth

Truth claims are ubiquitous. But truth is often elusive. What is the truth about the presidential election results from Florida in 2000? What is the truth at the heart of the Israeli-Palestinian conflict? Sincere and intelligent people identify and articulate different truths even when political events are analyzed continuously for weeks, months, and years. However hard we may try to be objective, our ways of sorting and processing information about complex issues are necessarily conditioned by many factors.

We do well to remember that religious truth claims concern issues and events about which we have far less tangible data than the two examples above. Human beings are subjective and conditioned in ways we do and don't readily perceive. The fact that I was born in 1950 and raised in Tulsa, Oklahoma, in the midst of the post–World War II baby boom—as opposed to Bombay or Cairo or Tokyo or Boston, as were my Jewish cousins—makes a substantial difference in my religious orientation to the world. My background and worldview shape the way I frame religious questions. This is not bad or wrong. It does mean that my experiences and understanding of God—however powerful and life changing these have been—do not exhaust all the possibilities.

The need for fixed stars, for certainty in the midst of our tenuous lives on a dangerously unpredictable planet, is real and understandable. Religious leaders who can package and deliver absolute truths find receptive audiences. Tune in religious broadcasting for a few hours, and you will hear preacher after preacher speak with absolute certainty that he (or occasionally she) has all the answers to life's most troubling questions. Evangelical Protestants in the West are not the only ones who propagate absolute truth claims. The rise in various forms of fundamentalism around the world is connected to the desire for clarity and guidance in a rapidly changing world.

It is much easier to know the truth than to seek it. But religious life is a journey through which we learn, unlearn, change, and grow. Religious truths are crucial; they are not easily bottled up or circumscribed by absolutist claims. On the contrary, the pursuit of religious truth is an ongoing process. For Christians, religious education in seminaries and Sunday schools, Bible studies, sermons, and retreats all point to the fact that there is always more to learn, that new information or ways of looking at things is good and healthy. It isn't all set in stone. Even those who devote their lives daily to learning and educating are constantly changing. To illustrate, ask a member of the clergy the following question: Do you ever go back and read your sermons from two or five or ten years ago? How have your views changed? Every clergyperson I know who does this admits it is a humbling discipline. They sometimes happily discover gems or insights that have slipped off the radar screen. More often, they find that continued growth and learning help them frame issues somewhat differently now. The same will be true five years hence. The greatest and most prolific evangelist of the early church, the apostle Paul, was not bashful about presenting his views on all types of issues. But even he acknowledged our human limitations:

> For we know only in part, and we prophesy only in part; but when the complete comes, the partial will come to an end. When I was a child, I spoke like a child, I thought like a child, I reasoned like a child; when I became an adult, I put an end to childish ways. For now, we see in a mirror, dimly, but then face to face. Now I know only in part; then I will know, even as I have been fully known. (1 Corinthians 13:9–12)

The New Testament writers used highly symbolic and metaphorical language when describing God: God is Spirit (John 4:24); God is light (1 John 1:5); God is love (1 John 4:8). Jesus frequently spoke in parables about God's relationship with creation. But we also find selected New Testament passages that, on the surface at least, appear to make definitive and exclusivist statements about Jesus in relation to God. The two most quoted passages are found in the Gospel of John and the Book of Acts: "Jesus said to him [Thomas], I am the way, and the truth and the life. No one comes to the Father except through me" (John 14:6); and, "There is salvation in no one else, for there is no other name [but Jesus] under heaven given among mortals by which we must be saved" (Acts 4:12).

Wesley Ariarajah, a United Methodist minister from Sri Lanka who served for a decade on the staff of the World Council of Churches in Geneva, addresses the question of truth claims posed by such exclusivist texts. He suggests that the key to understanding is found in discerning the language of faith and love. He reminds us that the Gospel of John deliberately uses events in Jesus' life to introduce theological discourses on the significance of Jesus to the community of faith.

> What we should remember, however, is that these are all statements of faith about Jesus the Christ. They derive their meaning in the context of faith and have no meaning outside the community of faith. They hold enormous significance for Christian people, today as in the past.[27]

Ariarajah argues that it is possible to embrace and affirm religious truth without defining truth for others. He suggests we can find our way forward by untangling the notion of absolute truth from confessional statements uttered in the language of faith and love. He illustrates the distinction in a way all parents can readily understand:

When my daughter tells me I'm the best daddy in the world, and there can be no other father like me, she is speaking the truth, for this comes out of her experience. She is honest about it; she knows no other person in the role of her father. But of course it is not true in another sense. For one thing, I myself know friends who, I think, are better fathers than I am. Even more importantly, one should be aware that in the next house there is another little girl who also thinks her daddy is the best father in the world. And she too is right. In fact at the level of the way the two children relate to their two fathers, no one can compare the truth content of the statements of the two girls. For here we are not dealing with the absolute truths, but with the language of faith and love. . . . The language of the Bible is also the language of faith. . . . The problem begins when we take these confessions in the language of faith and love and turn them into absolute truths. It becomes much more serious when we turn them into truths on the basis of which we begin to measure the truth or otherwise of other faith claims. My daughter cannot say to her little friend in the next house that there is no way she can have the best father, for the best one is right there in her house. If she does, we'll have to dismiss it as child-talk![28]

A human view of truth, one that is dynamic and relational, enables religious people to embrace and affirm foundational truths without necessarily solidifying the words into static, absolute, propositional statements. Conversely, religious convictions that become locked into absolute truths can easily lead people to see themselves as God's agents. People so emboldened are capable of violent and destructive behavior in the name of religion.

~ *Three* ~
BLIND OBEDIENCE

Few people knew anything about Asahara Shoko, the founder and leader of Aum Shinrikyo, prior to March 20, 1995. Asahara and his movement attracted world attention when his devoted followers simultaneously released sarin, the deadly nerve gas, in sixteen central Tokyo subway stations shortly after 8 A.M. that day. Within minutes of the stunning attack, Japanese television stations were broadcasting live pictures of disoriented rush-hour commuters coughing, vomiting, and collapsing as they emerged from the subway stations. The assault left twelve people dead, more than five thousand injured, and a nation in shocked disbelief.

Japanese police immediately launched a nationwide investigation centered on Aum Shinrikyo, a largely unknown religious sect. They discovered a movement of approximately 10,000 members spread among twenty-five centers in Japan and another 30,000 followers in Russia. The membership in Japan included an inner circle of 1,247 people who had renounced society and were living in one of the centers or communities. These devotees formed the core group that embraced the evolving teachings of Asahara with blind obedience. Less than two months after the subway attacks, the police found Asahara hiding in secret room filled with cash and gold bars at one of Aum Shinrikyo's major centers located in a village at the foot of Mount Fuji.[1]

Scholars and students of new religious movements in Japan have focused considerable attention on Aum Shinrikyo in the months and years since the chemical weapons were unleashed in the subway stations. The group was subsequently linked to an earlier sarin attack that killed six and injured six hundred in 1994 as well as several murders of "uncooperative" members, a lawyer who was working with disconcerted parents of Aum devotees, and others. The picture that emerged paralleled that of many other high-profile religious sects or cults. Aum Shinrikyo formed in 1986 as people gathered around a charismatic leader whose eclectic teachings drew from the deep well of established religious traditions: Buddhism, Hinduism, and Christianity. In the beginning, Asahara's teachings spoke to both the hearts and minds of his idealistic young followers. Less than a decade later, however, Asahara demanded unquestioning devotion to his destructive and apocalyptic vision. Those who had renounced society and were living in the Aum communities no longer needed to think for themselves. Master Asahara's views were all that mattered.

This is a pivotal point at which religion often becomes evil. Authentic religion engages the intellect as people wrestle with the mystery of existence and the challenges of living in an imperfect world. Conversely, blind obedience is a sure sign of corrupt religion. Beware of any religious movement that seeks to limit the intellectual freedom and individual integrity of its adherents. When individual believers abdicate personal responsibility and yield to the authority of a charismatic leader or become enslaved to particular ideas or teachings, religion can easily become the framework for violence and destruction.

RELIGIOUS SECTS AND CULTS

Religious sects and cults provide a helpful lens through which to observe and analyze distinctions between healthy and corrupt religion. They are typically small enough that one can focus meaning-fully on the primary leader(s) and the central tenets of the movement. And they reflect patterns common to most of the recognized religious traditions. It is important to address a built-in bias at this point. Most of us bring preconceived notions to the terms *sects* and *cults*, regarding them negatively. The terms and the groups they refer to, however, are not inherently sinister. Sects are simply alternative religious organizations with traditional beliefs and practices; cults deviate more from conventional religious organizations by virtue of novel beliefs and practices. While social scientists use the terms for description, in popular usage the terms, particularly *cults*, carry a pejorative connotation.[2] Contemporary negative associations stem largely from media images of individuals and groups in which something has gone dreadfully wrong. The case of Aum Shinrikyo is typical. There are dozens of new religious movements in Japan, the large majority of which pose no visible threat to Japanese people or society. Adherents in the various new religions make up approximately 10 percent of the population in Japan today. How and why this particular sect—and others we will examine below—veered off the path of esoteric Buddhism and traditional ascetic practices toward indiscriminate violence are the key questions.

Almost all religious traditions begin as what we today would call a sect or cult. They start out as small movements inspired or led by people experienced by others as highly gifted or insightful. The leader rarely brings a totally new message. Rather, the teachings are better understood as much-needed correctives or reforms or deeper insights into existing traditions. The majority community from which the sect or cult deviates predictably views the new movement as dangerous or heretical. We can see the pattern in the formation of major religions as well as in substantial groups within particular communities of faith: Christianity began as a movement within Jewish life in first-century Palestine; Siddhartha Gautama, the Buddha, was one of many such spiritual seekers within the classical Hindu tradition; the message of

Islam did not originate with Muhammad, whom Muslims understand to be the last in a long succession of prophets and messengers bringing God's message to humankind; John Wesley, the "founder" of the Methodist Church, was a reform-minded leader who never left the Anglican Church; and so on.[3]

Countless religious movements began as sects, cults, or offshoots of established religions. Most of them flourished and faded over a period of years or sometimes centuries. Those few that have developed into the major religions of the world continually spawn new movements and incorporate a wide variety of sectarian groups within the larger framework: several thousand different Orthodox, Catholic, and Protestant communities are included in the Christian church today; various Sunni, Shi'ite, and Sufi schools and sects are recognized within Islam; there are scores of Theravada, Mahayana, and Vajrayana Buddhist schools worldwide; hundreds of religious traditions make up what is generically termed Hinduism in the West; and many groups can be identified within the Orthodox, Conservative, and Reform branches of Judaism.

Students of comparative religion or of one major religious tradition or of a particular place or time in history know well how many religious sects, cults, and movements operate within their area of inquiry. Nonspecialists often know little or don't think much about the many groups present in any given place or religious tradition until the media spotlight calls attention to a particularly bizarre or extreme development. Viewing the group in question through the lens of its violent or repulsive behavior makes it difficult for most people to imagine how anyone could be drawn to or guided by the teachings of an Asahara Shoko or Jim Jones or David Koresh or a particular Shi'ite leader in Iran or Lebanon. The initial attractions, however, are often quite similar to what we find in nonthreatening groups. Closer inspection of particular sects helps clarify how charismatic leadership, the impulse to withdraw from society, and unwavering commitment to compelling ideas and teachings can work together to bring disaster on adherents and those around them.

CHARISMATIC AUTHORITY FIGURES

In the minds of many baby boomer and older North Americans, Jim Jones and the Peoples Temple constitute Exhibit A for religion becoming evil. The gruesome images of 914 bloated corpses sprawled in the communal clearing in the jungle of Guyana that was Jonestown are forever seared into our memories. How and why would so many people—with their children—line up to receive the deadly potion prepared for the suicidal end to this doomsday cult? Conflicting versions of events that led up to and precipitated the mass suicide-murder on November 18, 1978, continue to appear in books and articles and on Web sites devoted to understanding this group and assisting surviving members and families of those who perished. This much is clear: by the end, Jim Jones was highly unstable and addicted to several drugs; some members of the community were losing confidence in his authoritarian leadership, while many others followed his dictates to their deaths, or "revolutionary suicides"; a few people escaped the cataclysmic end, while the large majority perished voluntarily or were forcibly required to drink the deadly concoction.[4]

James Warren Jones was born in Indiana during the height of the Great Depression in 1931. He appears to have been influenced a great deal by both Pentecostalism and social idealism rooted in socialist and communist materials he read. Jones's ministry began in earnest in September 1954 when he preached at the Laurel Street Tabernacle in Indianapolis, an Assemblies of God church. His message of racial integration was too progressive for most members. In April 1955 Jones and a few members of the tabernacle left to form the Wings of Deliverance (later renamed the Peoples Temple Full Gospel Church). The deep commitment to racial equality and social justice led one of the most liberal Protestant denominations, the Christian Church (Disciples of Christ), to ordain Jones and include the Peoples Temple in its communion in 1960. This extraordinary development—ordaining a person without formal theological training and embracing a Pentecostal church as one of its own—reveals how some mainline Protestants viewed Jones as a courageous and visionary leader.[5]

The years in Indiana were tumultuous. Jones and his congregation endured many threats and faced great hostility, as did many others advocating change during the height of the civil rights movement. He preached a social gospel of human freedom, equality, and love. Jones also preached constantly about an impending nuclear conflagration that would end the world, and he conducted faith healing services in which people with ailments from cancer to arthritis were allegedly cured. By 1965 Jones had become convinced that the Peoples Temple should move to California, where, he believed, racial equality would be more readily embraced. Some seventy families—half African American and half Caucasian—made the move with Jones.[6] Clearly, this movement was distinctive. Its message involved a commitment to a religious community that transcended ties to home and jobs. The Peoples Temple grew steadily during the next decade, forming a second congregation in 1972. Members lived in a communal society, giving their income, real estate, insurance policies, and other assets to the temple to be shared equally by everyone. Jones's societal vision was increasingly communist. Serious problems began to surface as several disgruntled members spoke out about internal conflicts; some leveled charges of illegal activities within the temple. Public scrutiny and media exposés were relentless. Jones determined it was time to withdraw from the United States. The temple acquired a tract of land in Guyana in 1974. Less than three years later, fifty people were living in the Peoples Temple Agricultural Mission, a community literally carved out of the jungle.

Speaking from Guyana via telephone to temple members back in California on July 31, 1977, Jones made clear his hostility toward U.S. society:

> I know some of you are wanting to fight, but that's exactly what
> the system wants—they want to use us as sacrificial lambs, as a

scapegoat. Don't fall into this trap by yielding to violence, no matter what kinds of lies are told on us or how many. Peoples Temple has helped practically every political prisoner in the United States. We've reached out to everyone who is oppressed, and that is what is bothering them. We've organized poor people and given them a voice. The system doesn't mind corporate power for the ruling elite, but for the first time we've given corporate power to the little man and that's an unforgivable sin. And that's the whole problem in a nutshell.[7]

Jones's political disenfranchisement found expression in a self-reliant communal setting. He also broke away from his earlier version of biblical Christianity. He claimed the Bible was full of lies and contradictions. At Jonestown he attacked the "sky God" even as he claimed a form of divine status for himself:

You prayed to the sky-God and he never heard your prayers. You asked and begged and pleaded for help with your suffering, and he never gave you any food. He never provided a bed. He never gave you a home. But I, the socialist worker god, have given you all those things![8]

Life in Jonestown was very demanding: eleven-hour workdays; meetings or other duties occupying many nights; minimal food—mostly beans and rice. Though Jones was rarely seen during the final year, his lengthy discourses were frequently broadcast over loudspeakers. A key feature of his theological framework was what he called "revolutionary suicide." He would periodically test the loyalty and commitment of his followers by asking them to drink a liquid he said contained poison. These episodes no doubt served to desensitize some to the reality of mass suicide. Jones continued to speak of an impending apocalypse characterized by race and class wars and genocide in the United States, linking this to the need for his followers to make the "ultimate sacrifice" for "the cause."[9]

Jim Jones's fear of an external attack provided justification for armed guards around the compound. Having labored for months to clear land and build homes, a school, a hospital, and other structures, many People's Temple members were understandably alarmed at the prospect of a hostile assault on their community. The guards, however, also served another purpose: they prevented Jonestown residents from leaving. Concerned relatives in the United States often described Jonestown as a concentration camp. The mounting pressure from relatives led California congressman Leo Ryan to travel to Guyana on a fact-finding mission. Ryan arrived on November 17. He and his delegation were murdered the next day at the airstrip as their plane was preparing to depart. Jones then implemented the revolutionary suicide plan. Eyewitnesses who escaped reported many people voluntarily pouring the cyanide-laced purple liquid down their children's throats before drinking it themselves. Many others protested but were shot or forcibly poisoned by the armed guards. When investigators later reached the morbid scene, they discovered 638 adults and 276 children among the mass murder-suicide victims.

Jim Jones died at age forty-eight, some twenty-three years after launching his public ministry in Indiana. His charismatic leadership and message of social and economic justice touched the hearts and minds of many people, especially those who felt trapped at the bottom of the economic, political, and social ladder. He offered a message of hope and possible healing for people in search of both. The idealistic appeal of his communistic and egalitarian approach to life in the Peoples Temple was far more compelling between the mid-1950s and the early 1970s than many today might imagine. His vision was based not only in socialist and communist political theory, but also in the experience of the early Christian community. Like many other Christian cult leaders, Jones found inspiration in the communal living and sharing of resources practiced by the church under the apostle Peter's leadership.

Now the whole group of those who believed were of one heart and soul, and no one claimed private ownership of any possessions, but everything they owned was held in common. . . . There was not a needy person among them, for as many as owned lands or houses sold them and brought the proceeds of what was sold. They laid it at the apostles' feet, and it was distributed to each as any had need. (Acts 4:32, 34–35)

The passage continues with the stunning account of Ananias and Sapphira, a husband and wife who are struck dead at Peter's feet within three hours of withholding some assets from the church and lying about it. As with other examples cited in the chapter above, the story of Ananias and Sapphira and the communistic approach of the church led by Peter are somehow overlooked by most fundamentalist Christian ministers. They who insist that the Bible must be interpreted literally presumably don't imagine too many people will actually read and ponder the biblical texts. When people read and think for themselves they may discover provocative stories like this and then raise appropriate questions.

The story in Acts ends with a descriptive comment: "And great fear seized the whole church and all who heard these things" (Acts 5:11). I should think so. The story certainly gets your attention. In most churches people feel good about themselves for giving a tithe, or 10 percent, of their income.[10] In Peter's church, dire consequences awaited those who "kept back some of the proceeds, and brought only a part and laid it at the apostles' feet" (Acts 5:2). A biblical story like this is a powerful tool in the hands of a charismatic leader like Jim Jones.

Toward the end a growing number of followers were disconcerted by Jim Jones's ideas and increasingly erratic behavior. By that point, sadly, they were literally trapped far from their country of citizenship. An effort to bridge the gap created by their physical isolation, the official congressional fact-finding mission, proved to be the catalyst for disaster. At the same time, many other members of the

Peoples Temple behaved like sheep being led to the slaughter. They had long since shelved their individual intellectual integrity; they trusted Jim Jones to do their thinking for them. They were blindly obedient to a charismatic leader whose journey—theologically from Pentecostalism to the Disciples of Christ to scorn for the "sky-God" of the Bible; physically from Indiana to California to the jungle of Guyana—would seem to an outside observer too implausible to carry the story line of a fictional book or Hollywood screenplay.

Similar patterns are evident in the behavior and teachings of Asahara Shoko and his followers. While some journalists have described Asahara as little more than a delusional madman or a deceptive swindler seeking money and power, thoughtful scholars argue that the evolution of his eclectic teachings can be understood in context. His appeal to tens of thousands in Japan and Russia cannot be dismissed so casually. Shimazono Susumu traces Asahara and Aum Shinrikyo's early development (1984–87) in terms of esoteric Buddhist teachings and practices: freedom from *karma* through rigorous yoga and magical ritual processes; a teaching and training system for passing knowledge from master to pupil; and the achievement of liberation—absolute happiness, absolute liberation—by transcending life and death.[11] Asahara's focus on individual liberation, which was believed to be greatly facilitated by an initiation process involving the transfer of spiritual power from the master, widened into a vision of salvation for humanity. In the late 1980s he often spoke optimistically about his hope of establishing an ideal society based on the legendary utopia of Shambhala.

> Shambhala . . . , ruled by the god Shiva, is a world that only those souls who have penetrated the full truth of the universe may enter. There the world's saviors, whose goal it is to save all souls and lead them to *gedatsu* [salvation]. . . . Master Asahara has been reborn from that realm into the human world so that he might take up his messianic mission. Thus the Master's efforts to embody truth throughout the human world are in

accordance with the great will of the god Shiva. . . . The plan to transform Japan into Shambhala is the first step towards transforming the whole world into Shambhala.[12]

Asahara then outlined the "Lotus Village Plan," a vision for living communally in an independent society in which all needs—food, clothing, housing, places for religious practice, education, medical care—would be met. Twenty-five centers were thus established throughout Japan. Woven into his teachings one also finds prophetic utterances about an Armageddonlike war at the end of the century. There was a clear a shift in 1989. At that point Asahara believed that Armageddon was inevitable and one-fourth of the world's population would perish. His writings include references to the book of Revelation, and he cites conflicts in the Middle East as clear signs of the apocalypse. He acknowledged that his "plan for salvation [was] behind schedule and the percentage of those who will survive [was] getting lower and lower."[13] In a harbinger of things to come, his focus was changing from preventing catastrophe to living in survival mode. At about the same time, the group started getting negative press for its aggressive recruiting and fund-raising practices. From Asahara's perspective, time was short and the future of the world hung in the balance. The end he envisioned justified any means, including coercion and violence. A lawyer representing discontented families of Aum members suddenly disappeared along with his family. Well-founded suspicions of foul play led to more vocal opposition from other Aum family members. Fearing that time was running out for the plan of salvation and that the efficacy of their religious activities was insufficient, Aum leaders decided to run twenty-five members in the 1990 parliamentary elections. All of them were defeated. Asahara's movement turned inward; the Lotus Village Plan leading to Shambhala began to look more like a large version of the fallout shelter defense plan many Americans implemented in the 1950s and '60s.

In the early to mid-1990s, Asahara's teachings and some Aum practices were decidedly violent. Aum members participated in kidnappings, drugging, electric shock treatments, and even murder. People with no desire to join were sometimes forcibly brought to centers and drugged; members who tried to leave were locked in cells for long periods. This aggressive and violent posture appears connected to the certainty of an imminent, catastrophic war.[14] Asahara's later teachings also included a "compassionate" rationale for violence. Maekawa Michiko explains how Asahara's doctrine of *poa* led to the subway attacks:

Aum [members] interpreted *poa* to include killing certain persons in order to prevent them from accumulating more bad *karma* that would have to be worked out in future lifetimes; hence, it was a compassionate act. . . . The subway gas incident was simply another opportunity to extend an interpretation that had already been applied to earlier acts of violence. Anyone who stepped outside this faith and interpretive framework that legitimized violence faced the harsh reality that one had in fact committed what Buddhist teaching regards as the greatest sin—destroying life.[15]

As with Jim Jones and the Peoples Temple, this brief overview is far from a comprehensive analysis of Asahara Shoko's teachings and the development of Aum Shinrikyo. Several striking features are clear, however. A charismatic leader demanding total obedience stands at the center of this religious cult. Asahara was understood as the true guide who had already experienced enlightenment; for some he was divine. Veneration of a religious leader becomes dangerous when that leader has unrestricted power and total control. Aum Shinrikyo provided little room for independent opinions or debate among adherents. The guru knew all. Like Siddhartha Gautama, Asahara was embraced by followers as a path breaker. Clearly absent in Aum, however, was the traditional Buddhist emphasis on ethical training and a life of virtue along the path. The Buddha taught the Noble Eightfold Path and thus provided signposts along the way; the means are very much connected with the desired end. Not so with Asahara.

Charismatic religious leadership is not inherently bad. On the contrary, it is a vital and central feature of every religious tradition. Think of the contributions of Mahatma Gandhi and Martin Luther King Jr. during the twentieth century. They were extraordinary, charismatic leaders who changed their countries—and the world. But they were human beings, not gods. They were well aware of their human limitations and shortcomings. They did not command total obedience to their deeply held beliefs and teachings. Gandhi and King spoke in the context of their respective religious traditions, appealing to peoples' consciences and inviting participation in their noble causes. Their movements did not systematically manipulate or coerce followers. The integrity of their messages and movements did not prohibit intellectual scrutiny. Rather, their style of leadership and clear teachings spoke to the head and the heart. Those who embraced their movements did so voluntarily; they were free to withdraw or reduce the level of their participation if they wished.

Leaders demanding or expecting total obedience can and do find willing followers. Corrupt religion frequently includes coercive pressure tactics designed to keep members in line. In some cases, devotees are even "recruited" through overt manipulation. Various analysts focus on brainwashing tactics sometimes employed by nascent religious groups. The proliferation of sects and cults in the late 1960s and 1970s produced a corresponding cottage industry: deprogrammers. Family members of many who joined groups like the Children of God or the Unification Church, for instance, were often convinced that their relatives had been cleverly manipulated or brainwashed into joining the group. There is ample evidence that some religious groups, including the Peoples Temple and Aum Shinrikyo, used methods of isolation, physical deprivation, group pressure, and even drugs at certain points. Thus blind obedience is not always or necessarily a purely voluntary matter. It is nonetheless a sure sign of religion becoming evil.

While the examples considered above represent extremes, scores of charismatic leaders and groups in religious traditions around the world largely fit the profile. Dangers abound when people take direction uncritically from religious authorities. And as we have observed in the previous chapter on absolute truth claims, there is no shortage of self-appointed leaders who are confident they have all the answers; more than a few regularly claim to speak for God. While we have focused on highly visible figures, the same perilous dynamic is operating wherever a religious leader has excessive power and few restraints.

In contemporary Islam, a version of this phenomenon has been evident during major conflicts in Iran and Lebanon. In these turbulent settings the powerful influence of both highly visible and little-known religious leaders becomes clear. Although Sunni Islam technically has no clergy, the minority Shi'ite tradition features a hierarchical structure of religious leaders. The highest position is that of ayatollah.[16] In order to reach this position, a leader must have a large number of Muslims looking to him for guidance on all types of religious and personal matters. Such was the case with Ayatollah Khomeini, the leading cleric in the Iranian revolution of 1978–79.

Khomeini was a remarkable figure. He was a popular leader who boldly and consistently challenged the exploitation and brutal excesses of the Pahlavi regime. His opposition to what he and others experienced as injustice had come at a high cost over the years. Large numbers of his followers were tortured or killed, including his own son, and he himself was imprisoned and exiled. To most Iranians, Khomeini was a principled, moral Islamic leader around whom they could rally to remove an authoritarian regime. When I, along with six other Americans, met Khomeini at his home in Qum on Christmas Day of 1979, we encountered a soft-spoken, grandfatherly figure. Though he was eighty years old, he was, in my experience, very charismatic; his eyes were alive and engaging. Over the course of eight weeks in Iran during the next thirteen months, I saw him again in person and for many hours on television. My impressions from that first meeting remained the same. I met personally with four other ayatollahs during three trips to Iran. The level of their political activism varied substantially. They were all highly charismatic leaders. Two of them were warm and inviting; they rank among the most interesting people I've ever met. Two others were clearly cognizant of and pleased with their powerful positions; one, Ayatollah Khalkali, was truly frightening.

As we saw with the sinister figures of Jim Jones and Asahara Shoko, powerful, charismatic leaders defy simple analysis. There are many positive and attractive dimensions to their teachings. The same was true—indeed, much more so, in my view—with the Ayatollah Khomeini. But when religious leaders have great power over their followers, danger always lurks nearby. When they instruct followers to pursue violent actions and people follow those directions uncritically, the probability for abuse is extremely high. During the horrific, decade-long Iran-Iraq war, the Ayatollah Khomeini called on Iranian teenagers to charge across minefields shouting, "God is greatest." The call for action was accompanied by a promise of paradise for martyrs. Several thousand perished after accepting the directive obediently. Khomeini's famous *fatwa*, or legal ruling, that Salman Rushdie should die for his blasphemous book, *The Satanic Verses*, mobilized dutiful would-be assassins and forced Rushdie into hiding in England. Similarly, as discussed previously, several prominent Shi'ite leaders in Lebanon have called for the ultimate physical self-sacrifice of their faithful—suicide bombings or acts of martyrdom, depending on one's interpretative framework. Several hundred people have answered the call.

Powerful ideas and teachings—even destructive ones—frequently transcend the sphere of influence enjoyed by a particular charismatic leader. Suicide bombings as acts of martyrdom were inspired by particular religious authority figures in Lebanon. These heinous acts subsequently became a weekly occurrence among Sunni Muslim Palestinians as the conflict in Israel/Palestine escalated during the first half of 2002.

ENSLAVEMENT TO DOCTRINES

The dangers associated with the lack of intellectual scrutiny toward religious leaders are just as real when it comes to powerful religious ideas or doctrines. Both Jim Jones and Asahara Shoko spoke repeatedly about the approach of Armageddon. Dire apocalyptic doctrines were central components in their respective religious understandings. When the unquestioned authority figure declares a cataclysmic end is near, what else really matters? Everything about normal daily life pales by comparison. Public criticism of the group and family interventions simply reinforce the view that the evil world is hostile to the truth and the end is near. Typically, the group becomes even more introverted and withdraws even further from the larger society.

A distinctive feature for some apocalyptic groups, however, is a belief that somehow they can mitigate or at least survive the inevitable conflagration.[17] Both Jim Jones and Asahara Shoko continued to offer a measure of hope to their followers even as the end loomed just ahead. This, too, is a key ingredient. Rather than simply sit waiting for the inevitable,[18] the leader articulates specific things that can and must be done. Thus, many continue to follow instructions dutifully for months and years despite the dramatic shifts in doctrine and behavior being propagated. The obvious inconsistencies and reprehensible behavior visible from outside the group clearly are not obvious to those who are blindly obedient.

I teach a course at Wake Forest entitled Conceptions of the Afterlife. Students are intrigued by the course since they, like everyone else, have a vested interest in the question "What happens when you die?" The course explores the phenomena of near-death experiences and the various ways the major world religions have treated this question. The students discover that the question of afterlife is organically connected with larger understandings about the meaning of existence. They also discover striking similarities amid the rich diversity. Teachings about a cataclysmic war and savior figures at the end of time or a cycle of existence are woven into many traditions. They provide adherents symbolic ways of addressing ultimate questions of injustice and undergirding hope for a better future in a world to come. When those teachings are embraced as likely scenarios on the immediate horizon, otherwise bizarre behavior often becomes commonplace. Religion may not always be demonstrably evil in these contexts; it is frequently mindless and destructive.

The powerful allure of apocalyptic doctrines is as old as religion. Norman Cohn's classical study of Christian millenarian and mystical anarchists in the Middle Ages, *The Pursuit of the Millennium*, chronicles dozens of individuals and groups whose messianic and apocalyptic visions wreaked havoc all over Europe for centuries.[19] False messiahs and mystical teachings about dramatic and immediate change on the horizon wove their way through the Jewish tradition as well. One of the most famous messianic movements swirled around the seventeenth-century figures Nathan of Gaza and Shabbatai Zevi. In 1665 and 1666 Nathan promoted the messianic fervor by circulating extraordinary letters and starting astonishing rumors about Zevi. Mass hysteria broke out in Palestine and various parts of Europe and as far to the east as Iran. Zevi turned traditional teachings and customary laws inside out in anticipation of the Day of Redemption: June 18, 1666. If a rabbi protested, Zevi would denounce him as an unclean animal and the mobs of zealous supporters would often attack his house. Many sold all their possessions and began a pilgrimage to the Holy Land. The Jewish zealotry alarmed Muslim officials. Zevi was arrested in September of 1666 in Constantinople. Presented with the option of converting to Islam or facing death, Zevi converted and lived out his days on a modest government stipend. Remarkably, these events did not end the movement. Zevi's betrayal was interpreted by the faithful as a clever development. He was now a kind of Trojan horse within the empire of Islam. For over a century, a segment of the Jewish population in Europe and Palestine remained enslaved to the idea of Shabbatai Zevi as messiah.[20] Remnants of the movement continued into the twentieth century.

Jim Jones and Asahara Shoko joined a long line of religious leaders who have discovered the compelling power of this doctrine. The specifics vary over time and across traditions, but teachings predicting imminent catastrophe and a reversal of life as we know it are widespread. It is another form of the absolute truth claims we examined in the previous chapter. When people embrace this orientation, their brains often appear to stop working properly; they no longer rely on their judgment and common sense. In the next chapter we will explore one dimension of this further, trying to help God create an ideal time on earth.

Law enforcement authorities are well aware of the dangers posed by people in the grip of apocalyptic or millenarian fervor. While many people feared Y2K computer-related chaos as the year 2000 approached, the FBI was busily preparing Project Megiddo. Megiddo is a hill in northern Israel from which the name Armageddon is derived. The FBI prepared a strategic assessment of the potential for domestic terrorism in the United States in anticipation of or in response to the arrival of the new millennium. Its report sketches primary doctrines and practices under the following categories: Christian Identity, White Supremacy, Militias, Black Hebrew Israelites, and Apocalyptic Cults.[21] In a parallel development, the government of Israel detained or deported leaders from several dozen potentially dangerous religious groups during the final months of 1999. The U.S. and Israeli governments had good reason to be concerned about the dangers posed by small groups of true believers. The sarin gas attack in Tokyo was a wake-up call. The events of September 11, 2001, would later vindicate the need for vigilance. It doesn't take many people to wreak havoc on a large scale.

Apocalyptic doctrines illuminate a larger issue. Uncritical acceptance of popular or even conventional doctrines is never wise. All the more so when the teachings encourage or even demand violent or destructive actions. Sometimes the behavior is so shocking it gives rise to terminology recognized in many languages. The term *thug*, for instance, comes from "religious" behavior of a particular group of devotees of the Hindu goddess Kali. For more than a thousand years, the *thags* robbed and then murdered victims, offering the bodies and one-third of the proceeds to the goddess of death and destruction. Their methods of dispatching male victims (women were not supposed to be murdered) included poison, drowning, burning alive, and garroting; the shedding of blood was not permitted in their ritual murders. The *thags* were particularly active in the northern and central parts of India.

We can find parallels here with members of a Shi'ite sect, the Assassins, who terrorized Syria and Persia between the eleventh and thirteenth centuries. The designation comes from the Arabic word *hashashin* ("consumers of hashish"). The name was applied to an extremely militant group of the Nizari branch of Isma'ili Shi'ites. This esoteric sect controlled a number of fortresses in Syria and was, effectively, a kingdom within a kingdom. The Assassins struck fear in the hearts of their enemies through terrorism and targeted murder of selected political leaders. A favorite tactic involved infiltrating the ranks of adversaries. Once he gained trust, the Assassin would stab his intended victim. Many political opponents sought compromise with the sect out of fear. The group disappeared following the Mongul invasion in 1256. Their association with hashish is obscure at best. The appellation probably originated with stories about the use of drugs during initiation ceremonies or possibly as a disparaging reference to the group.[22] However faulty the etymology, the crusaders carried the term back to Europe, where it found its way into Latin, French, Italian, and other languages.

Examples of religious groups embracing teachings that support deplorable behavior are painfully clear when looking back on the doctrines in question. Reading through volumes of "Christian" sermons in support of slavery or apartheid today accentuates the point. Authentic religion encourages questions and reflection at all levels. When authority figures discourage or disallow honest questions, something clearly is wrong. Doctrinal positions supporting otherwise unethical behavior must always be challenged. This is much easier said than done, particularly when there is strong social pressure to conform within the community of faith. One of the most common ways such pressure is applied is when groups define themselves over against the larger society. Some groups physically withdraw from the perceived corrupt society around them.

WITHDRAWAL FROM SOCIETY

Our survey of both the Peoples Temple and Aum Shinrikyo high-lights a pattern common to many sects and cults. The movements initially included noble programs to help save people or reform societal ills; they ended in stages of withdrawal, even isolation, from the larger society. People in the movement viewed the larger society as corrupt, as uninterested in being "saved," and they cited individuals and institutions in the larger society that were becoming overtly adversarial. Both groups physically withdrew. The creation of Jonestown in the midst of a jungle on another continent shows clearly the level of hostility and depth of societal rejection Jones and his community perceived. How much of the societal reaction was warranted by Jones's dubious or even criminal behavior is not the point. Their perception of hostility reinforced a worldview that set the group over against the evil "system" that, in Jones's words, regarded their empowering of poor people as "an unforgivable sin." Congressman Ryan's visit to Jonestown was the last straw for Jones.

At some level, virtually every group within every religious tradition must ask about its proper relationship to the larger society. Every religion postulates that something is seriously awry in human life. Teachings about the nature of the human predicament and guidance concerning the paths that can lead to the desired goals are key ingredients in every community of faith. Armed with this knowledge, believers must ask how they can best function in a world in which most others don't share the same understanding. Put another way: How can people of faith—be they Jews, Hindus, or Christians—live in the world but not be conformed to it? This dilemma necessarily produces a serious tension. When a Christian gets "saved," he or she does not go immediately to heaven.[23] When a Buddhist becomes enlightened, he or she remains in this world. The image of a beautiful lotus blossom floating atop a grimy, mucky pond conveys symbolically the Buddhist perception of life in this world.

Classical Hinduism includes a world-affirming and world-renouncing approach simultaneously. On the one hand, the caste system connects with the law of *karma* and reincarnation to provide an ethically coherent and systematic way to live responsibly in this world. Proper behavior in line with one's station in life (understood as having been determined by one's own *karma*) offers the hope of incremental advancement on the spiritual path. At a deeper level of spiritual awareness, the entire phenomenal world is understood to be illusory, not ultimately real. Thus, at the final stage of the spiritual path you find the *sannyasin*, the wandering ascetic who has cut all ties to this world.

The ways different groups within and across religious traditions sort out this tension vary a great deal. At one end of the spectrum, we find examples of communities that live largely apart from society in healthy ways. Groups like the Amish and monastic communities in various traditions are visible examples. Less dramatically, churches whose weekly schedules fill much of the nonworking time of their congregants effectively create a community apart. Mega-churches in many cities across the United States today have become self-enclosed communities with every conceivable sports and recreational program and all kinds of social and educational activities in addition to religious programs and services. Many now include private schools as well. These communities even offer "Christian" alternatives on Halloween, New Year's Eve, Fourth of July, and so on.

The impulse to nurture and educate the faithful with minimal interference from outside is common and understandable. The potential for serious problems escalates proportionately in relation to how detached the group is from the surrounding society and how effectively it holds its own leaders accountable to ethical guide-lines. The examples we've considered above underscore the danger-ous combination of strict segregation and unlimited power in the hands of one leader.

Another highly publicized recent example involved David Koresh and the Branch Davidians in Waco, Texas. The Branch Davidians are an offshoot of the Seventh-day Adventists. In 1935 the sect established a community called Mt. Carmel near Waco, Texas, in order to follow the teachings of their leader, Victor Houteff, without interference from mainstream society. Houteff died in 1955, and his wife, Florence, assumed leadership of the group. She announced that April 22, 1959, would mark the beginning of a new era. Over nine hundred people moved to Mt. Carmel from around the coun-try to await the predicted end. When nothing happened most peo-ple became disillusioned and began departing. A small remnant of about fifty people moved to a new Mt. Carmel some ten miles out-side Waco. The fledgling group persisted under inept leadership until Vernon Howell joined the group in 1981. Within a few years Howell assumed leadership of the group, declaring his God-appointed role as "Lamb of God." He changed his name to David Koresh in 1990. The name David refers to the Israelite king from whose line the messiah will come; Koresh is a version of Cyrus, the Persian king who liberated Jerusalem from the Babylonians and is hailed as a messiah in the Hebrew Bible.[24]

Koresh's "inspired" teachings centered on the forthcoming Armageddon. He announced his role as the one who would open the seven seals and interpret the scroll mentioned in the fifth chap-ter of the book of Revelation. This would bring about the second coming of Christ. Koresh believed the Apocalypse would take place in the United States, not in Israel/Palestine. He began a survivalist program, stockpiling food and weapons. He also determined that he was responsible for establishing the House of David and began the practice of taking "spiritual wives." Koresh deciphered selected biblical passages to mean that only the seed of the Lamb of God was pure and that he alone should have sexual relations with all the women at Mt. Carmel. Everyone, including married couples in the community, apparently agreed that this was the will of God. Though couched in different theological contexts, sexual license for the charismatic leader is a common pattern in many sects and cults. It was a factor with Jim Jones and Asahara Shoko as well. That followers would willingly embrace such behavior is a clear sign of blind obedience and minimal independent thinking or reliance on one's conscience.

The details surrounding the conflagration at Mt. Carmel on April 19, 1993, are many and varied. Sharp criticism has been and continues to be leveled at the federal Bureau of Alcohol, Tobacco, and Firearms and the FBI for instigating the conflict and fire resulting in the deaths of Koresh and some 75 of his followers, including 21 children.[25] Many Americans who had no enthusiasm for the Branch Davidians were deeply offended and angered by what they deemed inappropriate U.S. government intervention. The magnitude of the frustration became crystal clear exactly two years later when Timothy McVeigh's devastating truck bomb attack on the Murrah Federal Building in Oklahoma City killed 168 people (including 19 children) and injured over 500.

Freedom of religion is a cherished cornerstone of American life. Why were the Branch Davidians denied that right? Is it a federal crime to propagate views on biblical prophecy or to have sexual relations with consenting adults? Government intervention in this case was based ostensibly on two allegations: the procurement and stockpiling of weapons (including illegal weapons) and the abuse of children within the compound. These are legitimate areas of societal concern. A well-armed and highly apocalyptic group of true believers poses a credible threat to the wider society. Furthermore, the state does have both the right and the obligation to protect children and others who are incapable of protecting themselves. Social services can remove children from abusive parents, for instance, when the courts deem it necessary. It is important to remember that freedom from religion is a corollary to freedom of religion. Many cases concerning state intervention to mandate medical care for children of Christian Scientists or to mitigate against harsh corporeal punishment in private Christian schools remind us of the difficulty of knowing how and where to draw appropriate lines. So, too, with the Branch Davidian tragedy.

Religious communities inevitably define themselves over against or in some kind of tension with the wider society. However removed from society a group might be, the key questions turn on issues of authority and accountability. The more the power and authority are focused in one or a few people, the higher the likelihood of abuse. As long as the sect poses no threat to anyone other than freely participating adult adherents, people should be able to practice their religion without interference. The behavior may be bizarre or even self-destructive. But bizarre and self-destructive behavior—religious or otherwise—occurs all the time.)

The odd case of Marshall Applewhite and Heaven's Gate comes immediately to mind. Thirty-nine men and women willingly "exited their bodies" over a three-day period in March 1997. The group rented a luxury home in San Diego. They carefully planned their physical exit—apparently timed with the arrival of the Hale-Bopp comet—and systematically dispatched themselves with phenobarbital, vodka, and plastic bags. Unlike with many other groups, there was no sexual scandal. On the contrary, sexual relations were prohibited; eighteen of the men had been surgically castrated well before the mass suicide. As sad and strange as the case appeared to be, the cult posed no threat to anyone except the seemingly willing participants. Their neighbors in the San Diego suburbs were as shocked as everyone else. Later reports indicated that many of these devotees were very intelligent people. Perhaps. But group psychology can be very powerful.

Learning to think for oneself, particularly in the face of peer pressure, is a lesson most children get early and often from parents. Who among us has not tried to persuade their mom or dad to let them do something on the grounds that "everyone else is doing it"? The predictable parental response is: "Just because everyone else is doing it doesn't make it right. Would you jump off a cliff if everyone else were doing it? You have to learn to think for yourself!" Intellectual freedom, personal integrity, and common sense are indispensable in authentic religion as well. Any religious group that largely withdraws from society needs to ensure that people can think and make important decisions for themselves. A segregated group in which the thinking and critical decisions reside with one or a few people, particularly when apocalyptic teaching is involved, is a disaster waiting to happen.

HUMAN RESPONSIBILITY

Religious traditions teach that ultimate meaning is both connected to and transcends physical existence in this world. They may share this understanding and yet differ substantially on the precise content of teachings and practices. Two key points of almost universal agreement relate directly to our focus in this chapter. One such point is that human beings are ultimately responsible as individuals for their behavior. And what one does during one's time on earth is connected to a larger understanding of existence. For Hindus and Buddhists, the *karmic* consequences of one's actions are one's own. For Muslims, the book he or she is handed on the Day of Judgment is filled with his or her own deeds.

The major religions also include the hopeful message that human beings are not without information on how to live responsibly in this less-than-ideal world. Though the particulars differ, the teaching is essentially the same: human beings are not left alone to stumble aimlessly in the dark. The truth of what we need to know may lie within us or be available through external manifestations or both. However conceptualized, knowledge and guidance are available for individuals and communities of faith. Jesus pointed the way through his life and his actions. It is telling that he often taught in parables, enigmatic stories that illuminated one or more points. He was a rabbi, a teacher, not a dictator who demanded blind obedience. Jesus welcomed honest questions. So, too, did the Buddha, who also frequently used parables in his discourse with followers. In fact, the Buddha's primary mode of teaching was in response to questions. We know from *hadith* materials that Muhammad also welcomed inquiry on all manner of things. Jews have a long tradition of questioning the most fundamental teachings or even debating with God.

As religious traditions develop, gifted leaders and central doctrines are vitally important. But these are at best "treasures in earthen vessels." It is all too easy to get swept up in the emotional wake of a charismatic leader or a compelling idea. Blind obedience to individuals or to doctrines is never wise. Such behavior effectively abdicates individual responsibility, and, as we have observed, that can be dangerous.

The opposite of blindness is sight. Of all the senses, sight is the one most closely connected with knowledge. When someone "sees" something, she or he "knows" in a powerful way. The most compelling testimony in court comes from an "eyewitness." One can build a circumstantial case, but someone who "saw" something happen "knows" in a more convincing way than someone who "heard" or "smelled" or "touched" something. Recall the famous story of four blind men respectively describing an elephant after having a chance to "feel" it. The descriptions vary wildly depending on whether they felt its trunk, its ear, its leg, or its tail. The sense of feel can be misleading. Only when there is trickery involved do our eyes deceive us. Idiomatic expressions in daily discourse illustrate the connection between sight and knowledge. When you get a point someone is making, you say, "I see what you mean." Someone who understands something deeply has great "insight." After a mistake or debacle of some sort, a predictable lament goes something like this: "Looking back, I see now where we made the wrong turn." We commonly revere people who have a "vision" for the future or whose "foresight" is proven to be accurate.

Vision and sight are naturally connected with knowledge and truth in the universal religious metaphor of light. In all religions, light dispels darkness, making things visible and opening the way toward understanding. But truth, as we discussed in the previous chapter, is not easily captured or contained. What may appear to be unquestionably true in a particular time or place may be far less obvious in a different setting. Affirming the role of ordained women in ministry, for example, is a relatively recent development in church history. I am grateful that some people had the courage to question the prevailing wisdom of Christian leaders on this and many other seemingly fixed truths. In some parts of the Christian church, the idea of women as fully equal leaders in ministry remains unthinkable.

I recall well my own declaration of independence in the realm of spiritual inquiry. As a sophomore in college at Oklahoma State University, I was enrolled in the College of Business and on my way to a promising career in accounting. I was active in a popular para-church organization, Campus Crusade for Christ. I had also been very involved with Young Life and in Baptist churches in Tulsa and Stillwater. Having read virtually all of the materials and books my friends and leaders in Campus Crusade had recommended, I decided I'd like to take a religion course in the College of Arts and Sciences. The reaction of most friends and religious leaders I knew was swift and decisive. "Don't do it," they warned. "Those professors will try to undermine your faith by confusing you with questions. They don't believe the Bible is true." The pressure was strong but not compelling. I was nineteen years old. I knew there was a great deal I did not know about my own religion, not to mention other traditions. Why were these people so afraid? Why would honest inquiry undermine my faith? Their protests served to convince me that my instincts were sound.

I enrolled in Introduction to the New Testament, a course taught by a young assistant professor named James Kirby. Dr. Kirby helped open up the New Testament to me that semester. Even more, he taught me to learn to think critically for myself. The first time I ventured into his office, I was dumbfounded to see hanging on his wall a framed certificate of ordination from the United Methodist Church. I had no idea he was a minister. I recall asking him what he thought personally about some of the critical questions we'd been exploring in class. He responded by saying, "Charles, what is important for you is what *you* think about these questions. I want to help you learn to ask good questions and know how to seek answers for yourself. In the final analysis, you are the one responsible for yourself." As I walked back to my room that day I felt both exhilaration and trepidation. I knew Dr. Kirby was right. I didn't want someone else to tell me what to think. In my religious life, as in the rest of my life, I knew that I would be responsible for what I thought and said and did. I thought about my Campus Crusade friends who were so worried about my faith and correct doctrine being in jeopardy. As I walked across the beautiful OSU campus that day my mother's sage advice came to life: "You have to learn to think for yourself!"

As a Christian, I look both outside myself and within for light to illuminate the path. I remain a Baptist in the South (which is no longer synonymous with being a Southern Baptist), in part because the tradition affirms individual freedom and responsibility before God. The priesthood of all believers is a foundational tenet of the Baptists and others in the free-church tradition.[26] But danger always lurks nearby. There are few checks and balances for individuals or congregations at this end of the Christian spectrum. Anyone who feels "called" to ministry can be ordained if a recognized church affirms that "call." In this tradition, seminary education is not formally required; the suitability of a person for leadership is not usually tested through a screening process or psychological exam. Individual leaders can and do preach and teach all across the theological spectrum. Take a look around the national scene in the United States and you will readily discover that Baptists are a varied lot.[27] Communal safeguards are built in through committees and congregational decision-making practices. But charismatic leaders often have extraordinary power and influence when there is no presbytery or bishopric to which they are accountable. It is not surprising, therefore, that many Christian cult groups spring from Baptist and Pentecostal churches.

Blind obedience is a sure sign of trouble. The likelihood of religion becoming evil is greatly diminished when there is freedom for individual thinking and when honest inquiry is encouraged. As the Buddha lay on his deathbed, he emphasized human responsibility and used the metaphor of light. He offered these poignant final words to his disciples:

> Do not accept what you hear by report, do not accept tradition, do not accept a statement because it is found in our books, nor because it is in accord with your belief, nor because it is the saying of your teacher. . . . Be ye lamps unto yourselves. . . . Those who, either now or after I am dead, shall rely upon themselves only and not look for assistance to anyone besides themselves, it is they who shall reach the very topmost height.[28]

Would that Asahara Shoko and his followers in Aum Shinrikyo had taken the final words of the Buddha to heart.

~ *Four* ~

ESTABLISHING THE "IDEAL" TIME

On the night of January 26, 1984, Palestinian guards stationed near the Dome of the Rock and al-Aqsa Mosque in Jerusalem confronted two Jewish extremists carrying several bags full of high explosives. The encounter thwarted what Israeli police later discovered was a detailed plan to blow up the sacred Islamic buildings. The two men were arrested. But that was just the beginning. First police found a huge arms cache and a bizarre hideout with religious graffiti covering the walls. Later they exposed an extensive, armed underground movement within Israel whose optional plans called for a reserve Israeli pilot to steal a military jet and bomb the Dome of the Rock. Yehuda Etzion, convicted in 1985 and sentenced to twenty years in prison as the chief architect of the plot, acknowledged his goal in a confession: "Four years ago, I began to contemplate the necessity to purify the Temple Mount from the grip of Islam."[1]

This was not the first attempt by Jewish extremists to "purify" this sacred space. There have been twelve efforts to destroy the Dome of the Rock and al-Aqsa Mosque or to kill and wound Muslim worshipers at the site considered sacred to both Jews and Muslims.[2] Why? What motivated these violent attacks? Removal of the

Islamic buildings was the first step in what these and their supporters believed was about to transpire. A key development in the divinely ordained sequence of events they envisioned was (and is) the rebuilding of the Jewish Temple on the site Muslims call the *Haram ash-sharif* ("Noble Sanctuary"), the site occupied by these cherished Islamic structures.[3]

A variety of Jewish groups and a vast network of fundamentalist Christian individuals and organizations continue to share the vision of an approaching day when the third Jewish Temple will rise again from the sacred precincts of the Temple Mount. This hope is tied to particular interpretations of selected biblical passages associated with the messianic age. For some Orthodox Jews, this will signal the coming of the longed-for messiah. For millions of mostly Protestant Christians, the texts and contemporary developments in Israel/Palestine are part of an eschatological scheme related to the second coming of Christ, a cataclysmic battle at Armageddon, and a subsequent thousand-year reign of peace.[4] The seriousness and certainty with which people embrace such views is manifest in several ways. In Jerusalem today, a small group of devout Jews is busily preparing the priestly vestments that will be needed once the Temple is rebuilt. At the Crown of Priests Yeshiva in Jerusalem's old city, students are engaged in a fifteen-year course of study in anticipation of their roles as temple priests.

Among evangelical Christians, premillennial dispensationalism became a dominant interpretive framework during the preceding century. This scheme divides time into defined segments or dispensations, the final one of which is preceded by cataclysmic events. We are thus in a time "before" the final dispensation. Popular preachers and turbulent global events—wars, natural disasters, and famine—helped fuel the notion that the world is fast approaching a seven-year period of great tribulation during which Satan's forces will rule under the leadership of the Antichrist. At the end of this time of great upheaval and suffering, according to this scheme, Jesus will come again to lead the forces of good at the battle of Armageddon.

He will then bind the forces of evil and establish his reign in the New Jerusalem for a millennium. This thousand-year reign is the final dispensation before the culmination of human history and the Day of Judgment. Thus proponents warn that the earth is exceedingly close to the tribulation, the end of history as we know it, and the millennial reign.

The Six-Day War in 1967 proved to be a catalyst for the spread of this perspective. Hal Lindsay's best-selling book, *The Late Great Planet Earth,* popularized the premillennial position by connecting many contemporary events with specific biblical texts.[5] Israel's decisive—he called it miraculous—victory in 1967, including physical control over all of Jerusalem, was interpreted as putting several critical pieces of the puzzle in place for the emergence of Antichrist. Commenting in the aftermath of several assaults on the Islamic buildings in the early 1980s, Lindsay said the following:

> For centuries, there have been well-meaning students of Bible prophecy that have sought to see signs from current events that indicate we are near the second coming of Christ. But none of them have been relevant in the past because the key to the whole predicted scenario is the rebirth of the state of Israel. So, before 1948 nothing was really significant for the second coming of Christ. . . . The next events we should look for are movements to restore the Temple, the ancient Temple of the Jews.[6]

This attitude reflects a level of certainty previously reserved for small fringe groups led by people who claimed to know the precise day and time Christ would return. From the beginning of the church, many Christians have lived in anticipation of Jesus' imminent return. In Paul's second letter to the Thessalonians, possibly one of the earliest New Testament documents, he addressed first-generation Christians who were so certain that Jesus was coming soon that they stopped working. According to Lindsay, whose books have sold over fifteen million copies and whose views are featured often on religious broadcasting, his interpretive framework after 1967 renders irrelevant the views of other "well-meaning" Christians through the centuries. The rapidly growing and widespread popularity of this approach to the Bible and history is readily evident in the overwhelming sales of Tim LaHaye's fictional, but ostensibly biblical, *Left Behind* series. Many popular movies and a high percentage of TV ministries broadcast worldwide every day build on this interpretive framework.[7]

Most Christians who embrace this worldview are not, of course, openly advocating the use of force to destroy the Dome of the Rock and al-Aqsa Mosque. Similarly, the large majority of Orthodox Jews who look forward to the reestablished Temple strongly oppose using force to help the process along. Traditionally, the Haredim ("the trembling ones") and Hasidim ("the pious ones") believe that the third Temple will come down from heaven in an act of divine intervention. But there are those who cross the line and become convinced that they are the ones God will use to accomplish the goal. It is a short step for some Christians as well. During the investigation following the 1984 plots, Israeli officials discovered connections, including direct and substantial financial links, between the Jewish extremists and fundamentalist Christian groups in the United States, South Africa, and Australia.[8]

Other very tangible consequences result from this worldview even if Western Christians provide no direct financial support for such overt actions. Linking the contemporary state of Israel with the kind of biblical interpretation described above has convinced many evangelical and fundamentalist Christians to support Israel uncritically. It makes no difference to them whether Ariel Sharon, Ehud Barak, Yitzhak Shamir, Yitzhak Rabin, Shimon Peres, Menachem Begin, Benjamin Netanyahu, or someone else heads the Israeli government. It makes a great deal of difference to Israelis and Palestinians. The vigorous political debates among Israelis—Jews and Arabs—are practically nonexistent among most premillennial

Christians. When the views of millions are colored by such theologically shaded lenses, there is little incentive to encourage the United States or other governments to work for a sustainable peace in the Middle East or effective arms control; some openly discourage such efforts on the grounds that active peacemaking mitigates against the coming conflagration they anticipate. The zealous allegiance to this eclectic theological scheme can easily become dangerously all consuming. In the process, Jesus' words from the Sermon on the Mount appear to fall on deaf ears: "Blessed are the peacemakers, for they shall be called the children of God" (Matthew 5:9).

The Impulse for the "Ideal" Time

On the positive side, the impulse behind the desire for a more hopeful future is normal and good. It is linked to one of the basic presuppositions informing all religious traditions, namely: something is badly awry. Every tradition is predicated on the notion that something is wrong. We are not living in the "ideal" time. The nature of the human predicament varies: pride and human sinfulness led to expulsion from the Garden of Eden; ignorance about the nature of reality ensnares Hindus and Buddhists in this illusory, phenomenal world; born with the knowledge of God, Muslims lament human forgetfulness and pride, which draw attention away from the source of life to the mundane. Similarly, the religious traditions identify various paths toward both short-term and ultimate goals. Often these are connected to understandings about life in society. The challenge becomes one of identifying the ideal and how one should strive for it, if at all.

There are many variations of the notion of an ideal time. Some religious traditions view the world with limited expectations for what is possible to achieve. The ultimate goal is often lodged in a version of an otherworldly hope: heaven, *nirvana*, *moksha*, and the like. In the meantime, one must find ways to live faithfully in this world. For some people in almost every tradition, this may require some type of communal life segregated from mainstream society. Different monastic groups, the Amish, and Orthodox Jews living in defined neighborhoods in Brooklyn or Jerusalem illustrate the point.

Some religious communities place a great deal of emphasis on a this-worldly hope. They may look back to a time when the ideal was achieved and yearn to recapture those circumstances. Whether or not the perceived ideal ever really existed is of little consequence. Others, as seen above, suggest the ideal is yet to come here on earth. When the hoped-for ideal is tied to a particular religious worldview and those who wish to implement their vision become convinced that they know what God wants for them and everyone else, you have a prescription for disaster.

An Islamic State?

The Islamic religious tradition is particularly susceptible to this volatile combination. The highly visible version of an Islamic state imposed by the Taliban ("the students" of Islam) in Afghanistan illustrates the danger not only for those unfortunate enough to have been born in that land, but also for the larger world community. For five destructive years, these self-declared guardians of true Islam enforced a rigid and extreme version of Islamic law. Their leaders also provided a safe harbor for Osama bin Laden and the *al-qaida* network. The Taliban are an unambiguous example of religion becoming evil. It is clear that predominantly Muslim nations also viewed this Afghan regime as dangerously extremist. Prior to September 11, 2001, only three countries—Pakistan, Saudi Arabia, and the United Arab Emirates—formally recognized the Taliban as the legitimate government in Afghanistan.

Al-qaida leaders, supported by their Taliban counterparts, were seeking to establish or reestablish an Islamic state or society in traditional Muslim lands. Their virulent language and violent actions were aimed at what they perceived as hopelessly corrupt governments considered propped up, if not controlled, by the United States. Stunned by the devastating attacks, the U.S. news media frequently asked one question after September 11: Why do they hate us? But the question was misleading. To begin with, it implied some monolithic "we" and "they," a superficial view at best. Sound bites will never explain the multilayered and convoluted dynamics at work, a task that requires much deeper thought and analysis. President Bush's repeated reference to the nineteen hijackers and their supportive network as "evildoers" rang true. But much more than labels is needed if we want to understand the powerful dynamics shaping many Muslim countries today and if we hope to help formulate constructive alternatives for the future.

Traditionally, Muslims have understood Islam as more than a religion. It is a comprehensive way of life including spiritual, social, economic, political, and military dimensions. Muhammad is viewed as the last, or "seal," of the prophets. He was also the political and military leader of the new *ummah* (community) established when the first Muslims left Mecca and traveled north to Medina in 622 C.E. Medina, under the leadership of the Prophet, theoretically presents an exemplary Islamic state. Its Constitution, coupled with qur'anic passages, and several volumes of authoritative sayings and actions of Muhammad (*hadith*) provide resources for structuring an Islamic society. Muslims in various settings throughout the centuries have sought to fashion governmental, social, legal, and economic systems with reference to a theoretical ideal.

It is difficult, however, to find sustained situations in which this ideal worked well. Strong disagreements, conflicts, and even civil war among the first generations of Muslims highlight the distance separating the ideal from the lived reality. The two large branches within Islam—the Sunnis and Shi'ites—trace their split to disagreement over who should lead the community immediately after the death of Muhammad in 632 C.E. The partisans (*shi'ah*) of Ali were those who believed Muhammad had designated his son-in-law and first cousin to be his temporal successor. The supporters of Ali were outvoted, and Abu Bakr was selected to be the first caliph. Although Ali did become the fourth caliph (656–661 C.E.), temporal power shifted away from the family of Muhammad on Ali's death. The Ummayad clan began a century of dynastic rule (661–750) based in Damascus. The civil strife within Islam hit a low point in 680 when a band of Shi'ites was massacred at Karbala (in southern Iraq today) and Hussayn, the grandson of Muhammad, was decapitated on the battlefield.[9] These events began a long history of disagreement about legitimate leadership and different legal and human sources of authority between and among branches of Islam.

The popular Western image of Islam as unsophisticated and anti-intellectual quickly disappears in the face of even a cursory survey of Islamic history. The error of this image is particularly ironic in view of the major ways Islamic civilization helped shape Western society as we know it. When Europe was languishing in the Dark Ages, Islamic civilization was thriving from Spain to India. For several centuries Muslims led the world in areas such as mathematics, chemistry, medicine, philosophy, navigation, architecture, horticulture, and astronomy. Muslims are proud of their history and civilization. But something went wrong.[10] From the sixteenth through the twentieth centuries most of the lands with a Muslim majority fell under the control of outside powers.

Islamic history parallels the history of other great civilizations. Some political leaders have been more flexible and benevolent than others. One can find encouraging and inspiring examples of tolerance and cooperation in multireligious settings during periods when Muslims ruled Spain, in Baghdad, and in Jerusalem, for instance. But these are more the exception than the rule. In the end, Islamic rule has included many remarkable achievements as well as all the foibles, power plays, internal strife, and ruthless behavior predictably displayed by leaders in positions of power throughout the world.

Many Muslims still embrace the hope that Islam can provide a way for the future in their societies. The formation of many new nations during the past sixty years provided hope for a new day. In the postcolonial era of nation-states, many Muslims dreamed of and worked for revitalized, contemporary versions of Islamic societies but faced frustration as their efforts were thwarted time and again. Although many Muslim lands now have indigenous leaders, few of those who govern are in power by virtue of popular choice. Instead, many states are ruled by dynasties of kings or military and political leaders who seized and now maintain power through force.

Movements for political reform have frequently been marginalized or crushed. Despicable human rights records in many Muslim countries add to the frustration. The details vary from country to country, but the pattern is all too familiar.[11] Economic disparity and perceptions of exploitation also frequently contribute to political instability. Extraordinary wealth enjoyed by a small percentage of the populace—often the ruling elite—coupled with omnipresent images of opulence in the West provide compelling, if oversimplified, evidence for those who argue that their countries are still very much controlled by external powers. Islamists often lament the visible erosion of cultural values in their societies. Without question, Western culture, with its seemingly innocuous as well as hedonistic and sometimes pornographic influences, is a source of considerable anxiety. But visit Cairo, Amman, or even Tehran, and you will see multiple influences. Western products, music, and entertainment are intertwined with traditional lifestyles and practices. While some are threatened by Western influences, many others line up at embassies and consular offices to seek visas to travel or study in the United States or Europe. Benjamin Barber, director of the Center for the Culture and Politics of Democracy at Rutgers University, frames the converging issues in terms of the conflicting movements toward globalism and tribalism.[12] People in many countries today are frustrated by their circumstances and the external, global forces that often appear to undermine traditional values. While the vast majority of Muslims reject the violent extremism of *al-qaida,* a substantial portion of the populace shares the frustrations that fuel this movement.

In many countries where Muslims constitute the majority, people tend to feel that existing political, economic, and social systems have failed. When most avenues for political change appear to be blocked, more and more individuals and groups are attracted to revolutionary Islamist movements. My work with the Middle Eastern churches and in public policy advocacy over three decades brought me into contact with some of the well-known Islamist groups: Hizbollah, Islamic Jihad, HAMAS, and revolutionary leaders in Iran, for example. If we wish to understand these complex movements more deeply, we will need to analyze the particular historical, political, social, and economic circumstances of each setting. A general understanding of the broad themes connecting these groups helps explain why many Muslims hope that Islam can provide the foundation for the future in their particular setting. Yet while many share the vision that Islam can provide the framework for their respective societies, there is no consensus on precisely what an Islamic state should look like. I've asked dozens of Muslim scholars, political leaders, professionals, and activists how they would fashion an Islamic state today and gotten dozens of answers. The disparate visions mirror the inconsistent patterns one can observe when contemporary Muslims have sought to create some type of Islamic state.

The Iranian revolution of 1979 led to an Islamic republic. Because the media focused intensely on the Iranian hostage crisis and the enigmatic figure of the ayatollah, few in the West noticed that the Iranians devised a governmental structure based largely on the model of a Western parliamentary democracy. Pakistan, the only country created explicitly to be an Islamic state, has had a tumultuous history for more than fifty years. Whatever the stated intentions, the outcome has not attracted others to repeat the experiment. No Muslims I know look to Pakistan as the model they seek to emulate in their country. In the Sudan, Hassan al-Turabi's concerted effort at Islamization—imposing Islamic political ideology—has not worked well. Despite accepting an open-minded and outwardly tolerant version of Islamic ideology, the country struggles with tribal histories and violent civil strife between multiple ethnic groups speaking over one hundred languages. The Islamist movement in Algeria, the FIS (Islamic Salvation Front), was poised to win elections in early 1992, but elections were canceled, the FIS leaders were jailed, and an already highly volatile situation descended into years of chaotic civil war.[13]

The distinctly different political versions of Islamic rule propagated in the Sudan, Algeria, and Afghanistan during the 1990s struck chords with some disgruntled and dispossessed Muslims in various lands. But there is no evidence to suggest many Muslims were interested in taking courses from such movements or regimes on how to organize an Islamic state in their setting.

It is important to understand that not all political leaders who employ religious imagery and rhetoric are actually seeking to draw upon Islam. Political leaders worldwide often consciously appeal to popular religious sentiment in an effort to bolster support for their policies. Saddam Hussein was a case study during the 1991 Gulf War. Hussein is certainly not a religious leader. He is a brutal secular leader who "got religion" when it served his purpose. He has used religious rhetoric in calculated and cynical ways, such as issuing repeated calls for *jihad* (often translated "holy war"), sewing the words "God Is the Greatest" (*Allahu akbar)* on the Iraqi flag, continually referring to the illegitimacy of the Saudi government for inviting masses of "infidels" to the Arabian peninsula and thereby somehow desecrating the sacred lands of Islam,[14] and pledging to liberate Jerusalem. The Iraqi leader knew that different constituencies would respond positively to different pieces of the rhetoric. Many of the same emphases are found in Osama bin Laden's broadcast interviews in the final months of 2001. The degree to which particular leaders or movements are genuinely grounded in their religious tradition is not always easy to discern. Western news media, with their shorthand analysis, rarely even make the effort to draw such distinctions.

While many Muslims call for some type of Islamic state, others work toward other goals. Given our pluralist, interdependent world, some Muslims argue for secular democratic states as the best model for the future. Many Muslims I know are deeply troubled by the very real problems of religious intolerance, persecution of minorities, and the poor treatment of women in Islamic societies. They suggest that guarantees for religious freedom and human rights are essential ingredients for any viable state today. Charles Kurzman's recent anthology includes thirty-two essays by influential Muslim scholars and political activists on the following topics: Against Theocracy, Democracy, Rights of Women, Rights of Non-Muslims, Freedom of Thought, and Progress.[15] Even so, open debates on these and other topics have been stifled far too often in predominantly Muslim countries. Muslims living in Western democratic countries have an especially important role to play in openly discussing and debating viable, alternative social and political structures for the future.

All of the above begs the question: Is it really possible to fashion an Islamic state in the twenty-first century? We will likely find out in the coming decade. Having spent a great deal of my professional life at the intersection of religion and politics in the Middle East, I have grave doubts. At some level, any state in which rights and status are tied to a particular religious tradition will relegate some of its citizens to second- and third-class status. Whatever the rhetoric or intentions toward people "protected" by those in power, the reality presents serious problems. A closer look at the distinctive dynamics in Israel illustrates the dilemma.

THE SPECIAL CASE OF ISRAEL

In the spring of 1987, the National Broadcasting Company (NBC) aired a startling one-hour documentary in prime time entitled *Six Days Plus Twenty Years: A Dream Is Dying*. The program, anchored by Tom Brokaw, marked the impending twentieth anniversary of

Israel's decisive victory in the Six-Day War in June 1967. The program set out to show two things: that the continuing occupation of the West Bank and Gaza was crushing the Palestinian inhabitants, and that it was also destroying the dream of Israel as a democratic, Jewish state. The documentary highlighted the evolution of Israeli policies regarding the occupied territories and the growing, disproportionate political power of groups like the Gush Emonim—religious zealots working aggressively to create government-sponsored and illegal settlements in the occupied lands. Many of these settlers enjoy dual citizenship in Israel and the United States, and their religious rhetoric has been unmistakable: "God not only gave us this land [meaning Israel and the occupied territories], but Abraham also paid for it."[16]

The program produced a swift and negative response from the Israeli government, headed at that time by Prime Minister Yitzhak Shamir. The reaction had little to do with the accuracy of the presentation; government officials were annoyed that, for the first time, a major American network had clearly revealed fundamental disagreements and a major dilemma within Israel during prime time. Most Israelis were well aware of the internal contradiction that the continuing military occupation presented. Quietly accepting governmental policies under the rubric of "security" was no longer acceptable to a growing portion of the Israeli citizenry. The 1982 invasion and subsequent occupation of Lebanon (dubbed the "Peace for Galilee" campaign) had mobilized the Israeli public and peace movement in unprecedented ways during the previous five years. Israelis were engaged in open discussion as the twentieth anniversary of the 1967 war drew near. The best-selling book in Israel during 1987–88 was David Grossman's *The Yellow Wind.*[17] Grossman's account of his journey into Palestinian camps and Jewish settlements, to kindergartens and military courtrooms, eloquently described the many ways the occupation humiliated and harmed the occupier as well as those occupied. NBC News presented a similar story. Lengthy excerpts from *The Yellow Wind* soon appeared in the *New Yorker*. Israel's difficult dilemma was out in the open. The Palestinian *intifada* ("uprising"), which began in late 1987, exposed the contradictions even further.

Since 1967, U.N. Resolution 242 has provided the basis for an Israeli-Palestinian peace process. The resolution doesn't address all the key issues; it does, however, highlight the sine qua non: land for peace. Israel must return the lands it captured in return for a guaranteed, lasting peace. The NBC documentary, *The Yellow Wind*, and various other programs and events revealed the fact that the settlers, a substantial and powerful segment within Israel, were effectively undermining the possibilities of a meaningful peace process based on land for peace. Moreover, a closer look showed how the settlement process had been encouraged and subsidized all along by various Israeli governments, both Labor and Likud.[18] At the same time, the different governments in Israel displayed no discernible desire to annex the occupied territories and make them part of Israel. Why? Annexation would require citizenship for the inhabitants. Israelis of all political persuasions knew that demographics mitigated against such a move. In a period of years, the Palestinian Muslims and Christians living in the West Bank and Gaza, together with the Israeli Arabs (Muslim and Christian Arabs who remained within the borders of Israel in 1948 and thus became Israeli citizens), would outnumber the Jewish citizens in Israel. Since Israel is a democracy, the Palestinian Arabs in the not-too-distant future might simply take over the government at the ballot box. Thus the fundamental character of the Jewish state could be lost to a democratic, secular state in Palestine—the original goal of the Palestine Liberation Organization!

For two decades Israel had been in the awkward position of defending vigorously both the necessity of a Jewish state and an unshakable commitment to democracy. The earlier Camp David process included the return of the Sinai to Egypt as part of the permanent peace between Israel and Egypt. The extraordinarily strong and disturbingly violent response of some settlers to Menachem

Begin's concessions exposed the depth of division within Israel in the early 1980s.[19]

What was Israel going to do? While the large majority sat on the fence, several prominent religious leaders on the right end of Israel's political spectrum were painfully honest and forthcoming about the dilemma. One of the most flamboyant and boisterous leaders, Rabbi Meir Kahane, spoke for his KACH movement as well as many within the Gush Emonim. He saw the problem clearly and presented a solution by posing a rhetorical question: How can Israel be a Jewish state and a democracy and still retain control of Judea and Samaria (biblical names for the territories captured in 1967)? It can't do all these things, he argued. So Kahane and others who shared his views opted publicly for a Jewish state, stating unapologetically that most of the Arabs in Judea and Samaria simply had to leave. Kahane advocated first trying to buy them off. If that didn't work, Israel had to find effective ways to force them out. Once the population was small enough, Israel could then annex the lands permanently. When asked whether Arabs who had lived there for centuries had any rights or claims to a state, Kahane always quickly retorted: They have one; it is called Jordan.[20]

The vast majority of Israelis rejected Kahane's extremism. Even so, he enjoyed enough support to win a seat in the Knesset. Although his positions were deeply offensive, most Palestinians I know and many within Israel suspected that the official policies in the occupied territories effectively coincided with his goals and those of the Gush Emonim. Without question, even a cursory examination revealed how the indigenous Palestinian population was suffering under the rapid increase in settlements, targeted deportation of Palestinian leaders, administrative detention of thousands of people, continual exploitation of limited natural resources, long and unpredictable closure of schools and businesses, even whole towns, and other forms of collective punishment.

I have spent a great deal of time in the occupied territories, including various refugee camps and settlements. I have witnessed frequently the daily indignities and physical harassment Palestinians have endured at the hands of well-armed, extremist settlers. The tragic cycle of violence continues as some Palestinians lash out violently against those who humiliate and brutalize them as well as, in some instances, innocent Israeli civilians. I, along with the large majority of Jews, Christians, and Muslims I know and have worked with in Israel/Palestine, do not condone such violence in either direction. On the contrary, many individuals as well as religious and humanitarian organizations continue to work tirelessly to find ways to end these horrific and counterproductive patterns of behavior. As bad as it has been, I have always been amazed that more people didn't snap in the midst of such untenable living conditions.[21]

The convoluted history of the Israeli-Palestinian and larger Israeli-Arab conflict defies simple analysis. Many major factors complicate the situation, including the necessity for security, a long history of suffering and victimization, dehumanizing of the adversary, confusing and conflicting voices among leaders, and the disproportionate influence of extremist individuals and groups, as well as constantly shifting political, economic, and military priorities among international and regional powers. The point here is not to argue for a particular resolution for this sad, tortured conflict.[22] Our concern relates to the fundamental dilemma and explosive tension inherent in the status quo. When we inquire about pernicious ways religion can be used or can easily contribute toward violent and evil ends, the behavior of zealous Jewish settlers cannot be overlooked. The Israeli-Palestinian conflict remains one of the most explosive flash points in the world. The uncompromising biblical claim for all the land and the powerful political role played by Jewish extremists are like a lighted match in a room full of high explosives.

Jewish zealots are not the only religiously motivated people complicating the picture at the eastern end of the Mediterranean. Palestinian Islamist extremists within the Islamic Resistance Movement (HAMAS) and Islamic Jihad emerged as major forces in the past two decades. These groups reject PLO leadership and the negotiated peace process symbolized by the Oslo Accords and the famous handshake between Yasser Arafat and Yitzhak Rabin after they signed the Declaration of Principles on the White House lawn on September 13, 1993. HAMAS and Islamic Jihad leaders declared this a betrayal of their struggle for liberation and vowed to continue their *jihad* against Israel.[23] These organizations advocate an Islamic state in Palestine. Some individuals connected to these groups have gained international attention through violent attacks and suicide bombings. Their harsh rhetoric and violent actions play a similar role in the violent exchanges between and among Israelis and Palestinians virtually every week. We have discussed suicide bombers in the context of chapter 2. We will return to the larger issues involved in *jihad* in chapter 6.

The deeper dilemma of a state tied to a particular religious tradition is also evident within the pre-1967 borders of Israel. Israeli Arabs, who account for 15–20 percent of the population in Israel, certainly enjoy many more rights and privileges than their Palestinian relatives and friends living nearby under military occupation or in refugee camps in Lebanon or Jordan. Even so, they remain second- and third-class citizens within Israel.[24] Many studies, books, and articles over the years have detailed ways Arabs in Israel experience discrimination from the government. In the long run, as stability and security become more the rule than the exception in Israel, these matters must be addressed more forthrightly. The viability of Israel's democracy depends on it.

A CHRISTIAN AMERICA

Self-proclaimed "Bible-believing" Christians became a powerful presence on the U.S. political landscape during the final two decades of the twentieth century. The Moral Majority, headed by the Reverend Jerry Falwell, and the Christian Coalition, founded by the Reverend Pat Robertson, have been the most prominently visible among a number of organizations making up the New Religious Right. The groups vary in focus and structure. They tend to converge and cooperate on a variety of issues—against abortion, homosexuality, and gun control; in support of prayer in school, school vouchers, and capital punishment—often grouped under the rubric of "family values."

Christian groups making up the New Religious Right are united in their commitment to change laws and government structures in light of their biblical ideals. As with Muslim and Jewish examples discussed earlier, these Christian organizations did not form in a vacuum. For most of the twentieth century, conservative evangelical and fundamentalist Protestants tended to eschew politics. The rapid social changes during the 1960s and the perceived threat of secular humanism catalyzed them into activism.[25] Supreme Court decisions related to abortion rights and clear separations between church and state became key rallying points. The literature and rhetoric of groups in the New Religious Right reveal nostalgia for an ideal time that has been lost—usually connected somehow with the founders of the country—and warnings about the danger awaiting this nation if it continues to turn its back on God.

Public education is one arena where the battle lines are clearly drawn. For almost two decades federal and state legislators as well as thousands of local school board officials have fought over the appropriateness of prayer in school (in the classroom, before football games, at commencement, and so forth), teaching evolution and creationism, posting the Ten Commandments, and the provision of vouchers for private schools. Having studied these issues and engaged in public debate with leaders in the New Religious Right over many years, I have been disturbed to find out to what extent their argument is predicated on generic assumptions about the founding fathers or the notion that the Supreme Court somehow "kicked God out of school in 1963." It is a curious theological perspective that contends God's power and presence are circumscribed by Supreme Court rulings. As I've tried to explain to people who fear the lack of formal prayers in public schools, as long as there are math tests, there will be prayer in schools.[26]

These matters, while highly charged, appear to be far removed from religiously motivated violence in the Middle East and elsewhere. There is a direct link, however. They share a religious conviction that the perceived ideal has been lost and must be restored through institutions of the state. In this country the plan for restructuring the state—the federal government or the public school system—is somehow to be gleaned from a particular understanding of the Christian religion. A closer look at Pat Robertson and the Christian Coalition, the most powerful force in this movement for a Christian America, reveals the dangers inherent in this theological orientation.

Pat Robertson embraces a reconstructionist theological position. This orientation challenges the mechanisms of the state and seeks to bring all of life under God's rule.

> For reconstructionists there is no neutral ground, no sphere of activity outside God's rule. One is either following God in all aspects of life or not following God at all. One is either engaged in godly politics or is participating in the anti-God structures that now threaten the home, the school, and the church. . . . Like their premillennial cousins, reconstructionists wait for a dramatic change in history. But they are not merely waiting.[27]

Reconstructionists seek "to remove the political and institutional barriers to God's law in order to impose the rule of God's law."[28] Robertson's approach is well documented. With a vision for transforming the government and the country, he ran for the top office in the country during the Republican presidential primary season in 1988. He surprised most pundits with strong finishes in the Iowa caucuses and the New Hampshire primary, outlasting most other candidates in his party. When his hope for a victory faded in 1988, he regrouped. Rather than choosing a top-down political strategy, he organized a grassroots, bottom-up approach under the auspices of the Christian Coalition. With surprisingly little effort, Robertson revealed how small numbers of committed Christians could literally take over school boards and city councils and control Republican precincts in many states.[29]

The political sophistication and rapid success of the Christian Coalition during the first half of the 1990s was stunning. In addition to controlling school boards and city councils, these activists effectively commanded the political power among Republicans in twenty states.[30] As their positions translated into official planks in party platforms and policies in local school districts, many people and organizations they targeted began to look more closely at the theological underpinnings of Robertson's movement. They didn't have to look long or hard. Robertson's daily television program, *The 700 Club,* and his books spelled it out: the structures of government and the legal and educational systems were effectively under the dominion of Satan. Complete overhaul was needed to establish God's rule in this land.

> Satan has established certain strongholds. He goes after areas of our society which are crucial. He has gone after the education system and has been very successful in capturing it. He has gone after our legal profession and has been successful, through the ACLU and others, in capturing large portions of the legal system. He's gone after the government and moved it away from the more free enterprise system we've known and turned it into a socialist welfare state. He's gone after the family, the church, etc., with less success, but nevertheless he's battering away. These places control society. . . . I don't know if Satan has been able to get to the military yet, but he's tried. . . . Satan hates people. He desires to destroy people. . . . We need to do spiritual warfare.[31]

Robertson's religious and political battle plan envisioned the Christian Coalition working in tandem with a wide array of church-related community action councils across America. They enjoyed tax-exempt status under section 501(c)(3) of the IRS code. Such organizations can only direct a small portion of their budgets to political activities. There are limits on participating or intervening in political campaigns, including making statements for or against candidates for public office. These groups did just that through the distribution of millions of thinly disguised "voter guides." The guides rated local, state, and national candidates—often erroneously—for public office on eight or ten hot-button issues. The "guides" were conveniently sized to fit as church bulletin inserts; they were distributed in thousands of churches the Sunday before Tuesday elections. The tactic was highly effective in many instances; it was also blatantly deceitful and probably illegal. Few public officials, however, dared challenge the process in court lest they be seen as somehow beating up on "religious" institutions.[32]

On several occasions I asked Ralph Reed and other leaders in this movement to explain and clarify how they were not violating the spirit, if not the precise letter, of the law. Were they not deliberately spreading sometimes false and misleading information about candidates in order to influence voters? Did they not actively promote a strategy of running "stealth" candidates, that is, people who deliberately hid their real agenda until after they were elected and in position to change the system? How do these tactics square with responsible Christian witness or tax-exempt status? The responses were predictably weak and couched in legalese. But a deeper message always resided in Robertson's theological statements. He saw the battle in cosmic terms of good and evil. God's rule must prevail against the principalities and powers controlled by Satanic forces. The end, in effect, justified the means.

In 1997, even as the IRS was reviewing the tax-exempt status of the Christian Coalition and the Federal Election Commission was examining its campaign-related activities, Pat Robertson revealed his objectives in a taped message to the top one hundred leaders of the state organizations. Robertson jokingly addressed his audience as "fellow radicals" who were "dangerously seeking to overturn the established order and take power away from a bunch of liberals and give it to those who love this country."[33] Robertson made clear his role in shaping the future for this country and how he expected both to "select the next president of the United States" and to have the undivided attention of the Republican Party leaders:

> We just tell these guys, "Look, we put you in power in 1994, and we want you to deliver. We are tired of temporizing. Don't give us this stuff about you've got a different agenda. This is what we are going to do this year. And we're going to hold your feet to the fire while you do it."[34]

The mixing of God, a narrow understanding of Christianity, and country lies at the heart of this powerful movement. Small wonder that Pat Buchanan, another Republican presidential candidate, chose the Christian Coalition's national convention in 1993 to state his position clearly: "Our culture is superior because our religion is Christianity and that is the truth that sets men free." However deeply that view is held by those with an agenda for a Christian America, it appears that a great deal of work remains to be done. Eight years later, in the immediate aftermath of the September 11 attacks, Jerry Falwell appeared on Robertson's *700 Club* and revealed, as we noted in chapter 2, his belief that pagans, abortionists, feminists, and gays and lesbians had helped the attacks happen. Pat Robertson's response to Falwell: "Well, I totally concur."

When we begin to connect the dots, a larger picture comes into view. Christian reconstructionists in America are only one step removed from their counterparts with a concrete, divinely ordained plan for an Islamic state or the reconstituted, expanded biblical state of Israel. The gap begins to close when the agenda includes denigration of Islam or direct action against abortion clinics. It is not too surprising to hear some detractors of leaders like Robertson and Falwell refer to them sarcastically as American ayatollahs or leaders of the American version of the Taliban.

RELIGION AND THE STATE

Theocratic models for government have never worked well for long. At the zenith of Israel's power under Kings David and Solomon, the mechanisms of the state and its leaders were far from ideal. The biblical record of the following four hundred years depicts a downward spiral culminating in the destruction of Jerusalem by the Babylonians in 587 B.C.E. The prophets—from Nathan to Jeremiah—were central religious figures during these centuries. They spoke their understanding of truth to power, calling on the political and religious leaders of their day to turn away from repressive, self-serving, and hypocritical policies of exploitation. Prophetic witness centered not on dogma but on foundational principles of justice, honesty, compassion, and humility.

The early Christians did not control governmental structures. Rather, they were often on the receiving end of brutal government persecution. Everything changed in the fourth century when Constantine made Christianity the official religion of the Roman Empire. Some of the negative consequences flowing from this dramatic reversal and the corrupting influence of political power will be discussed in the next two chapters. Many experiments to fashion Christian government structures fill the pages of church history. While a few Protestants look back to Calvin's Geneva or the Puritans in New England for guidance, there is little enthusiasm for church-related states today. On the contrary, contemporary remnants of such models in parts of Europe include virtually moribund "official" churches.

Muslims often point to Muhammad's ten-year rule in Medina (622–632 C.E.) and the period of the Rightly Guided Caliphs (632–661 C.E.) as the golden age that provides the model to emulate. The system worked well for its time and place. Even so, there were many serious problems, including the treatment of Jews in Medina and the prosecution of military campaigns. Muslims explain such matters within their context. Our contemporary context, however, is vastly different. How well can this governmental model work today?

Institutional structures shaping social, political, and economic life vary dramatically across the globe and through the centuries. Some systems have worked better than others; all are fraught with problems and inequities. Challenging government and societal structures seen as unjust and oppressive is a valid, if not imperative, feature in most religious traditions. Within and among the descendants of Abraham, however, there is no consensus on how best to do this and to what end.[35] People of faith and goodwill must continually wrestle with the most appropriate and constructive ways to structure institutions in light of fundamental principles and changing circumstances. The biblical model of prophetic witness remains powerful and relevant. There are strong parallels in qur'anic insistence on social and economic justice as well as compassion for the most vulnerable members of society—the poor, widows, and orphans. Prophetic witness in the Abrahamic tradition calls attention to injustice and to oppressive practices; it offers an alternative vision for life in community, and it offers hope. The prophetic witness of Dr. Martin Luther King Jr. and the civil rights movement illustrates the point.

We live in a world of nation-states. Borders are real, and national identities constitute an important component of our human identities. But, to borrow Thomas Friedman's image, nationalism is not the only root that anchors and feeds our respective olive trees. Even the zealots described above see themselves as part of larger communities—Jewish, Christian, or Muslim—that transcend national boundaries. The challenge facing governments today is to address both the interdependent dynamics of nation-states and the pluralism within each nation. Although theocracy is not a tenable model for the nation-state today, some type of formal religious connection to the structures of state may be necessary for the foreseeable future in some countries.

The particular history and tenacity of the Jewish people provide a compelling argument for Israel as a modern nation. A safe haven for

Jews remains a pressing need in the face of continuing hostilities. Yet Israel's security must be based ultimately on peaceful coexistence and on political and economic cooperation with neighboring states. Israel's internal strength rests directly on its strong democracy. Anyone who has visited Israel's parliament, the Knesset, in session knows how vigorously Israelis practice democracy. Over time, Israelis and those who support Israel must face more squarely the tensions inherent in being a democracy and a self-defined Jewish state in which a substantial minority is not Jewish.

The challenges facing Muslim countries are many and complex. Yet the hope that Islam can provide the basis for nation-states cannot and should not be dismissed casually. Integrating all parts of life—religious, political, economic, and social—remains a deeply embedded goal in Islamic thought. But the multiple problems permeating many countries cause understandable frustrations. Muslims living under repressive, unrepresentative regimes are justifiably angry and have every right to demand change. The turbulence in many parts of the Muslim world is hardly surprising when you add to the picture deplorable human rights violations and minimal chance for economic improvement. The hope that Islam can provide the societal structure for a way forward runs deep, but the actual shape and form an Islamic state might take, as noted above, is far from clear.

The best hope lies in serious and concerted efforts to address the major sources of frustration and, in the process, change existing government structures. No easy answers or quick fixes are visible on the horizon. Perceptible movement toward self-determination and meaningful participation in government is a crucial step. Contrary to popular images in the West, Islam and democracy are compatible. Benjamin Barber may be on the right track in wanting to move beyond nation-states to more global democratic institutions, but that remains a distant dream.[36]

In the immediate future, steps toward democratization and self-determination will surely include experiments with some forms of

Islamic government. Hopefully, new and viable structures can be fashioned over time. One such potentially positive experiment is the Islamic Republic of Iran. The basic Iranian government structure is a Western parliamentary democracy, a republic. Unlike citizens in most Muslim countries, Iranians elect their president and representatives in the *majlis* (parliament). The revolution did not produce a return to the time of Muhammad or Ali's caliphate. Rather, it resulted in a new form of government that endeavored both to draw on tradition and to adapt to the contemporary circumstances. Iran is not a pure democracy. The government structure includes distinctive and powerful roles for Shi'ite clergy leaders. Nonetheless, clear signs of moderation among many elected leaders over two decades suggest that democracy is alive and functioning in the Islamic Republic.[37]

Efforts to establish an "ideal" time discussed above illustrate clearly what doesn't work. Those who narrowly define ideal temporal structures of the state and determine that they are God's agents to establish a theocracy are dangerous. Religion is easily corrupted in this context. Beware of people and groups whose political blueprint is based on a mandate from heaven that depends on human beings to implement.

~ *Five* ~

THE END JUSTIFIES
ANY MEANS

The *New York Times* headline on March 1, 2002, "Hindu Rioters Kill 60 Muslims in India," announced the beginning of a series of horrific events unfolding in the northern part of the world's second most populous country. Graphic photographs of rampaging mobs and grieving mothers accompanied the story, indelibly capturing images of a religious conflict propelling India and Pakistan toward war. Eyewitness descriptions of the day included Hindus burning Muslim families alive in their homes and cars, setting fire to restaurants and shops—the sickening details of another deadly day of brutal conflict in India. During the first half of 2002 there were many such days, which resulted in more than one thousand deaths and many military skirmishes across the disputed border in Kashmir.

Three months after the rioting began, over one million troops had been mobilized along both sides of the India-Pakistan border. The prospect of war brought many interventions by world leaders, including trips to the region by U.S. secretary of state Colin Powell and secretary of defense Donald Rumsfeld. While many analysts predicted that a war between India and Pakistan might quickly involve nuclear weapons, Pentagon officials estimated that twelve million people could die from the initial detonations; untold millions more would become casualties from the continuing effects.[1]

These images and possible outcomes are gruesome—and all too real. Sparked by a controversy over sacred space, this particular conflict has become a conflagration of ferocious animosity and taken on perilous dimensions. Here we see clearly that religion has become a force for evil. Why? How? What possible justification could there be for such behavior by "religious" people? Some background information is necessary to explain this tragic and dangerous manifestation of corrupted religion.

Conflict between segments of India's Hindu majority and Muslim minority populations did not begin in 2002. Their long history of coexistence in South Asia has included considerable distrust and periods of open hostility. The epic, Academy Award–winning film *Gandhi* conveyed the depth of anger related to long-standing tensions between Hindus and Muslims, which erupted during India's movement toward independence. The clashes were not then and are not now simply about religion. As is almost always the case, political, economic, and social factors weave in and out over time, shaping the contours of conflict. But religion has always been squarely in the center of this escalating tragedy, and the catalytic events leading the march toward war in 2002 had deep religious roots. These events and their roots reveal a common way religion is corrupted: religion becomes a force for evil—with potential global consequences—when the ends justify any means.

The violence in 2002 was ignited by a ghastly episode linked to a decade-long clash over a sacred site in the city of Ayodhya. On February 27 Hindu zealots were returning home to Gujarat from a mission to build a temple on the site revered as the birthplace of Ram, an incarnation of the Hindu deity Vishnu. As the train carrying them home reached the station in the town of Godhra, a fight erupted between taunting Hindu fanatics on the train and Muslim vendors on the platform. One of the passenger cars was set ablaze, resulting in the death of fifty-eight Hindus. In the next few days Hindus in thirty towns and villages across northern India unleashed ferocious attacks, killing more than six hundred Muslims.

The behavior of the Hindu extremists, regardless of the justifications or charges of provocation they offered, directly contradicted the most fundamental truths informing religious life in India. The Hindu tradition is, by definition, tolerant and respectful of diversity. There is no structured hierarchy or single sacred text or designated day of worship each week. The rich diversity of religious life in India attests to the widespread understanding that there are many paths for people with widely differing aptitudes and dispositions. At the same time, common themes run through the many tributaries of the river called Hinduism. Chief among these are the affirmation of one ultimate essence in the universe, the Brahman, and the immutable law of *karma* and transmigration. In this world of illusion, the Brahman is that which is real. The soul essence of each person, the *atman,* in the final analysis is understood as part of the Brahman. The *atman* is what Hindus believe transmigrates during the process of reincarnation, a process that continues until the soul is liberated and fully reunited with the Brahman. The end goal, *moksha,* or liberation, may be achieved through various paths, all of which include high moral and ethical standards for behavior on earth. The law of *karma,* the deed and its result, animates the ethical system of this worldview.

At its heart, the Hindu tradition affirms what we have described as a central feature in all authentic religions, namely, an orientation toward the transcendent that is inextricably linked with compassionate, constructive relationships with others in this world. Hindu teaching offers a seamless blend of Jesus' two great commandments—to love God and to love your neighbor as yourself—informed by the central monistic and pantheistic tension at the heart of its worldview. The divine essence animating creation is no different from the divine essence in every living thing. When Hindus greet someone with folded hands and a bow, they are affirming the divine essence in that person. From this basic understanding grows the doctrine of nonviolence. Mahatma Gandhi embodied these fundamental Hindu teachings.

For Hindus as well as all other people of faith, the ultimate focus of religion—liberation or salvation—cannot be disconnected from life in this world. In authentic, healthy religion the end and the means to that end are always connected. But it is often easy for religious people to lose sight of the ultimate goal and focus instead on one component of religion. When a key feature of religion is elevated and in effect becomes an end, some people within the religion become consumed with protecting or achieving that end. In such cases, that component of religion functions like an absolute truth claim, and zealous believers become blind in their single-minded defense of it. As we will see, this corruption takes many forms, but the pattern is unmistakable. The end goal of protecting or defending a key component of religion is often used to justify any means necessary.

The most obvious sign of this corruption is visible when compassionate and constructive relationships with others are discarded. In the case of the temple commemorating the birth of Lord Ram in Ayodhya, the goal of protecting sacred space was used to justify unspeakable violence against Muslims. Regrettably, corruption of religion in the context of protecting or defending something considered sacred is all too common.

DEFENDING SACRED SPACE

All religious traditions distinguish between the sacred and the profane. Space, time, objects, and people are set apart and approached differently based on their role in the sacred stories in each tradition. We have underscored the powerful attachment to sacred space in previous chapters and will observe it again in connection with holy war. The role of sacred space in Islam is evident five times each day when pious Muslims orient themselves toward Mecca for *salat,* the ritual prayers. Sacred space is a prominent feature in the Hindu tradition as well, as each year millions of Hindus make pilgrimages to sacred places and bathe in sacred rivers. Thus sacred space is a key component of religious life and practice.

The traditional burial site of Abraham is located in Hebron (in Arabic, al-Khalil) on the West Bank. Two sites, the Cave of the Patriarchs and the Mosque of Ibrahim (the Arabic name of Abraham) hallow this space, which is considered sacred by Jews, Christians, and Muslims alike. Periodically during the past sixty years conflicts and tensions have intensified at this site. On February 25, 1994, however, the sacred space became the venue for mass murder. It was the Jewish holiday of Purim, a day commemorating the deliverance of Jews from extinction by their oppressors. As hundreds of Palestinian Muslim men and boys were gathering for prayer at the mosque, Baruch Goldstein, an American medical doctor living in the nearby Jewish settlement of Kiryat Arba, entered the mosque disguised as an Israeli soldier. He opened fire with an automatic weapon, killing twenty-nine and wounding many more before being killed by those he sought to murder. Were the repulsive story of a devout and deranged man to end here, it would not be cited in this book. Many individuals in all religions have perpetrated horrific acts of violence. But, sadly, there is much more. In the view of some extremist Jewish settlers and activists, Goldstein became a hero. His grave became a pilgrimage site complete with streetlights, a sidewalk and paved area for people to gather, and a cupboard with prayer books and candles. The marble plaque on his grave reads, "To the holy Baruch Goldstein, who gave his life for the Jewish people, the Torah, and the nation of Israel." On the sixth anniversary of his attack in the mosque, the BBC reported on a celebration by extremists who gathered at his grave "dressed up as the gunman, wearing army uniforms, doctors' coats, and fake beards." The story concluded by noting that an estimated ten thousand people had visited his grave in six years.[2]

The overwhelming majority of Israeli Jews find the behavior of

Goldstein and those who venerate him as repugnant as do all people of goodwill. Extremist settlers, however, exhibit a religious zeal that can be frightening. I know; I have met with some of them. Many Israelis note that this zeal is one of the largest obstacles to a negotiated peace with the Palestinians, and yet the settlements in the occupied territories have continued to grow as the government of Israel subsidizes them with more than $300 million each year.

The settlement of Kiryat Arba sits right in the middle of a large Palestinian population precisely because of the sacred space associated with Abraham and the patriarchs. Goldstein was a devoted follower of Rabbi Meir Kahane. Goldstein recognized Israel (including the occupied territories he called Judea and Samaria) as sacred space for Jews. He openly advocated forcing the Palestinians out of these lands. He gave his life for this goal, an end whose means included murdering Muslims as they gathered for prayer at the tomb of their common patriarch.

The contrast between this behavior and the well-known teaching of Hillel, the celebrated first-century rabbi for whom Jewish campus organizations today are named, could not be starker. In a scene paralleling the query posed to Jesus, a heathen man approached Hillel and said, "If you can teach me the whole of the Torah while I stand on one foot, you can make me a Jew." Hillel replied, "What is hateful to you, do not do to your neighbor. This is the whole Torah; the rest is commentary. Go and study."[3] Hillel's version of the golden rule reflects the clear biblical imperative found in Leviticus 19:18: "You shall love your neighbor as yourself."

When violence is used to defend sacred space, political machinations are usually involved. We have already seen this in connection with attempts to destroy the Dome of the Rock and al-Aqsa Mosque in Jerusalem. In some instances extremists with political and religious goals initiate confrontation. In many cases political leaders, people who are keenly aware of the powerful attachment to sacred space, deliberately provoke the passions and elevate the cause of defending sacred space among zealous adherents. Blatant abuse of religion for political expediency may be deplorable, but it is often effective. Political figures would not try such manipulation of religious sensitivities if malleable and often gullible believers did not regularly take the bait.

Such was clearly the case on September 28, 2000, when Ariel Sharon, then leader of the opposition Likud Party in Israel, decided to visit the Temple Mount. Although Sharon claimed he intended no provocation, few people believed him. He announced his visit days in advance, summoned the media, and took along hundreds of police in riot gear. Sharon admitted he intended to make a bold statement about every Jew's right to walk on the Temple Mount. Since most rabbis believe Jews should not go on the Temple Mount precisely because of its sanctity, Sharon's visit was not a religious pilgrimage. Rather, most Israelis and Palestinians interpreted his actions as a political provocation using jointly revered sacred space to stir deep passions. The ploy worked. He strengthened his position among the hard-liners on the right in the Likud, blunting the growing strength of former prime minister Benjamin Netanyahu. And he provoked an angry response, a violent "uprising" from Palestinians. Within two days of the highly visible trip to the Temple Mount, more than one hundred Palestinians had died as Israeli forces responded to their angry reaction. As the situation deteriorated, increasingly frightened Israelis rewarded Sharon's hard line toward Palestinians: he was elected the new prime minister.

Overtly political manipulation of religious sentiment connected to a sacred space was also at work in the Hindu-Muslim clashes in Ayodhya. In 1991 political and religious organizations promoting Hindu nationalism combined energies in a provocative campaign to build a temple on the site traditionally associated with Lord Ram. Whipped into frenzy for months, throngs of Hindus marched into Ayodhya in 1992 and destroyed the Babri Mosque, a structure that had been on that site since 1520. Muslim response was swift and deadly. More than 1,100 people in both communities perished in the subsequent fighting. Religious sensitivities were continually inflamed during the 1990s, as periodic clashes ensured the open wound would not heal.

The man who spearheaded the initiative to tear down the mosque and build the temple in 1991–92 was L. K. Advani. It was a deliberate effort to rally support for Advani's Hindu nationalist party in Uttar Pradesh, India's largest state, where Ayodhya is located.[4] Advani's party aligned with the World Hindu Council, consolidating support that had traditionally split among several caste-based parties and the main rival, the Congress Party. By 2002 Advani had become India's second most powerful political leader, the home minister. In order to reach the top level of political power in the world's largest democratic country, Advani's party abandoned support for constructing the Ram temple in order to build political coalitions. Most Muslims have been predictably wary of a leader who rode the wave of Hindu nationalism to power. Many have charged that the government was slow to send in forces to protect the Muslim minority during the riots in late February 2002. Many Hindu extremists also became annoyed with Advani's party for withdrawing support for building the Ram temple. But the goal of reclaiming this sacred space had now taken on a life of its own.

People of faith routinely want to connect physically with the places associated with the sacred stories of their religion. Sacred spaces represent an important component in religious life, one of many means facilitating movement toward the goal. But if protecting the sacred space at any cost becomes paramount, the results can be deadly. When people are called on to do violence to their neighbor in the service of a righteous cause, they should know that something is dreadfully wrong. In the end, human beings remain responsible for their actions. In the examples we've considered, political manipulation, nationalist agendas, and group identity are also bound up with the defense of sacred space. Maintaining or reinforcing group identity is another component of religious life that can easily be elevated to an end that justifies any means.

REINFORCING GROUP IDENTITY
AGAINST OUTSIDERS

Concern for the well-being of one's religious community is normal. The positive impulse can turn violently negative when group identity is defined in ways that dehumanize people outside the community; the "other" is seen not as a person but as an object posing a threat. Once this dynamic is in place, otherwise unthinkable behavior can be justified as a means to the end of reinforcing and protecting group identity. This orientation helps explain, for instance, the horrific phenomenon known as ethnic cleansing. The most extreme and vile example of dehumanizing the other occurred during the Holocaust, the systematic extermination of more than six million Jews during Hitler's reign in Nazi Germany. The policies of Nazi Germany were not officially Christian, but they were the product of a long and deplorable history of Christians' behavior toward Jews.

From its beginning, Christian identity was closely linked with the Jewish tradition. Jesus was a Jew. The disciples were Jews. Paul, the most successful first-century missionary, was a zealous Jew who saw the nascent Christian movement as a threat before he had a dramatic experience of conversion near Damascus. The New Testament texts, which were written twenty to seventy years after the time of Jesus, tell us a good deal about the interplay among different factions of the Jews and the new religious community emerging in Palestine. Historian James Carroll begins his comprehensive study of the relation between the church and the Jews with these interchanges, citing many positive as well as negative dimensions to this often confused and confusing relationship. The earliest documents, the letters of Paul, reflect the apostle's own inner struggle. Paul contrasts Jewish "works" with Christian "faith"; he writes of Jewish "law" and Christian "freedom"; and yet he also makes clear that God has by no means abandoned the Jewish people (Romans 9–11). Carroll draws on a wide range of scholarly resources to argue that the Gospel accounts reveal different stages of Christian identity vis-à-vis the Jews. The final canonical Gospel written, the Gospel of John, reflects the growing friction in several passages harshly critical of Jews. Many Christians have quoted these texts over the centuries as a basis for demonizing the Jews as a group. As we have already seen, absolute truth claims based on selective reading of sacred texts is often a sign of corrupted religion.[5]

Despite considerable tension and conflict, Christians and Jews continued to interact positively in a variety of ways prior to the fourth century, when "the cross of Jesus became a sword in the hands of Constantine." When Christianity became joined with state power, attitudes and behavior toward Jews deteriorated. The rancor evident in the polemics of some New Testament writings "mutated into a more virulent strain of rhetoric in subsequent centuries."[6]

In the fourth century prominent Christian leaders like John Chrysostom, bishop of Antioch, and Ambrose, bishop of Milan, defined Christian identity in sharp contrast with the Jews. Theologian Rosemary Radford Ruether's powerful study *Faith and Fratricide* recounts how their vitriolic incrimination of Jews led directly to attacks on synagogues. In a series of eight "Sermons Against the Jews," John Chrysostom sought to chasten both Christians who were still embracing forms of Jewish practices and the Jews themselves:

> I know that many people hold a high regard for the Jew, and consider their way of life worthy of respect at the present time. This is why I am hurrying to pull up this fatal notion by the roots. . . . [A] synagogue is not only a whorehouse . . . it is also a den of thieves and a haunt of wild animals.[7]

Ambrose declared synagogues "a place where Christ is denied . . . a haunt of infidels, a home of the impious, a hiding place of madmen, under the damnation of God Himself."[8] From there it got worse. Much worse. The checkered history includes sporadic examples of vicious attacks on Jews and synagogues in different parts of Christendom during its first millennium. At times Jewish life flourished. After the rise of Islam, many Jews prospered as merchants who could move freely in both Islamic- and Christian-controlled lands. Jews shared in government and in the rich life of arts and sciences during a golden age lasting over two centuries in Islamic Spain. But ominous developments were also taking place. The charge of deicide, the accusation that Jews as a people were responsible for the death of Christ, began to take hold. Restrictions on occupations, residency, and sometimes clothing foreshadowed other deplorable dimensions of many Christians' attitudes and behavior toward Jews.

Beginning with the Crusades, a phenomenon we will examine in the next chapter, brutal assaults on Jews and Jewish communities occurred systematically throughout Europe. Sociologist of Religion Rodney Stark catalogs dozens of collective anti-Semitic outbursts in Germany, France, England, and Spain, resulting in tens of thousands of documented deaths during the Middle Ages.[9] The now-familiar pattern continued in various manifestations throughout the centuries. Many Western Christians shared the view that Jews somehow endangered Christian identity. Whatever the perceived threats—real or imagined, from Islam or within Christendom—the Jews as a group were often the convenient target. As I said in the introduction, my family story includes Jewish great-grandparents who fled the Poland-Russia area just over a century ago during pogroms.

The long history of Christians' dehumanizing Jews reached the lowest point with the Holocaust. Such massive violence would not have been possible apart from the history leading up to Nazi Germany. It would not have happened without the active participation of, sympathetic support of, and relative indifference exhibited by large numbers of Christians.[10] The genocide was so grotesque it defies comprehension. Jews, Christians, and others are right to say continually, we must "never forget." A somber visit to a concentration camp in Germany or Poland or to a Holocaust Memorial in Jerusalem or Washington, D.C., places a haunting question squarely in front of followers of Christ: How could a gospel of love be connected with such hateful and evil behavior—not once but consistently for many centuries?

Our focus is on signs of religion becoming evil. Even a cursory survey of Christians' hostility and brutal treatment of Jews reveals several of the signs we've considered already: absolute truth claims about God and the meaning of selected sacred texts, blind obedience to influential leaders and unquestioned doctrines, and misguided efforts to reinforce or defend group identity over against the other. During the sixty years since the Holocaust, many Jews and Christians have worked hard to gain understanding, build bridges, and find constructive ways to work together on common concerns. But remnants of anti-Semitism are visible and audible as various Christians continue to define themselves over against Jews as a group.

In early March 2002 a private conversation between evangelist Billy Graham and then-President Richard Nixon appeared on the thirty-year-old Oval Office tapes that were released to the public. Graham told the president that Jews had a "stranglehold" on the media that needed to be broken because it was "ruining the country." Nixon replied, "You believe that?" "Yes, sir," Graham responded. "Oh, boy. So do I," Nixon agreed, adding, "I can't ever say that, but I believe it." At this point Graham replied, "No, but if you get elected a second time, then we might be able to do something." Graham also confides to Nixon, "A lot of Jews are great friends of mine. . . . They know I'm friendly to Israel and so forth. But [Jews] don't know how I really feel about what they are doing to this country, and I have no power and no way to handle them." Nixon's reply: "You must not let them know."[11] On hearing of the tapes, Billy Graham immediately issued an apology saying that he did not recall making the remarks when he was fifty-three years old.

When I heard this news story, I thought of many other examples of stereotyping, dehumanizing statements I've heard over the years. I thought, too, of a poignant comment made by my friend Rabbi

Balfour Brickner fifteen years ago as he and I left a U.S. senator's office. We had been meeting with several senators on the Foreign Relations Committee, advocating for U.S. policies that we both believed were appropriate and in the best interests of all parties to the Middle East conflict. The joint advocacy of two New Yorkers—a prominent rabbi and the director of the Middle East Office for the National Council of Churches—was causing, we believed, some senators to think about U.S. policies and religious constituencies in new ways. As we left one office and were walking together in the hallowed halls of Congress, Bal paused and said to me, "I'm very glad we are doing this together. We are very much on the same wavelength. What we are saying must be heard by these senators. But, Charles, you need to know that this is not easy for me. It is hard for us Jews to fully trust most Christians, even those we are convinced have the best intentions. You have to realize that two thousand years of Christian 'love' is almost more than we Jews can bear."

Jesus' teachings, like those of Hillel, are a reliable guide for authentic religion: love God and love your neighbor as yourself; treat other people as you would like to be treated. Far too many Western Christians have failed to appropriate that central tenet, separating their religious community by dehumanizing others—Jews and people of color, in particular. They often have failed to ask, "What is the end or the goal we are seeking? How can it be realized in ways that are consistent with the central teachings and requirements of our faith?" The good news is that change is both possible and happening. Long-standing patterns of behavior can and must change.

Reinforcing Group Identity from Within

Failure to apply the golden rule, to love your neighbor as yourself, is not only an external problem. Sometimes religious communities reinforce group identity or protect the status quo through forms of discrimination and dehumanization within the group. This can take the forms of racism, classism, and sexism. In recent decades major strides in gender and women's studies—particularly, but not exclusively, within Judaism and Christianity—have illuminated some of these long-darkened corners of religious life and practice. A great deal more work remains to be done if concerned people of faith hope to clarify and effectively rectify ways religion has been and is being used against women as a group. Examples of this form of corrupt religion within Islam and the Hindu tradition illustrate the problem.

Media attention on the restrictive and harshly repressive policies affecting Muslim women in Afghanistan brought serious issues into a wider public discussion. Under the extreme version of Islamic law instituted by the Taliban, women had to be covered in the full *burqa* outside the home. A female discovered to be less than "properly" covered in public was subject to a beating on the street by self-appointed guardians of Islam. No exceptions were permitted; the few women doctors who continued working even had to perform surgery from behind the mesh cloth eyepiece in the head cover, which allows only limited visibility. Educational opportunities were severely curtailed for girls and young women; books were confiscated; access to the outside world was largely blocked. Many Muslims—men and women—objected to these policies as extreme, yet the laws differed in degree rather than kind from Islamic laws in other Islamic lands, notably several prominent countries in the oil-rich region of the Arabian Gulf.

I have pursued many dimensions of these issues personally with Muslim women and men as well as thoughtful and knowledgeable non-Muslims. Were we to gather one hundred Muslims in a room to talk about what the Qur'an and *hadith* teach and how best to interpret and implement those teachings today, we would hear a wide range of opinions. Many would insist that men and women are absolutely equal before God but that they have different roles and responsibilities; some would point out that the specific injunctions applying to women focus on dressing modestly. The way such basic premises are manifest in practice varies significantly.[12] In

Tunisia, a North African country where Muslims make up over 98 percent of the population, there are few notable restrictions: women enjoy educational opportunities; women vote; women have choices in matters of reproduction. In Saudi Arabia, on the other hand, many restrictions apply: women cannot go out in public unless accompanied by a male relative; women cannot drive cars; women cannot vote. Many Westerners would be surprised to learn that Iranian women have considerably more freedom and opportunities than women in most other nearby Islamic countries. In the first elections after the Islamic revolution in 1979, for instance, three women were elected to the *majlis,* the Iranian parliament.

The point is that there are legitimate options, authentic ways to address and change "religious" policies and laws that subjugate women as a group. In all traditions many historical and cultural factors shape current practices. Some examples illustrate the depth of the problem and specific ways some Muslim men claim to protect the integrity of the community of Islam at the expense of women within the tradition.

Perhaps the most egregious example is that of "female circumcision," or female genital mutilation. This horrific practice is thought to have originated in central Africa long before the arrival of Christianity or Islam. Some Christians and people in tribal cultures still practice forms of female genital mutilation, but it is much more widespread in Islam. The painful procedure is done on young, pre-pubescent girls. The degree of mutilation varies, but it involves scraping away all or part of the clitoris and sometimes the labia. While the large majority of Muslims worldwide do not practice or endorse this procedure, it remains a common feature, sanctioned as Islamic, in parts of Africa and elsewhere. The rationale varies, but it is usually connected to the belief that women cannot easily control their sexual urges. This procedure, along with veiling and seclusion, is justified as a way of protecting both the women from their lusts and the honor of the male in the family. Serious, painful, and long-term medical problems often accompany this crude practice, most obviously in relation to intercourse and childbirth. The destructive psychological impact is difficult to quantify but not hard to imagine. Many who have studied and advocated against the practice believe it has nothing to do with Islam and a great deal to do with perceptions about increased sexual pleasure for men and male control over women. It is estimated that today "one in five Muslim girls lives in a community where some form of clitoridectomy is sanctioned and justified by local Islamic leaders."[13]

At times, protecting the so-called honor of females and their families becomes truly absurd. Such was the case on March 11, 2002, when fire broke out at a school for girls in Mecca. Male firefighters and paramedics arrived on the scene, only to be prevented from entering the building by religious police. The guardians of public decency blocked the rescue on the grounds that some of the girls inside were not wearing the clothing deemed appropriate in public. Fifteen girls perished in the fire. This episode produced an outcry within Saudi Arabia, resulting in King Fahd's decision to reassign oversight of girls' education in the kingdom.

Gender-related practices effectively discriminate against women as a group in a number of ways, sometimes with deadly consequences. Although numbers are difficult to obtain with any precision, several hundred Muslim women are killed each year by family members under the rubric of honor killings. Islamic law includes many strict rules and harsh punishments for illicit sexual activity outside of marriage, including capital punishment when there is a confession or there are four male eyewitnesses to adultery.[14] At times the legal processes are ignored and fathers or brothers who believe their family honor has been besmirched take matters into their own hands through vigilante-style "justice." Frequently, the killers disguise the woman's death by fire or some other type of "accident" in order to limit the likelihood of an investigation by the police. The practice occurs mostly in poor and remote locations, but not always. In 1977 a major controversy erupted when the BBC in England and the Public Broadcasting System in the United States

announced plans to air a documentary about the honor killing of a
Saudi princess entitled *Death of a Princess*. A Muslim friend once
described an honor killing he witnessed on the streets of Baghdad
in the early 1970s. He was drinking coffee when he heard a young
woman screaming, running down the street. He looked up and saw
a nineteen- or twenty-year-old being chased by a middle-aged man
with a knife in hand. The man, who turned out to be her father,
caught her by the hair, slashed her throat, and dropped her on the
street to die. Despite feeling instant nausea from the grisly scene,
my friend joined others trying to get assistance for the young
woman. But it was too late. When I asked what happened to the
killer, he replied, "Nothing. It was an honor killing."

Following the war in the former Yugoslavia, the U.S. State
Department began publishing extensive reports on atrocities and
war crimes. Along with reports on forced expulsions, looting, and
burning, the documents record thousands of cases of "systematic
and organized mass rape" and summary executions. The evil of
mass rape and murder perpetrated on women, children, and other
noncombatants is incomprehensible. How could human beings so
dehumanize and objectify other human beings, in this case people
with whom they had lived as neighbors for decades? Subsequent
stories about the additional plight of Muslim women compounded
the tragedy. Many women raped by Serbian soldiers were "tainted";
their own communities later abandoned them. These victims were
being victimized yet again.[15]

The deeply troubling stories are reminiscent of a scene described
by theologian Harvey Cox in *Many Mansions*, his story of encounters with other faiths. During a visit to the holy city of Vrndavana in
India, Cox discovered that a quarter of the city's population con-
sisted of widows living wretchedly in hovels carved out of back
alleys. They had come there to live out their lives since their auspiciousness had died along with their husbands. In traditional India,
widows could retain their auspiciousness by voluntarily joining
their departed husband on his funeral pyre, a practice known as *sut-*

tee. The British first outlawed the practice of *suttee,* and it remains illegal in India today. As Cox wrestled with the issues raised by the plight of these destitute widows, he concluded that once again, "the patriarchal control of the myths and practices of religion—this time Hinduism—has succeeded in making life miserable for women."[16]

It is important to underscore that the examples cited here offend the religious and moral sensitivities of many Muslims and Hindus as well as others. And other traditions have overt and subtle ways of reinforcing group identity or the status quo by means of subjugating or dehumanizing women as a group. The examples are intended to make two points. First, people in all traditions can and do employ horrific means to achieve traditionally accepted goals—not the ultimate goal, but goals that are intentionally or unintentionally elevated and considered sacrosanct. When these result in dehumanizing patterns of behavior toward others—in this case, women within the tradition—something is clearly wrong.

The second point is one of hope. Change is possible. After more than 2,500 years, the caste system in India is now illegal. The Hindu tradition is alive and well and adapting in the world of the twenty-first century. Significant changes related to gender issues and long-established perceptions about women are occurring in all traditions. As communication and global interdependence continue to grow, it will be increasingly difficult to justify, in the name of religion, behavior that fails to meet the standard of the golden rule. Men and women of faith can and should be at the forefront of the long-overdue struggle to stop religion from being used as a vehicle to oppress and dehumanize groups of people.

PROTECTING THE INSTITUTION

People also use the end to justify any means when they wish to protect religious institutions and teachings they feel are at risk. Institutions and central doctrines are necessary components in all enduring religious systems; they are essential to propagate the tradition and nurture each generation of adherents. Institutions and authoritative teachings provide structures that help religious communities move toward their goals. In the case of Christianity, the process of institutionalization began in earnest in the years after Jesus was no longer physically present. As long as he was with them, followers could seek his guidance on all types of issues. Jesus' disciples and apostles assumed primary leadership roles in the emerging community, but in time more structure was necessary. In the New Testament book of Acts, we can see the process of institutionalization taking shape:

> Now during those days, when the disciples were increasing in number, the Hellenists complained against the Hebrews because their widows were being neglected in the daily distribution of food. And the twelve called together the whole community of the disciples and said, "It is not right that we should neglect the Word of God in order to wait on tables. Therefore, friends, select from among yourselves seven men of good standing, full of the Spirit and of wisdom, whom we may appoint to this task, while we for our part will devote ourselves to prayer and to serving the word." What they said pleased the whole community, and they chose Stephen, a man full of faith and the Holy Spirit, together with Philip, Prochorus, Nicanor, Timon, Parmenas, and Nicolas, a proselyte of Antioch. They had these men stand before the apostles who prayed and laid their hands on them. (Acts 6:1–6)

This short passage tells us a great deal. The earliest church included "Hellenists," Greek-speaking Jews or Jews who had embraced Greek customs, as well as "Hebrews," believers who spoke Aramaic. We have already discussed the communal sharing of resources in connection with the startling story of Ananias and Sapphira. Here we learn that some people are grumbling about perceived inequities in the daily distribution of food. The successful growth of the new movement has put a severe strain on the energies of the apostles, so they propose ordaining or calling out seven "men of good standing" to "wait on tables" in order that the apostles might devote themselves more to "prayer and serving the word," that is, proclaiming the gospel. The plan sounds good to everyone, and a simple process follows whereby authority is symbolically transferred through an ordination ritual consisting of prayer and the laying on of hands.

This passage shows the earliest followers of Jesus adapting and creating institutional structures to further key components of their mission. They couldn't simply go ask Jesus what to do; they had to formulate a plan to meet the growing needs of the community in ways that allowed for further proclamation of the gospel message. Some of the later New Testament documents show more sophisticated structures within the churches. As the early community continued to grow, a larger system of parishes and bishoprics developed, largely along the lines of governmental structures evident in the Roman Empire. In time, the bishop in Rome was affirmed as having primacy among the hundreds of bishops. The basic institutional structure of what would become the Roman Catholic Church, by far the largest Christian communion among thousands today, was in the process of forming.

Although the institutional structures vary considerably in different traditions, the need for decision-making authority and established vehicles to carry out the work of the religion is a common feature of all major religious systems. Typically, first the teacher and then, after the teacher's death, his or her words become the foundation for such authority. In Buddhism, the first disciples of Siddhartha Gautama could approach him with questions for the first forty-five years. Jesus was available to his disciples for only a few years, and then they had to form the lines of authority noted above. For twenty-two years the Muslims could look to Muhammad for guidance on religious, political, economic, and social matters. In addition to the Qur'an, as mentioned previously, Muhammad's sayings and actions became the second primary source for a system of Islamic law. The methods differed widely, but all three of these traditions over time had to find institutional ways of clarifying what was authoritative teaching and practice, what variations were allowed, and what things were unacceptable.

Institutional structures develop to meet and serve real needs—religious, political, economic, military, recreational, and so on. As needs change, so, too, must institutional structures. This often does not happen easily. Rather than being a means to an end, protecting the religious institution sometimes becomes the end that justifies any means. When this corruption occurs, negative consequences are sure to follow.

An unsettling example has been visible within the Catholic Church for the past two decades. Between 1985 and 1993, a number of shocking stories emerged alleging sexual abuse of children by predatory priests. The simmering scandal erupted in January 2002 with disclosures in Boston about a number of incidents tied to Father John Geoghan. Reports in the *Boston Globe* indicated that this priest had been moved around parishes during the 1980s *after* the leaders in the archdiocese knew he had abused children in at least three different parishes. The report disclosed that the archdiocese had paid out over ten million dollars to settle some fifty lawsuits against him.[17] Within days, other stories flooded out of Boston, Chicago, Los Angeles, and elsewhere. By June, reports indicated more than two hundred charges against Geoghan, who turned out to be one of twelve priests in the Boston area with charges pending. Another alleged pedophile who had been knowingly moved among parishes for three decades, Father Paul Shanley, was arrested in California and extradited to Massachusetts on charges of child rape.

Media attention was white hot for months. Hundreds of newspaper stories and television reports and talk shows covered various dimensions of the unraveling scandal. The U.S. cardinals and leaders of the National Conference of Catholic Bishops were summoned to Rome to meet with Pope John Paul II and cardinals in the Roman

Curia. Two months later, in mid-June, the U.S. Catholic bishops met in Dallas, Texas, to debate and adopt a uniform policy for past and future offenses. They also issued public apologies to victims of sexual abuse. Within the span of five months, a total of 177 priests suspected of molesting minors had either resigned or been relieved of their assignment in twenty-eight states and the District of Columbia.[18] Two American priests committed suicide, and one was murdered by a person who claimed to be a victim of the priest's sexual misconduct.

Sordid details retracing particular events will continue to emerge for several years as legal actions against alleged perpetrators unfold. The fact that there are pedophiles among the clergy is deeply distressing, to be sure. But it is not beyond imagination. We all know stories of sexual predators who work in various professions. And sexual misconduct among clergy is not exactly a new phenomenon. Priests or any other men who sexually abuse children are not only criminals; they are ill and in dire need of help. Whatever punishment and treatment program may be appropriate, one thing is absolutely clear: people who are known to abuse children must not be allowed to work in situations where more unwitting victims may be put at risk. So the larger and more haunting questions raised by this scandal pertained to the leadership in the various dioceses where the 177 (or more) priests were working. Why on earth would bishops, archbishops, and cardinals continue to move so many people around or try to deal with these problems without recourse to the criminal justice system? Was it simply negligence? Was it a matter of unwarranted confidence in treatment programs? In some cases, these were surely factors. Whatever the excuses or explanations, however, a tellingly systematic pattern points to a larger issue, an overriding concern, an "end" that apparently justified secrecy, duplicity, and even criminal negligence as means to achieve it.

The answer lies in an overriding commitment to protect the institution of the church. When you listen carefully to the explanations and read the documents closely, this end is obvious. Many church leaders feared that scandals regarding sexual misconduct would undermine the many good ministries within their diocese. If people could not trust a priest with children, who and what in the church could be trusted? Indeed. So, behind a veil of secrecy, priests were moved and lawsuits filed by some victims were quietly settled without public awareness. Not only did this corruption of religion victimize and traumatize untold numbers of individuals and their families, but the long years of cover-up will almost certainly do far more harm to the institution of the Catholic Church and its ministries than might have resulted from the honest and transparent action warranted at the time the heinous behavior was substantiated. Although the percentage of priests involved was relatively small, the impact of unconscionable decisions made by responsible leaders continues to loom large. The largest Christian body in the United States will spend years seeking to recover from the damage done by leaders whose concern for the institution sometimes outweighed the concern for children whose nurture and growth in faith the church existed to serve.

Authority figures have tried to protect religious institutions and essential doctrines from perceived threats in many ways throughout history. The church-sponsored Inquisition stands out as a prime example. For more than six centuries, church officials in Western Europe used a wide range of now legendary and horrific techniques as means to goals. The ostensible ends were two: to "save" people from eternal damnation and to protect the church from various threats related to heretical doctrines.

The Office of Inquisition began in 1215 at the Fourth Lateran Council, when Pope Innocent III put forth guidelines for persecuting heretics. This set in motion the first of a series of initiatives whereby inquisitors would secretly collect information about possible heretics in a given region. Proof was not required, just enough hearsay evidence. The rules varied over time and in the different lands most actively involved: Italy, France, Germany, Spain, and Portugal. But the patterns were strikingly similar. Charges were brought against suspects, and they were given an opportunity to recant or face severe punishment. The accused may or may not ever have known the charges against them. They often had to guess at the alleged offense if they wanted to "confess." Torture was an acceptable means to "get at the truth." The rack, water torture, and leg screws were among the most effective techniques. The "confession" rate hovered near 90 percent. Under these conditions, it was possible to get almost anyone to confess to almost anything. The penalties for those who recanted might include public scourging, fines, and being forced to wear unmistakably distinctive clothing—often a garment with huge yellow crosses on the front and back—as a mark of shame. Those declared guilty on the prescribed Day of Judgment often were burned slowly at the stake. The families were made to suffer even more as all the property connected to the guilty party was confiscated.

Many people associate the Inquisition with the reign of King Ferdinand and Queen Isabella, who decreed in 1492 that all Jews had four months to convert or leave Spain. Approximately forty thousand, one-half of the Jewish population, fled; the other half "converted." However, this was only one of several major phases of the Inquisition. The process began with a crackdown on dissenting groups like the Waldensians and Cathars in France. Then for several centuries the Inquisition took the form of witch hunts.[19] Attacks on Protestant reformers and creative thinkers like Galileo marked other phases of the Inquisition through the centuries. In Spain, the Inquisition a century after Ferdinand and Isabella was aimed largely at the *conversos,* Jews who had converted under threat of persecution; inquisitors claimed that *conversos* were "Judaizers," people who were secretly practicing Judaism. Similar charges were later applied to *moriscos,* Muslims who embraced Christianity under duress. In 1609, just over a century after Muslims were forced to convert or leave Spain, the government decided that Muslims were incapable of truly converting and so all *moriscos* were expelled. A similar conviction about *conversos* permeated the Spanish Inquisition during the sixteenth century. Although the official reasons for the Inquisition were to save people from hell and to protect the church from heresy, other motives were often involved. In the case of King Ferdinand, the Inquisition was a tool for confiscating fiscal resources many Jewish merchants had acquired. It also turned out to be a source of slave labor for his fleet of ships. Instead of death, Ferdinand sentenced many to work as galley slaves.

The most notorious practices of the Inquisition largely died out by the nineteenth century, but the office remained until 1965, when Pope Paul VI officially changed the institution to the Office of the Congregation for the Doctrine of the Faith during Vatican II. In October of 1998 Pope John Paul II summoned a large group of scholars and church leaders for an "unprecedented examination of conscience" during the Year of Jubilee. In particular, he advocated a painful exploration of the Inquisition, which he termed "a tormented phase in the history of the Church." The pontiff then ordered the opening of secret Vatican archives for scholarly scrutiny.[20]

PRESERVING THE CONNECTION BETWEEN THE MEANS AND THE END

One common warning sign appears in all of the examples contained within this chapter. A particular goal or end was articulated as essential or paramount, and in defense of that goal people ignored the call to compassionate, constructive relationships with their neighbors. When people are dehumanized or treated as objects, the purported goal immediately should be called into question. In each religious tradition, foundational figures provide clear guidance that it is essential to treat others with love and respect, just as you would like others to treat you.

Various components of religious life—including sacred space and time, communal identity, and institutional structures—are vitally important. But they are not the ends of religious life. They facilitate the life of faith in community. Jesus illustrated this in a dramatic way when he apparently defied one of the Ten Commandments, much to the chagrin of people focused on the letter of the law. Jesus picked heads of wheat to eat (Mark 2:23–28) and healed people (Luke 13:10–17) on the Sabbath, and both acts were considered work and thus violations of the commandment to "remember the Sabbath day and keep it holy." When challenged by religious authorities, Jesus responded by saying, "The Sabbath was made for humankind, and not humankind for the Sabbath." In other words, sacred time was a benefit, a means to facilitate religious life, not an end in and of itself. Jesus was concerned first with the human interest. The principle applies to sacred space and objects as well. As with Islamic law, Jewish law allowed for death by stoning when people were guilty of adultery. Jesus, on the other hand, repeatedly reached out to prostitutes and others in need of his compassionate, healing touch. In the famous story of the woman caught in adultery and about to be stoned, Jesus intervened and challenged the assembled executioners: "Let anyone who is without a sin among you be the first to cast a stone at her" (John 8:1–11).[21]

In recent years, many evangelical Christians have worn cloth bracelets with the letters *WWJD* prominently displayed. "What Would Jesus Do?" is meant to remind the person to reflect continually on his or her behavior in light of Jesus' teachings. If all who follow Jesus would pause, reflect, and ask that simple question, a number of presumably vital ends might look different. There might well be a great deal more attention on the most basic commandments to love God and love your neighbor as yourself.

So, too, examples of corrupt manifestations of religion in Islam cry out for change. Many Muslims today argue convincingly that Muhammad did a great deal to elevate the status and protect the rights of women, particularly in view of the prevailing customs in seventh-century Arabia. For instance, Muhammad forbade female infanticide, the cruel practice of burying unwanted female infants alive in the sand. Many passages in the Qur'an and *hadith* materials stress the absolute obligation of Muslims to provide for the needs of widows, orphans, the poor, and the needy. The Five Pillars of Islam all remind believers that everything one has comes from God, and generosity toward others, particularly those in need, lies at the heart of Islam. On the Day of Judgment, people will be given a book containing the record of their life on earth. Do many Muslims really imagine that an honor killing or the shunning of rape victims or silence when presented with horrific information about female genital mutilation in the name of Islam will be recorded as positive deeds in that book?

Long-held views and customs are woven into the fabric of these various patterns of behavior. Change is not easy or painless. But it is possible. It is entirely possible to change one's way of understanding even teachings apparently set forth in the Qur'an. The Qur'an allows, for instance, Muslim men to marry up to four women. This practice still occurs in some parts of the Muslim world. In some Muslim countries it is illegal. The most common argument against the practice is found in the related requirement that any man with more than one wife must treat each wife equally. I've heard dozens of thoughtful Muslims conclude that this latter requirement effectively nullifies the provision since no man can ultimately treat two or three or four wives absolutely equally. The point here is that Muslims have the resources and the flexibility within their tradition to modify teachings and practices that clearly need to be changed in the twenty-first century. And many Muslim women and men as well as non-Muslim students of Islam today are reexamining the Qur'an, *hadith,* and other recognized sources to seek new ways of understanding and reframing the tradition where forms of misogyny have too often prevailed.

When historians of the future look back on the extraordinary events of the twentieth century, they will have much to say about one its most towering figures, a poor, frail Indian man named Gandhi. Here was a saint, a deeply religious man who challenged the political and religious status quo on many levels. On the basis of his understanding of religious truth, he successfully led a nonviolent revolution against British colonial rule even as he rejected and helped abolish the Hindu caste system. His writings and life deserve to be studied and discussed much more widely than they are today.

Why? Gandhi articulated clear ends; he had definite goals for his many pursuits. But he refused to allow these ends to be in conflict with their means. Above all else, he affirmed the guiding principle of nonviolent "soul-force," or *satyagraha*. He was committed to treating others, even the British and some Muslims who opposed him, with love and compassion, trusting that God's truth would prevail.

Gandhi was speaking on communal relations on March 26, 1930, when a Muslim youth asked him about serious problems between Hindus and Muslims that threatened the struggle for independence. Gandhi replied,

I never dreamed I could win merely through my effort or assisted only by Hindus. I stand in need of assistance of Muslims, Parsis [Zoroastrians], Christians, Sikhs, Jews, and all other Indians. I need the assistance even of Englishmen. But I know too that all this combined assistance is worthless if I have not one other assistance that is from God. All is vain without His help. And if He is with this struggle no other help is necessary. But to realize His help and guidance in this struggle I need your blessings, the blessings of all communities. The blessings of thousands of men and women belonging to all communities that have attended this march are to me a visible sign of God in this struggle. . . . The question was put by a Muslim representing a powerful interest. But had a little Parsi girl representing but one hundred thousand Parsis asked the question, I should have given the same answer and said, "Without the help of Parsis, there is no 'home rule.'"[22]

~ *Six* ~

DECLARING HOLY WAR

For many people in the West, Osama bin Laden has become the face of religious evil in the world today. Television, newspaper, radio, and other media have reported frequently on bin Laden's calls for *jihad* against the United States and Israel as well as against "infidel" Muslim leaders who support those governments. Repulsive videos showing the Saudi-born leader of *al-qaida* laughing smugly as he described the "successful" attacks on the World Trade Center and the Pentagon are forever juxtaposed in our minds with the horrific and haunting images of airplanes hitting the twin towers and the towers' eventual collapse. As soon as the U.S. government was confident that bin Laden and *al-qaida* were responsible for the attacks, President George W. Bush dubbed him "the evil one" and his network of operatives "evildoers"—terms historically used for Satan and those who do his bidding. Few people objected publicly to personifying Osama bin Laden and his terrorist organization in this way as evil.

The U.S. responded to bin Laden's call for a "holy war" with the "war on terrorism," beginning with the military attack in Afghanistan. The initial name for the U.S.-led military operation—Operation Infinite Justice—had to be changed, however, since many felt the term *infinite* was too presumptuous for any person or nation to claim; only God or the law of *karma* has the capacity to dispense infinite justice. President Bush also encountered significant opposition—at home and abroad—when he extended the highly charged language of evil to nation-states, referring to Iraq, Iran, and North Korea as the "axis of evil" in his 2002 State of the Union address.

The clear lines separating the forces of "good" from the forces of "evil" were further blurred in the first few months of 2002 when intense, daily fighting broke out between the Israel Defense Forces (IDF) and the Palestinians. Israeli prime minister Ariel Sharon repeatedly invoked President Bush's unequivocal push for a war on terrorism to defend harsh military action against Palestinian "terrorists" living and operating in the West Bank and Gaza. A rash of suicide bombings, including one massive explosion that killed more than twenty people who were enjoying a Passover meal, further bolstered Sharon's position. While the Bush administration remained squarely in Israel's corner, it did not embrace such a clear demarcation between the forces of good and evil in this situation. Secretary of State Colin Powell worked directly with the involved parties to find ways to defuse the escalating crisis and resolve the conflict, which is causing both sides to suffer enormous physical and psychological losses.

Meanwhile, Pakistan and India approached the brink of war several times as Muslims and Hindus continually clashed in Kashmir. Both Hindus and Muslims perpetrated atrocities as world leaders repeatedly intervened between these two nuclear-armed countries. The depth of hostility between Hindus and Muslims in this disputed region is crystal clear. Questions about who initiated the latest round of fighting or the legitimacy of retaliation for a particular event fade rapidly into the background as the specter of nuclear conflagration looms squarely before us.

Coverage of all these events appeared day after day, week after week, month after month on the front pages of newspapers all around the world. On page three or four, one could often find stories about deadly clashes between Christians and Muslims in Nigeria or the Philippines. Periodically, the media provided an update on the war crimes tribunals in which Serbian Christian leaders were standing trial for atrocities committed against Bosnian Muslim civilians in the former Yugoslavia. An objective reader might well conclude that religion and war are inextricably linked. That same observer might perceive that the battle lines are drawn sharply and distinctly at times, while at other times being much less clear. But the pattern is unmistakable: wars all over the world are being framed by and fought with reference to religious worldviews.

We have said that more wars have been waged, more people killed, and more evil perpetrated in the name of religion than by any other institutional force in human history. The sad truth continues in our present day. In somewhat different ways, leaders and combatants continue to depict their war as a holy cause. In doing so, they compound the grave mistakes of those who went before them, and they distort the very heart of the religion they claim to be defending. Declaring war "holy" is a sure sign of corrupt religion. In fact, at the center of authentic religion one *always* finds the promise of peace, both an inner peace for the adherent and a requirement to seek peaceful coexistence with the rest of creation.

Perilous situations, at times, may indeed warrant the decisive use of force or focused military action. But such action must not be cloaked in religious language or justified by religion. There is no doubt, in my view, that the attacks of September 11 and the prospect of additional mass murder through terrorism required swift and decisive action. The immediate potential for catastrophe—from the loss of life to widespread suffering resulting from economic and political instability—was, and remains, a real and present danger. While there are legitimate bases for collective military action in the community of nations, an appeal to religion is not one of them. Moreover, in a world with a growing number of sinister weapons of mass destruction, declaring and prosecuting a holy war is not only a corruption of religion; it is also potentially suicidal.

Both Christians and Muslims claim that peace lies at the heart of their religions. Both Christianity and Islam, however, have a long and checkered history in which their respective adherents fought for causes declared holy. Many of those conflicts, moreover, involved fighting each other. Not only are these the two largest and most geographically dispersed religious communities; they also head the list of those who have corrupted the heart of their religion by linking it confidently to war. How did this happen? What can be done to stop and reverse the self-righteous march toward destruction?

FROM PACIFISM TO JUST WAR

A survey of Christian history reveals three distinct attitudes and approaches toward war and peace: pacifism, the just war doctrine, and the Crusade. A brief exploration of these three approaches helps us see how the religious ideal is easily compromised and anti-thetical behavior justified, particularly when a community of faith feels threatened by external powers.

Many passages in the New Testament point to the example of Jesus and the beliefs and practices of the first generation of Christians. Jesus rejected the mantle of a military savior that many zealots were anticipating and some would-be followers urged on him. Jesus' teachings, in fact, moved in another direction. The Sermon on the Mount begins with the Beatitudes, teachings that include a promised blessing for the peacemakers; those who work earnestly to make peace will be called "children of God" (Matthew 5:9). Jesus challenged conventional wisdom, telling his disciples to "love your enemies, and pray for those who persecute you" (Matthew 5:43). As Jesus was arrested in the Garden of Gethsemane, one of his followers drew a sword and struck the servant of the High Priest. Jesus immediately said to him, "Put your sword back into its place; for all who take the sword will perish by the sword" (Matthew 26:52). The letters of Paul speak frequently about the centrality of love and the call to a ministry of reconciliation. Writing to the Christians at Rome, Paul underscored their responsibility:

"Do not repay anyone evil for evil, but take thought for what is noble in the sight of all. If it is possible, so far as it depends on you, live peaceably with all. . . . Do not be overcome by evil, but overcome evil with good" (Romans 12:17–18, 21).

The overwhelming evidence suggests that the followers of Jesus were pacifists for the first three centuries.[1] Many early church leaders and documents underscore the unwavering commitment to nonviolence. The first hint of a Christian serving in the military appears between 170 and 180 C.E. The records are sporadic, but it appears that only a handful of Christians were soldiers prior to the fourth century.

> Christianity and war were incompatible. Christians were charged with undermining the Roman Empire by refusing military service and public office: they answered that human life was sacred to them, that they were . . . given over to peace, that God prohibits killing even in a just cause, without exception, that the weapons of the Christian were prayer, justice and suffering.[2]

The major turning point in church history came with the rise to power of Constantine early in the fourth century. Engaged in a multisided contest for leadership in the Roman Empire, Constantine prevailed in a decisive battle the day after reportedly having a vision of a white cross with the Greek inscription "In this sign you will conquer." In the shadow of two of the worst waves of Roman government persecution, Christianity was suddenly on its way to becoming the official religion of the Roman Empire. The dramatic change occurred over two decades as Constantine was able to consolidate his rule.[3] As the religion became linked with state power, the tables were turned. Threats to the state became threats to the church. The pacifist tradition did not disappear, but it was largely suppressed as most church leaders sought to redefine the roles and responsibilities of Christians within the state.

Some early writers began to distinguish between clergy, whose vocation required total dedication, and laity, whose duty as citizens included military service. Later in the fourth century, Ambrose furnished the first ingredients of what would develop into the Christian doctrine of the just war: the conduct of war must be just, and monks and priest should abstain.[4] Augustine (354–430), the highly influential thinker and prolific writer, then developed elements of the code of war, drawing on Plato and Cicero as well as his own theological understanding. Augustine's writings reflect his views on sin and punishment, the challenge of living in this world and not yet in the city of God, and the very real threat posed by barbarians storming the gate. Historian Roland Bainton summarized Augustine's views in this way:

> The war must be just in its intent—which is to restore peace. . . . Those wars may be defined as just which avenge injuries. . . . The war must be just in its disposition, which is Christian love. . . . Love does not preclude a benevolent severity, nor that correction which compassion itself dictates. . . . [War] is to be waged only under the authority of the ruler. . . . The conduct of the war must be just. . . . Faith must be kept with the enemy. There should be no wanton violence, profanation of temples, looting, massacres, or conflagration. Vengeance, atrocities, and reprisals were excluded, though ambush was allowed.[5]

Christian approaches to war and peace during the following centuries, the so-called Dark Ages, are anything but coherent. A variety of texts, edicts, and oaths reflect the conflicting influences.[6] In some cases people were clearly following New Testament teachings and requirements of penance for the shedding of blood, even for soldiers who kill an enemy in battle under orders. The overall picture one gets, however, is of a chaotic era in which various religious views were intertwined with military campaigns waged against and sometimes with the peoples on the fringes of the empire: Visigoths, Vandals, Franks, Saxons, Norse, Slavs, Berbers, and others. For centuries, Europe was beset with major wars and local conflicts. At times people completely reversed early church understandings and practices, as did Clovis, military hero of the Franks, who said about the crucifixion of Jesus, "If I and my Franks had been there, it never would have happened!" Clovis and the Franks continued their ruthless activities following their conversion to Christianity. The examples of militant Christianity from that time are many: One of the oldest known German poems actually praises Peter for drawing the sword in defense of Jesus in Gethsemane. The Saxons were converted by force. Charlemagne fought against "pagans and infidels" with the papal blessing. Many clergy engaged in battle.[7]

The convoluted story includes efforts to refine the criteria for Christians' participation in war. A monk named Gratian is credited with introducing the concept of the just war into legal discourse during the middle of the twelfth century. Others developed and refined criteria regarding the nature of the war and the status of the combatants. The doctrine of the just war was finalized in the sixteenth century.

> There were four basic criteria: (i) it must be proclaimed by lawful authority; (ii) the cause must be just; (iii) the belligerents should have a rightful intention, to advance good or avoid evil; (iv) the war must be fought by proper means. Additional criteria are sometimes found: (v) action should be against the guilty; (vi) the innocent should not suffer; (vii) war must be undertaken as a last resort; (viii) there must be a reasonable chance of success.[8]

Historian John Ferguson points out that this doctrine served to support those in temporal and ecclesiastical positions of power since violence against them was, by definition, unjust. There was also no effective way to determine if a war was just; it was by definition just if the authority figure declared it so. The doctrine also had no obvious connection with the Christian faith:

> The arguments . . . are a replacement of the teaching of the New Testament by Greek philosophy or Roman law. There is nothing, literally nothing, distinctively Christian about the result. Yet these are the considerations which have dominated the majority of Christians for most of the history of the Church.[9]

Among the many positions put forward during these early centuries were arguments that pagans, heretics, and infidels were people who effectively opposed the law of God. Conventional law or admittedly flexible norms of behavior did not automatically protect people identified as enemies of the Church. Such ideas circulating within Christendom became powerful weapons during the centuries when the behavior of many Christians was furthest removed from the teachings and example of Jesus: the era of the Crusades.

THE CRUSADES

In March 1095 Pope Urban II received an appeal from Alexius asking for help against the Turks, who were within striking distance of the Byzantine capital, Constantinople. This appeal set off a chain of events leading to the first Crusade. In late November of that year, at a meeting in Clermont, France, the pope delivered an impassioned sermon in which he called on the Franks to march to the East for the two purposes of helping the Byzantines turn back the Turks and liberating Jerusalem from Muslim control:

> You are obligated to succor your brethren in the East, menaced by an accursed race, utterly alienated from God. The Holy Sepulcher of our Lord is polluted by the filthiness of an unclean nation. . . . Start upon the road to the Holy Sepulcher

to wrest that land from the wicked race and subject it to your-
selves.[10]

The appeal produced a strong response that day with the crowd
reportedly shouting, "God wills it!" In the next few months the
message spread through sermons, papal letters, and word of mouth
in France, Italy, and parts of Germany. Far from being a just war
declared by a king, the Crusade was a war instigated by the church.
Neither Alexius nor Urban could have anticipated the popular
response. Before the scheduled departure in the summer of 1096,
large numbers of poor people decided to answer the call without
delay. With little preparation or adequate provisions, many began
marching toward Jerusalem under the banner of the cross. From the
outset of this "peasant's crusade," righteous zeal spurred horrific
behavior. Before leaving Germany, some crusaders massacred large
numbers of Jews, whom they determined were also enemies of
Christ.[11] The vast majority of those in this first wave of crusading
pilgrims died of hunger, exposure, or disease, and in battle far from
Jerusalem. The "official" First Crusade got under way with several
organized groups taking different routes toward Constantinople
and eventually Jerusalem.

A compelling four-hour documentary produced for the British
Broadcasting Corporation traces the shocking violence perpetrated
by "savage fanatics convinced they were on a sacred mission from
God." Christopher Tyerman of Oxford University notes how this
new approach to war represented a dramatic reversal: "Whereas in
1066 soldiers who fought at Hastings had to do penance for their
slaughter, on the first Crusade the slaughter itself was considered a
penitential act." Crusaders often returned to camp carrying the
heads of Muslims on spears or forcing prisoners to carry the heads
of their comrades on spears. The savagery descended even further,
into cannibalism, as the crusaders neared Antioch. Eyewitnesses
included Fletcher of Chartres, who "shuttered" as he reported on
crusaders consuming Saracens, and Radulf of Caen, who described

how "our troops boiled pagan adults in cooking pots. They impaled children on spits and devoured them grilled."[12] All along the routes to Jerusalem, crusaders terrorized and massacred Jews and many Orthodox Christians as well.

The First Crusade ostensibly set off to expel the Turks from Jerusalem. By the time crusaders reached their destination, however, the Turks were no longer in control. Egyptians ruled the city of one hundred thousand, where Jews, Christians, and Muslims were functioning well in a multicultural setting. Nevertheless, on July 15, 1099, the crusaders breached the defenses of Jerusalem and began slaughtering wantonly. They set fire to the Great Synagogue, where the Jews had gathered for safety, burning them alive. They stormed the Noble Sanctuary (or Temple Mount), where thousands of Muslims had gathered that Friday for prayers. Fleeing into the al-Aqsa Mosque, the Muslims paid a huge ransom in return for guarantees of their safety. It didn't matter. The next day they were all slaughtered. Raymond of Agiles summarized the "triumphant" scene:

Some of our men (and this was more merciful) cut off the heads of their enemies; others shot them with arrows, so that they fell from the towers; others tortured them longer by casting them into flames. Piles of heads, hands and feet were to be seen in the streets of the city. It was necessary to pick one's way over the bodies of men and horses. But these were small matters compared to what happened at the temple of Solomon, a place where religious services are ordinarily chanted. What happened there? If I tell the truth, it will exceed your powers of belief. So let it suffice to say this much at least, that in the temple and portico of Solomon, men rode in blood up to their knees and the bridle reins. Indeed, it was a just and splendid judgment of God, that this place should be filled with the blood of unbelievers, when it had suffered so long from their blasphemies. Now that the city was taken it was worth all our previous labors and hardships to see the devotion of the pilgrims at the Holy Sepulcher. How they rejoiced and exulted and sang the ninth chant to the Lord.[13]

If the macabre scene exceeded the "powers of belief" for Raymond's intended readers, it is even harder to fathom today. Nearly eleven hundred years after Jesus explicitly rejected the use of the sword in his own defense and warned "all who take the sword will perish by the sword," fanatical holy warriors waded through blood-drenched streets, stepped over dismembered body parts, and walked past the charred remains of the Great Synagogue in order to rejoice and sing at the traditional site of Jesus' burial. Those who used extreme violence to advance Christ's kingdom understood their actions in terms of "holy war." Horrific consequences resulted from the convergence of authoritative, charismatic leadership; absolute truth claims; and an end that justified any means.

The marches toward and capture of Jerusalem set in motion a series of countercrusades and new crusades that continued for centuries. In addition to the organized initiatives focused on the Holy Land, various lesser crusades were mounted with other destinations as the clashes with Muslims played out from Spain to central Europe to the eastern end of the Mediterranean. The leadership of the Roman Church was intimately involved in this dynamic process, organizing and often motivating crusaders with the promise of an indulgence.[14] This complex history shows that political and economic factors intersected with religious motivations in ways that defy simple analysis.[15]

The Crusades represent the third type of response to war and peace among Christians, joining the just war and pacifist traditions, which remained ongoing. The just war doctrine evolved between the fourth and seventeenth centuries, and it continues to provide a basis for some Christians' response to the legitimacy of war. During the same period, the pacifist tradition of the early church was suppressed but not eliminated. It continued through the centuries, particularly among some monastic groups, the most notable being the

Franciscans. St. Francis of Assisi, after his conversion to a life of poverty, was a pacifist, and his followers rejected the view that the Crusades were an appropriate way to spread the gospel. In the later Middle Ages a number of pacifist groups surfaced among the Waldensians, the Hussites, and some followers of John Wycliffe. In the sixteenth, seventeenth, and eighteenth centuries prominent individuals advocated a pacifist stance, and we see also the rise of the historic peace churches: the Anabaptists (mostly known today as the Mennonites), the Brethren, and the Quakers.

Our brief introduction to the Crusades draws attention to the violent savagery of this extended era, an unpleasant lesson most Western Christians never fully grasp. This point is important: for most Christians growing up in the West, the Crusades are a part of ancient history, an episode often viewed in a detached way through the popular lens of *The Canterbury Tales;* not so for Muslims, Jews, some Eastern, and most Oriental Orthodox Christians.[16] Their memories of the Crusades are vivid and certainly not relegated to ancient history. In my interaction with these communities of faith over the past twenty years, I have been struck time and again by the way many Muslims, Jews, and Middle Eastern Christians speak about the Crusades as if they happened recently. The historical roots run deep, as does the mistrust of powerful "Christian" nations in the West. In the Middle East, the legacy of the Crusades merges with their more recent experiences of domination by European colonial powers and post–World War II superpowers. This history creates the backdrop against which attitudes and actions are perceived in present-day conflicts. The Gulf War of 1990–91 provides a lens through which we can observe contemporary approaches to war and peace among Christians in the United States. It also clarifies some of the behavior and rhetoric emanating from certain quarters in the Middle East.

THE GULF WAR OF 1990–91

On January 16, 1991, less than twenty-four hours after the United Nations' deadline for the Iraqi withdrawal from Kuwait, U.S.-led military forces launched a massive air assault on targets in Iraq and Kuwait. That day is now firmly fixed in the minds of millions of Americans who sat mesmerized in front of televisions while reports of the war and pictures from Baghdad began flooding the airwaves.

The Gulf War was not religiously based. The sources of conflict were primarily political and economic. Even so, religion figured prominently in the many ways the conflict was framed, supported, and opposed.[17] From the beginning, President George H. W. Bush used religious language to rally public support for his policy decisions. When he announced plans to deploy troops to the region on August 8, 1990, he concluded his remarks with these words:

> And, I ask that in churches around this country prayers be said for those who are committed to protect American interests. Standing up for our principles is an American tradition. . . . Thank you, and God bless the United States of America.[18]

President Bush's appeal to popular Christian sentiment was less blatant than Saddam Hussein's self-serving appeal to Islam, as we noted earlier, in chapter 4. Nonetheless, it was obvious: virtually every speech ended with the words "God bless the United States of America"; several Sundays were designated as national days of prayer and marked by ringing of church bells; and the Reverend Billy Graham was the president's highly visible overnight guest in the White House on January 15, 1991.

President Bush and other administration officials underscored time and again the moral basis for the war as the means to halt aggression and tyranny. In the weeks leading up to the war and during the actual combat, the president spoke passionately about good versus evil, right versus wrong, the moral use of force, and God's blessing on the U.S.A. While some protesters chanted, "No blood for oil," the administration acknowledged but played down the underlying economic crisis precipitated by Saddam Hussein's takeover of Kuwait, a country whose oil fields are adjacent to Saudi Arabia.

Many prominent church leaders and organizations were visibly active in the months prior to, during, and immediately after the six weeks of the U.S. offensive. Virtually all agreed on the cruelty of Saddam Hussein's aggression and the need to halt and reverse it. The debate turned not on whether but on how best to do so. Christian voices were audible in support of each of the three different historical approaches to war and peace. On one extreme, religious broadcasting stations featured a host of TV preachers poised in front of enormous American flags—the size normally reserved for display by foreign car dealers. With this imposing backdrop, these modern-day proponents of holy war offered seemingly uncritical support for any and all U.S. policy decisions. The line between church and state was practically nonexistent.[19] Many evangelical and fundamentalist Protestants focused intensely on Armageddon scenarios, concentrating their intellectual energies on tedious efforts to interpret tidbits of information as pieces of the biblical puzzle for the end times.

To a surprising degree, however, a large number of Protestant, Orthodox, and Catholic leaders took a decidedly different approach: they were visibly united in their opposition to the massive military buildup and the prosecution of the war. Their positions were often strong and sometimes controversial, particularly in the face of seemingly strong popular support for the war among the general public. Why did so many church leaders oppose the Gulf War? First, many within the churches raised a fundamental moral objection to armed conflict as an acceptable basis for resolving conflicts. The pacifist position was evident not only among the historic peace churches but within the Roman Catholic Church and many Protestant communions as well.

Other Christian leaders, less certain of a pacifist stance, argued on moral and pragmatic grounds: violence begets violence. They advanced the same arguments for seeking diplomatic and political means (including boycotts and sanctions) that had been pursued in relation to the conflict in South Africa. Why, they asked, was it necessary for the United States and others to resort to military options so quickly in this case? The fact that Allied forces were successful militarily did not prove that this was the only or even the best way to deal with Iraqi aggression. Many feared that the middle- and long-term consequences of a military victory would only complicate and exacerbate already precarious regional dynamics. The history of the twentieth century suggests that durable peace and stability in the Middle East is not likely to be secured through war. More than a decade after the Gulf War, its legacy in Iraq and the region still speaks to this concern.

Catholic bishops in the United States and many Protestant leaders tried to focus debate on the specific requirements of the just war doctrine. In mid-November 1990 the U.S. Conference of Catholic Bishops released a statement that asked specifically if the proposed war with Iraq met the just war criteria. The bishops raised serious doubts about several of the points, including the issue of proportionality. Their doubts turned out to be well founded. While casualties on the Allied side were far below initial Pentagon estimates, more than 150,000 Iraqis and several thousand Kuwaitis perished; the number of civilian casualties in the decade following the war was much higher. Six months after the war, when media investigations revealed that various types of misinformation had been issued during the war, journalists asked Pentagon spokesman Pete Wilson about reports that some eight thousand Iraqi soldiers had been deliberately buried alive during the ground offensive. Wilson did not dispute the report. He agreed that this image was horrible, saying, "There is no nice way to kill people."[20]

The question of right intention was also challenged. If the reason for mobilization and war centered on the naked aggression of Saddam Hussein toward the hapless people of Kuwait, why did the United States not respond with military force to the desperate pleas for assistance from Iraqi Shi'ites in the south and Kurds in the north, who were also being crushed by the forces of Saddam Hussein? The tragedy befalling the Iraqi civilians, according to Bush administration officials, was an "internal" matter for the people of Iraq.

Many objected strongly to the rush to war as an apparent first, rather than last, resort. Had all the options been exhausted? Clearly many church leaders as well as many in Congress, several former secretaries of defense, and former military leaders said no, offering congressional testimony on this point in the fall of 1990. An unexpected array of conservative writers and leaders—including H. Ross Perot and Patrick Buchanan—also opposed the sequence of events that placed the military option at the head of the list. After the fact, it is all too easy to forget that church leaders arguing on the basis of just war criteria found strong support in Congress. When the U.S. Senate voted on definitive resolutions on January 12, 1991, forty-six senators voted in favor of giving sanctions more time, while fifty-three voted against; forty-seven voted against the authorization to use force, while fifty-two were in favor.

The growing ecumenical movement was another major factor shaping the thinking of many Christian leaders who opposed the Gulf War. Protestant, Catholic, and Orthodox leaders were in close contact with Christian communities in the Middle East, and the overwhelming majority of indigenous Middle Eastern Christians[21] urged them to work actively for peace. Many, including the Right Reverend Edmond Browning, the presiding bishop of President Bush and Secretary of State James Baker's own Episcopal church, responded to the challenge. Returning from a trip to Cyprus, Jordan, and Iraq, Browning met privately for nearly an hour with the president and secretary of state in order to share his views and concerns.[22] After the meeting, the president acknowledged that he "hated to see his bishop in opposition."

Even as the war raged and patriotic fervor ran high, more than one hundred leaders from different Protestant, Catholic, and Orthodox communions issued "A Call to the Churches," which included these words: "Let our churches embrace the bereaved, maimed, and homeless of the Middle East through a generous response to the ministry of compassion. . . . Let our churches reach out in a spirit of dialogue and seek ways to bring Muslims, Christians, and Jews together to address our fears, concerns, and hopes for peace."[23]

The Gulf War was not about religion, but religion figured prominently into the swirl of events. While no major Christian leaders in the United States came forward to defend Saddam Hussein, a wide range of leaders sought ways to say, "War is not the answer." There is a hopeful message here. Many Christian leaders stood up in the face of patriotic zeal to say we all must find a better way to live together. Christians not only must learn from the past and draw on their best resources, notably the New Testament mandate to be peacemakers and ministers of reconciliation; they must also make future decisions in partnership with others who share the planet, not just their country.

ISLAM: A RELIGION OF PEACE

In the days following September 11, many Muslim leaders denounced the attacks on New York and the Pentagon as un-Islamic. Time and again, the media featured Muslims saying, "Islam is a religion of peace," a common refrain reinforced by President George W. Bush's affirmation that Islam is a good and peaceful religion. A long history of enmity between Christians and Muslims, images of hostages in Iran, hijacked airplanes, suicide bombers, and other violent extremists claiming inspiration from Islam clearly presented a very different image of the religion. What does it mean to say Islam is a religion of peace? How does this connect to *jihad*, the Islamic term that has now entered the English lexicon as "holy war"?

A brief Arabic lesson helps demystify the issues. Like Hebrew, Arabic is a Semitic language built on a consonantal root system. Most words are derived from three consonants that convey one or more basic notions. The letters *k-t-b*, for example, relate to the idea of writing. When different vowels, prefixes, or suffixes are added, distinct but related words are formed. Thus *kataba* means "he wrote," a *kitab* is a "book," a *maktabah* is a "library," and so forth. The root meanings of the letters *s-l-m* in Arabic have to do with "submission to the will of God" and "peace." Three familiar words are derived from this root: *salam, Islam,* and *Muslim. Salam* means "peace, well-being"; it originates from the same root as the familiar Hebrew word *shalom.*[24] Israeli Jews traditionally greet people with the word *shalom;* Arabs greet people with a parallel phrase, *salam alaykum* ("peace be with you"). The term *Islam* literally means "submission to God" and "peace." The ideas are linked in the notion that submission to the will of God brings peace. Those who submit themselves in obedience to God are "Muslims"; they are, by definition, people "at peace" in creation. At one level, "peace" in Islam refers to the inner state available to individual Muslims who seek to know and do the will of God.

How does one know the will of God? The answer begins, as we've noted earlier, with God's revelation, the Qur'an. The sacred scripture in Islam includes a great deal about love, justice, compassion, and other virtues that are close to the heart of God and are required of Muslims. Every *surah* ("chapter") in the Qur'an, save one, begins with the words, "In the name of God, the Most Merciful, the Most Compassionate." Many Muslims can be heard uttering these words before beginning a public lecture, sermon, or presentation. Human beings are responsible before God, and high standards apply in all types of human interaction.

The requirement for Muslims to seek "peace" in their communities and beyond involves both avoiding conflict when possible and the even more challenging task of establishing a stable social order characterized by peace and justice. Various passages in the Qur'an allow or sometimes call for Muslims to fight in defense of attacks on Islam. There are also verses setting forth the requirement of making peace, including: "If your enemy inclines toward peace then you too should seek peace and put your trust in God" (Qur'an 8:61), and "Had God willed, He would have made them dominate you and so if they leave you alone and do not fight you and offer you peace, then God allows you no way against them" (Qur'an 4:90). Many passages deal explicitly with relations between Muslims, Jews, and Christians. The Islamic self-understanding is that all three religions are direct results of the same revelation God had given through many prophets and messengers. The Qur'an enjoins the People of the Book to align with Muslims, affirming the "common word between us and you, that we worship none but God" (Qur'an 3:64). Many passages exalt Jesus as one of the greatest, even unique among God's prophets.[25] But the Qur'an also includes a harsh critique of those who followed Jesus with doctrines about his divinity and the Trinity. Grave warnings against doctrinal error notwithstanding, the revealed religions have salvific value: "Behold! Those who have faith, and those who are Jews, Christians and Sabaeans—those who trust in God and the Last Day, and do what is righteous, they shall have their reward; no fear shall come upon them, neither shall they grieve" (Qur'an 2:62 and 5:69).

The different communities can and should exist in harmony. Muslims should invite others to embrace Islam, but a well-known verse declares, "There shall be no compulsion in matters of religion" (Qur'an 2:256). In fact, the different communities are explained as part of God's plan. The diversity among religious communities provides a kind of test, with the emphasis falling on responsible behavior here in this life: "If God had so willed, He would have made all of you one community, but [He has not done so] that He may test you in what He has given you; so compete with one another in good works. To God you shall all return and He will tell you the truth about that which you have been disputing" (Qur'an 5:48).

In his new book, *The Heart of Islam,* internationally known Muslim scholar and writer Seyyed Hossein Nasr elaborates on the inextricable link between Islam and peace.

> For Muslims, the idea of living at peace while denying God is totally absurd, because only God can put the chaos and strife within the human soul in order, and when there is no peace within, there will be no peace without. Islamic teachings contain many injunctions for settling disputes between people and nations with the aim of establishing peace. But the highest goal of Islam is to lead the soul to the "abode of peace" by guiding people to live a virtuous life and to establish inner harmony with the help of Heaven. For Islam, as for all authentic traditions, the goal of religion is to save the human soul and consequently establish justice and peace in society so that people can live virtuously and live and die "in peace," which in the deepest sense means in the blessed state that leads to the experience of celestial peace.[26]

The deeper call to building peaceful and just societies presupposes an Islamic religious, political, and economic framework. Muslims are thus expected to carry forth the message of Islam so that others may hear the message of God and join in the noble task of building a just and peaceful social order.

THE MEANINGS OF *JIHAD*

Jihad literally means "striving" or "struggling in the way of God." All Muslims are enjoined to engage in *jihad.* The term *holy war,* which is widely used in Western media and among some Muslims, includes one of the ways this obligatory duty has been and is being promulgated. But this is not the primary focus for a term rich in meaning throughout Islamic history. A word of caution is necessary for non-Muslims. While there are many violent extremists among

Muslims calling for and carrying out despicable acts under the banner of *jihad,* these represent a small minority on the fringe of Islam. It is important to remember that the media always tend to gravitate toward the most dramatic and sensational events. As a result, we run the risk of interpreting the larger religious tradition through the narrow lens of extremists' behavior. In the course of my twenty-five years of study about and personal interaction with Muslims, I can say without hesitation that the overwhelming majority of Muslims are as horrified and disgusted by violent extremism as are most Christians, Jews, Hindus, Buddhists, and people who do not identify with any religion.

The degree to which the narrow "holy war" meaning of *jihad* has become entrenched in popular understanding was manifest in the 2002 commencement ceremonies at Harvard University. Zayed Yasin, a biomedical engineering senior and former president of the Harvard Islamic Society, sparked an outcry when the title of his graduation-day speech was announced: "The American Jihad." A number of graduating seniors at Harvard, the bastion of intellectual freedom and cultural diversity in America, immediately launched a petition drive demanding that university officials allow them to read and assess his speech in advance. They also called on Yasin to "publicly condemn violence in the name of *jihad.*" One senior, the head of a group called Jews for Conservative Politics, wanted "some guarantees from Harvard that this is a speech that we'll be proud of." In response to the outcry, Yasin explained,

> *Jihad* in the Muslim tradition represents a struggle to do the right thing. This is not a speech about *jihad* as war, or 9/11, or Israel and Palestine, or politics. I want to use the idea of struggle to say that we, as graduating seniors from Harvard, who have been incredibly blessed, have a duty and responsibility to the world to struggle against injustices, and to struggle for social justice.[27]

Zayed Yasin is correct. At the most basic level, *jihad* is the constant struggle to be virtuous and moral, to do good works on behalf of others and for the betterment of society. A well-known saying attributed to Muhammad emphasizes this meaning in contrast to its military connotation. On the way home from a battle, Muhammad told the Muslims that they were returning to the "greater *jihad*" from the "lesser *jihad*." The outward struggle in defense of Islam is not the biggest challenge. The greater *jihad* is the inner struggle to overcome selfish and sinful desires, the strong tendencies that inhibit human beings from doing what they know to be right.

A wonderful illustration of *jihad* manifest in good works that are pleasing to God is depicted in a popular video series on world religions, *The Long Search*.²⁸ As the host explores the basics of Islam, he spends considerable time with two medical doctors, a husband and wife, in Cairo. At one point she takes him to a free clinic literally in the shadow of the great pyramids. Dr. Abdeen and others created this charitable institution for young children with serious, chronic heart problems. In a gentle, self-effacing, and yet deeply moving way she explains that this work is her *jihad*, a help to the children for the betterment of society. She clearly doesn't want any praise or special recognition. Her demeanor reveals her faith that "God knows our intentions" and assurance that "God loves this mercy toward children." I often use this video in my world religions and introduction to Islam classes. Late in the semester, I send the students out into the community to locate and interview people who embrace the religions we are studying. When the interview teams present their findings in class, the stories reveal the diversity all around us. Invariably, several of the students return deeply impressed after meeting and spending time with a Muslim very much like Dr. Abdeen.

When we can get past the media focus on violence and extremism, when we begin to put a human face on Islam, we find the large majority of Muslims living their lives and talking not about holy war but about the *jihad* of the heart, of the tongue, and of the hand.

Jihad can also refer to two types of struggle or self-exertion in the military sense. The Qur'an and the *hadith* materials make clear that Muslims can and sometimes should take up arms in defense of Islam. At other times, strategic withdrawal, or *hijra* ("flight"), is a better course of action. John Esposito, a world-renowned scholar of Islam, identifies these alternatives in response to various types of attacks in Islamic history. Muhammad and the first community of Muslims exemplified the patterns; they withdrew to Medina and later fought the Meccans who had persecuted them.[29] The Qur'an makes clear that war may be "hateful," but it is at times necessary:

> Sanction is given unto those who fight because they have been wronged; and God is indeed able to give them victory; those who have been driven out from their homes unjustly only because they said: Our Lord is God—for had it not been for God's repelling some men by means of others, monasteries and churches and oratories and mosques, wherein the name of God is often mentioned, would certainly have been pulled down. Truly, God helps one who helps Him. God is strong, Almighty. (Qur'an 22:39–40)

There are a number of so-called sword verses, passages that either allow fighting or call upon Muslims to fight aggressively. These passages have been interpreted in different ways through the centuries. Some Muslims look primarily to the specific circumstances being addressed and carefully seek to draw conclusions about contemporary applicability; others have found justification for attacking anyone deemed an unbeliever or infidel. Osama bin Laden stands in this latter tradition, but he is by no means alone in Islamic history or among Islamists today.

The second major military application of *jihad* relates to the expansion of Islam. Muhammad and the first *ummah* ("community of Muslims") provided a model that brought religious, political, social, economic, and military dimensions of life together. Whereas the marriage of religion and the state occurred in Christianity's fourth century, the two have always been intertwined in Islam. As adherents of a missionary religion, Muslims sought to spread their message and societal system through proclamation, diplomacy, and military expansion. Here we come back to the idea of peace, or submission to God's will, in relation to a stable and just social order. Thus the expansion of Islam was understood as the establishment of God's rule. And the rapid spread of Islam—going west across North Africa and into Spain; north through the Fertile Crescent; and east through the Tigris and Euphrates Valley, across Persia and into northern India—within the first hundred years following Muhammad's death was an unprecedented and stunning development in world history. For most Christians, the advent and phenomenal success of Islam was clearly a threat; for Muslims, it was an unmistakable sign of God's favor.

Many traditions attributed to Muhammad set forth guidelines about what is permissible and what is unacceptable in combat. The safety of women, children, and noncombatants, for example, is paramount. In the absence of a unifying, hierarchical authority structure, various Sunni legal scholars articulated rules and judgments in response to particular issues that arose over time. Professor of comparative ethics at Florida State University, John Kelsay traces these developments and concludes that the formal parallels between Islamic "rules of war and the Western just war criteria are rather striking. Just cause, right intent, competent authority, a reasonable hope of success, the aim of peace . . . and discrimination in targeting."[30] In another parallel with Christian history, one finds many examples of particular leaders and soldiers appearing little concerned with the rules. For Muslims, Genghis Khan mirrors Clovis and the Franks, only on a much larger scale. Frequently, the savage attacks and murderous intrigue took place among Muslims vying for power. Groups practicing violent extremism or religious terrorism appear in the early decades following Muhammad. The thread of fanatical extremism weaves through the Assassins in Syria and up to groups like Islamic Jihad, the organization responsible for murdering Anwar Sadat and perpetrating other terrorist attacks in Egypt.[31] The most visible manifestation of such holy war in the name of Islam occurred on September 11, 2001.

RENEWAL AND REVOLUTIONARY ISLAMIST MOVEMENTS TODAY

Reform movements are not new in Islam. Islamic history, like the histories of other world religions, includes a continuing process of renewal and reform. Charismatic leaders, Sufi masters, learned scholars, and others have organized and led movements to renew the community, to return to core teachings and values during periods of decline. My personal experience corroborates the general sense that movements for renewal are gaining strength in many parts of the Muslim world today. Traveling and living in various Middle Eastern countries for many years, I've observed many indicators of change, such as more women wearing traditional Islamic clothing, more people fasting during Ramadan, and more open discussion about Islam providing answers to various societal problems.

At the political level, the landscape is clearly changing in many countries. Muslims constitute the majority in more than fifty countries. In many places, people react out of high frustration against political, economic, and social structures they believe have failed. Collective anger is near the boiling point in many lands where citizens experience debilitating problems of economic disparity and exploitation, human rights abuses, crumbling cultural values, and political marginalization in systems headed by unrepresentative leaders. Islamist groups demanding change are visible, active, and gaining strength in the midst of such conditions. Follow the news closely in any of the major U.S. newspapers or on the daily broadcasts of the BBC, and you will hear stories of serious religious and political unrest in Algeria, Afghanistan, Lebanon, Pakistan, Egypt,

Indonesia, Saudi Arabia, the Philippines, the Sudan, Israel/Palestine, and other countries.

Some Islamist groups pressing for change are trying to work within a political system, while others have abandoned that approach and openly advocate violent means to their revolutionary ends. Many leaders of such groups have declared a holy war in an effort to legitimize their cause. While many such emotional calls to action ring hollow, as with Saddam Hussein's efforts during the Gulf War, John Esposito's insightful book *Unholy War* documents how some extremists are effectively rallying substantial support. Our earlier discussion on Islamic suicide bombers explained the allure of this distorted form of *jihad*, particularly among poor and impressionable youth.

Muslim leaders must take a strong and visible lead in articulating constructive alternatives to holy war. They must work strenuously to name and address real problems that currently serve as the breeding ground for terrorists in different lands. Margaret Thatcher, the former British prime minister, provoked a storm of controversy in the weeks following September 11 when she publicly lamented the relative silence of Muslim leaders and then challenged them to denounce terrorism in all its forms. Some critics argued that the press was at fault for failing to cover moderate and progressive Muslim leaders. Others pointed to the very difficult, potentially life-threatening, circumstances facing Muslim leaders in many lands who challenge violent extremists. The points had merit. The Western media don't usually consider carefully measured religious pronouncements to be news. At the time of the Gulf War, for instance, Saddam Hussein's push for religious legitimacy received a lot of press attention, while one could scarcely find news about the many Muslim leaders who denounced him.

It is also true that Muslim leaders who reject violent extremism in favor of nonviolent means to rectify injustices are, in some settings, taking huge personal risks. When levels of anger and frustration are high, violent actions can be and sometimes are focused on people whose loyalty to particular interpretations of revolutionary Islam is called into question. But Thatcher, too, had a point. Now, more than ever, the world needs visible, vocal, and principled leadership from within Islam. Like the many Christians who looked deep into their tradition for guidance during the Gulf War, Muslim leaders today must do the same in their respective settings. They must articulate and finds ways to model the message of peace they affirm as the heart of their religion. The future of their countries and the integrity of Islam itself are ultimately at stake. Political instability in the Muslim world places an additional responsibility on the shoulders of Muslims living in open, democratic societies to provide clear and courageous leadership. Even so, some who reject the way of the sword may themselves pay a high price. As we know all too well, both Mahatma Gandhi and Martin Luther King Jr. were assassinated.

Non-Muslims also have a responsibility to address the dangerous challenges posed by violent extremist groups within Islam. We in the United States have a particular responsibility since the behavior of our government, the world's superpower, often has a major impact on the daily lives of people all over the world. In a democracy, the government represents the people. The health of a democracy is dependent on an informed citizenry. Put another way, we bear responsibility for what is done in our name. One of the unmistakable messages from September 11 is that the United States is the object of considerable anger from many Muslims. While nothing justifies indiscriminate violence, it is also true that terrorism doesn't occur in a vacuum. Violent extremists calling for *jihad* against the West may be on the fringe, but substantial numbers of Muslims resonate with the deep frustration fueling the extremists. In answer to the question "Why do they hate us?" we must continue searching for constructive answers, not just the sound bites provided in five-minute segments between commercials on a television talk show.

The need for clarity about the Islamic connections to turbulent forces is obviously an urgent item on the world's agenda. Bringing the picture into focus requires both an awareness of widespread aspirations among Muslims and a lot of hard, painstaking work in the dense thickets of specific situations.[32] It also requires a sober assessment of U.S. government policies in each of these countries. Alongside many constructive policies, the U.S. government has sometimes pursued shortsighted policies that contradict the ideals most Americans believe we espouse. Regrettably, many Americans don't pay much attention to the inconsistencies in U.S. foreign policy. People in other parts of the world who feel the impact of those policies pay close attention. And they take notes.

In the media coverage following September 11, General Norman Schwarzkopf, who led U.S. military actions in the Gulf War, acknowledged several times that the United States had helped train bin Laden and his forces. In the late 1970s they were considered freedom fighters, since the enemy in Afghanistan was the U.S.S.R. Muslim revolutionaries next door in Iran at the same time were labeled fanatics by the U.S. government.

During the 1980s the U.S. supported Iraq in the ten-year war of attrition against Iran. Many public policy advocates, including me, publicly opposed support for Saddam Hussein. His human rights record was among the worst in the world, and he used chemical weapons against his own people as well as the Iranians. More than a decade later, on October 11, 2001, President Bush labeled Saddam "an evil man," noting that he "gassed his own people." True. Where was the official outrage when these events were taking place? Fear that the Iranian revolution might spread prompted the United States to look the other way while it supported Iraq in the 1980s.

The operative policy for the world's superpower is often simple: the enemy of my enemy is my friend. The fallacy of such short-term, expedient policies is increasingly clear. When these policies include the use of military force to counter an immediate threat, the long-term consequences may be catastrophic. Osama bin Laden's history is a tragic case in point. After years of revolutionary struggle against the U.S.S.R. in Afghanistan—a "good *jihad*" in the view of

U.S. and Saudi governments—bin Laden returned to Saudi Arabia and his family business in 1989. John Esposito picks up the story from there.

> When Iraq invaded Kuwait in August 1990, bin Laden quickly wrote to King Fahd, offering to bring the Arab Afghan *mujahidin* to Saudi Arabia to defend the Kingdom. Instead, the deafening silence from the palace was shattered by the news that American forces were to defend the House of Saud. The admission and stationing of foreign non-Muslim troops in Islam's holy land and their permanent deployment after the Gulf War, bin Laden would later say, transformed his life completely, placing him on a collision course with the Saudi government and the West.[33]

Despite the stated ideals informing U.S. policy decisions, when we look closely we often find serious inconsistencies in the areas of human rights, economic development, military policies, support for self-determination, and democratization. Some of the anger directed toward the United States is a reaction to what are perceived as self-serving U.S. policies that effectively shore up repressive regimes and block avenues for reform. Trying to understand the deep sources of frustration and the ways in which we—and our own government—may be culpable is a painful but essential step if we hope to stop the flow of new recruits into the ranks of violent extremists. Such work is essential for people—Muslims and non-Muslims alike—who seek to contain and begin extinguishing the raging fires being stoked by violent extremists committed to fight and die in a holy war.

Pursuing Peace with Justice

We look back in order to learn how best to move forward. This much is crystal clear: holy war is not holy. However deep the grievances and perceived injustices may be, holy war is not the answer. Whatever religious justifications Christians or Muslims put forward in the past, the results of "holy" warfare were consistently catastrophic. To pursue holy war today is to rush headlong down a dead-end street. Healthy religion speaks not of war but the promise of peace with justice. People of faith, today more than ever, must look deep into their traditions for clarity and guidance about the paths that will lead toward peace and justice.

Some extreme circumstances may call for military force, but we must all be wary when political leaders seek to justify policies on religious grounds. The multiple dynamics and continuing fallout from the Gulf War stand as a powerful reminder that military action must, at the very least, meet the high standards of just war criteria. But even this is highly dubious. Given the nature of modern weapons and the dangerous ways regional conflicts can ignite a wider conflagration, Christian and Muslim versions of just war criteria may no longer be applicable.

The only intelligent way forward is the route laid out by authentic religion: we must be peacemakers. Yet working for peace and justice is exceedingly difficult. Passivity, isolationism, wishful thinking, or holding hands, lighting candles, and singing "We Are the World" may provide an illusion of peace, but hard work in the dense thicket of the particulars is required. We must try to understand and address those factors that lead to holy war. The religious communities—Christians and Muslims in particular—can lead the way by affirming the promise of peace in their respective traditions and committing themselves to nonviolent resolution of conflict.

For Christians, the historic peace churches and well-established groups within various denominations have been working diligently to develop resources and models for ministries of reconciliation. A relatively new and promising initiative among Christian ethicists, theologians, and experts in conflict resolution has produced an alternative to pacifism and just war theory: the just peacemaking paradigm. In this paradigm the focus shifts to initiatives that can help prevent war and foster peace. Working during the 1990s, the scholars and activists developed ten key practices and detailed guidelines for peacemaking:

1. Support nonviolent direct action.

2. Take independent initiatives to reduce threat.

3. Use cooperative conflict resolution.

4. Acknowledge responsibility for conflict and injustice and seek repentance and forgiveness.

5. Advance democracy, human rights, and religious liberty.

6. Foster just and sustainable economic development.

7. Work with emerging cooperative forces in the international system.

8. Strengthen the United Nations and international efforts for cooperation and human rights.

9. Reduce offensive weapons and weapons trade.

10. Encourage grassroots peacemaking groups and voluntary associations.[34]

Jews, Muslims, and Christians with particular concern for peace and justice in the Middle East can find many groups and resources working strenuously for peace.[35] The casual observer may conclude that peace with justice is not possible in the Middle East, but many people in all three communities have been striving and will continue to strive for the only future that can work, a shared future. The long-standing Israeli-Palestinian conflict defies simple solutions. If the past teaches us anything, however, it is that peace, justice, and security cannot be achieved and maintained through violent means. A Palestinian Jew two thousand years ago warned that violence begets violence and that "those who live by the sword will perish by the sword."

For Muslims, the challenge is most formidable. Many Muslim individuals and groups have clearly rejected the military meaning of *jihad,* most notably Sufis, who have emphasized its spiritual meaning. But these have been more the exception than the rule. For most Muslims, the military dimensions of *jihad* have been a legitimate feature of their religious tradition. The religious and political dynamics in the world today require Muslims of goodwill to place their emphasis—personally and publicly—on "greater *jihad,*" the struggle with the self and the good works of the heart, hands, and tongue for the betterment of society. In the face of those who would wage holy war in the name of Islam, Muslims who embrace their religion as a religion of peace must find the resources to live out the call for peace and justice in society.

Raymond of Agiles's grim description of the crusaders' attack on Jerusalem amounted, in his words, to "small matters" in comparison with what he didn't report. The unspeakable horror perpetrated by "holy" warriors at the portico of Solomon on the Temple Mount defied "powers of belief." The attacks on September 11 are the modern-day parallel to his description. The potential use of chemical, biological, or nuclear weapons by self-proclaimed zealous warriors for God or in response to them tests our "powers of belief." Grave dangers facing the world community demand focused, intentional, and persistent "striving" together for peace and justice.

Seven

AN INCLUSIVE FAITH
ROOTED IN A TRADITION

Our awareness of the complexities and dangers of global conflicts has grown significantly since the sobering events of September 11, 2001. Our knowledge concerning the causes and possible solutions to these conflicts lags behind, but we are learning important new lessons each day. We know that religion remains one of the most powerful forces in human society and that religious ideologies and commitments are often directly linked with violent conflict. We know with certainty that well-organized groups of motivated people are capable of wreaking havoc on a global scale. At the beginning of this book, I offered the edge of a cliff as a metaphor for the precarious place where we find ourselves standing today and suggested that progress is best defined as taking one step back. This book represents an effort to step back, by identifying clearly the major warning signs of corruption in religion that invariably lead to violence and evil in the world.

The complicity of religious persuasions in global conflicts today is undeniable, but understanding this complicity requires that we clearly grasp the difference between what we have called corrupt forms of religious commitment and the authentic forms that offer hope. Throughout much of the book we have described the five tell-tale signs of corruption in religion. As we have seen, one or more of these five signs always precedes any instance of religiously sanctioned evil. Knowledge of such corruption is invaluable in today's world, yet it is not sufficient in itself. Whether one is a true believer or a die-hard secularist, it remains necessary to take the next step from the knowledge of these factors that predict *when religion becomes evil* to a clear understanding of *how religion can remain true to its authentic sources* and a force for positive change.

As we have explored each of the warning signs of corrupted religion, we have seen how correctives were always present within each tradition. Our study of the pathological has helped to elucidate the healthy. At the heart of every major religious tradition we find abiding truths and principles that provide the first antidote to violence and extremism. It is important to recall that violent extremists are on the fringe of these traditions for a reason: the large majority of adherents recognize that the extremists violate the most basic teachings and values within the tradition. But as our examples have shown, many sincere people are susceptible to authoritative claims made by charismatic leaders. It is all too easy to lose sight of the most basic teachings in one's religion, particularly when oppressive social, political, or economic conditions figure prominently into the arguments advanced and sacred texts quoted by authoritative leaders. Fear, insecurity, and a desire to protect the status quo can foster a tribalism in which otherwise sincere people engage in dehumanizing patterns of behavior, even war.

Nevertheless, in my view, people of faith offer the best hope both for correcting the corruptions leading to violence and for leading the way into a more promising future. At the outset, we affirmed that religious ideas and commitments have inspired individuals and communities of faith to transcend narrow self-interest in pursuit of higher values and truths. Throughout history religion has often been connected with what is noblest and best in human beings. Now, perhaps more than ever, religious people must transcend narrowly defined self-interest and seek new ways to live out what is noblest and best in their faith traditions.

We have seen truths common to each of the major religious traditions. These same traditions that have nurtured millions of people have also inspired adherents to rediscover, redefine in contemporary terms, and deepen these truths amid changing circumstances over the centuries. Such an impetus for reform is urgently needed today. All the resources needed for reform can be found at the heart of the major religious traditions. Even in the face of the worst examples of religious extremism, a strong and clear voice for change always sounds from the center of those traditions. Scott Appleby, who coedited the five-volume *Fundamentalism Project* with Martin Marty, has been studying religious extremism for more than a decade.[1] Appleby argues convincingly that deeply committed religious peacemakers provide a major source of hope. He, too, suggests the respective religious traditions can once again serve us well.

The religious tradition is a vast and complex body of wisdom built up over many generations. Its foundational sources— sacred scriptures and/or codified oral teachings and commentaries—express and interpret the experiences of the sacred that led to the formation of the religious community. A religious tradition is no less than these sources, but it is always more. The deeper meaning and significance of these sources continues to be revealed throughout history. In each of the major religious traditions of the world, prophets, theologians, sages, scholars, and simple believers, exalted by the holy lives they led, refined and deepened the tradition's spiritual practices and theological teachings in support of peacemaking rather than war, reconciliation rather than retaliation. To be traditional, then, is to take seriously those developments that achieved authoritative status because they probed, clarified, and developed the insights and teachings contained in the foundational sources.[2]

The challenges today include and move beyond those that religious people have always faced. Like those generations who have gone before us, we, too, must look deep into our traditions for the wisdom and resources that support peacemaking rather than war, reconciliation rather than retaliation. But we must do this in a global context. Albert Einstein, whose name is synonymous with innovative thinking, once noted, "The significant problems we face cannot be solved at the same level of thinking we were at when we created them."[3] His observation remains apropos. Today's call for reformation is *both* an imperative within the different traditions *and* an imperative at the interfaith level. We need new paradigms, new ways of understanding and living out our particularity in the midst of pluralism. We need new paradigms both for the ways we function within existing traditions and for our multicultural and interfaith engagement.

A Compass for the Journey Ahead

A common religious metaphor for life in this world is that of a journey or a pilgrimage. The religious traditions provide a worldview to orient the adherents; they teach of origins, purposes, and ultimate goals. The religious traditions provide symbolic maps for the journey. They present different paths and identify different obstacles blocking the way toward the goals. As a Christian, for instance, I can approach the Bible with this orientation. The cumulative tradition from Genesis to Revelation provides a frame of reference for me and for nearly two billion others who make up the largest religious community in the world. The sacred texts indicate where we come from and where we are going. While we recognize that the specific landscapes evident in the journeys of faith recorded in the Bible are often different from the terrain we encounter today, the biblical stories continue to offer invaluable insights from the successes and failures of pilgrims seeking and discerning God's guidance along the way. So, too, we can learn from the journeys of those throughout history who have faced similar, and distinctly different, challenges as well as perilously unfamiliar landscapes. The Bible provides no detailed map for the terrain of the twenty-first century. For us, the Bible is more like a globe, showing us the big picture. If one could have taken a picture of the Earth from the moon in Jesus' day, it would look very much like the picture of the Earth from outer space we see today. A detailed map of Europe or Palestine from Jesus' day, however, would not be very helpful today in trying to reach one's destination in those lands.

More than a map, we need a compass. This need has been reflected clearly in American culture in recent years, especially in the profusion of values-based inspirational publishing. In his perennial best-seller, *The Seven Habits of Highly Successful People*, Stephen Covey offers one of the clearest arguments for this need for reorientation:

> We are more in need of a vision or destination and a compass (a set of principles or directions) and less in need of a road map. We often don't know what the terrain ahead will be like or what we will need to go through it. . . . But an inner compass will always give us direction.[4]

Covey believes that one's inner compass is a set of core principles, what he terms "deep, fundamental truths that have universal application." Covey includes fairness, integrity, honesty, human dignity, service, growth, patience, nurturance, and encouragement among the universal principles he suggests are "part of most every major religion, as well as social philosophies and ethical systems." He goes further, arguing that these principles are self-evident: "It's almost as if these principles or natural laws are part of the human condition, part of human consciousness, part of the human conscience."[5] Covey is writing primarily for people functioning in organizational settings, especially businesses and families. In 1993 Stephen Covey and I discussed his view that these fundamental principles are innate and reflected in the major religions. I agreed then and still affirm his basic assessment. But I believe the core principles in the major religious traditions go deeper. They include faith, hope, and love. We will return to these components of the religious compass after an additional comment on the metaphor of the globe.

In the introduction to his book *Why Religion Matters,* Huston Smith alludes to this innate human compass without using the term. "The reality that excites and fulfills the soul's longing is God by whatsoever name. Because the human mind cannot come within light-years of comprehending God's nature, we do well to follow Rainer Marie Rilke's suggestion that we think of God as a direction rather than an object."[6]

On the compass of each enduring religious tradition, God or the transcendent is true north. Jeff Rogers, my former faculty colleague at Furman University and now the senior minister at First Baptist Church in Greenville, South Carolina, affirms this image but adds a helpful caveat. Rogers reminds us that the needle of a compass points to magnetic north, not geographical north. Depending on where you are on earth, there can be several degrees of variation, or magnetic declination. He suggests that our needles point in the right direction but that we must be careful lest we assume the needle on our particular compass points directly to the sum total of the reality of God. Rogers echoes the message of chapter 2, on absolute truth claims; he warns us to beware of those who speak and behave as though magnetic declination does not exist on their compass.[7]

Faith, hope, and love are also guiding principles on the spiritual compasses provided by the enduring religions. Faith is not the same as belief. Belief is connected to particular ideas, ways of conceptualizing religious systems. Faith is sometimes linked with belief, but it is deeper and richer. Wilfred Cantwell Smith wrote extensively on human faith over several decades. In his book *Faith and Belief,* Smith examines the phenomenon of faith in the Hindu, Buddhist, Islamic, and Christian traditions. As a result of his meticulous, historical exploration, Smith concludes that faith is an essential human quality.

> It is an orientation of the personality, to oneself, to one's neighbor, to the universe . . . a capacity to live at a more than mundane level; to see, to feel, to act in terms of, a transcendent dimension. . . . It is engendered and sustained by a religious tradition, in some cases and to some degree by its doctrines; but it is a quality of the person, not of the system. . . . Faith, then, is a quality of human living. At its best it has taken the form of serenity and courage and loyalty and service: a quiet confidence and joy which enable one to feel at home in the universe and to find meaning in the world and in one's own life, a meaning that is profound and ultimate, and is stable no matter what may happen to oneself at the level of immediate event.[8]

Hope is another vital point of orientation on the compass. Hope sustains people when the immediate circumstances are less than ideal. Hope is forward looking. Even when obstacles seem insurmountable, the religious traditions orient adherents toward a more promising future. Theologically, hope is not merely wishful thinking; it is much deeper, more profound. Hope calls us to act in pursuit of a better future. Hope and faith were points on the compass that guided and sustained Moses as he led the children of Israel on the extraordinarily difficult journey for forty years in the wilderness of Sinai. Faith and hope sustained Muhammad when powerful leaders in Mecca mocked him and persecuted those who abandoned the multiple tribal and local deities in order to worship the God of all creation. Like Moses, Muhammad and the community of faith also had to embark on a journey, a perilous pilgrimage to a new location. So, too, did Martin Luther King Jr., who had every reason for pessimism as the forces of prejudice, injustice, hatred, and death assailed him and others on their journey to the promised land. How did Gandhi and Nelson Mandela find their way on their respective, dangerous, and seemingly impossible journeys?

In each of these cases, we can identify with the metaphor of a compass. None of these well-known leaders had a detailed map from which to chart each step on their long and arduous sojourns. But each had a spiritual compass; whatever the obstacles blocking their path, they were oriented toward true north and guided by faith, hope, fairness, integrity, honesty, human dignity, service, and encouragement. They neither retreated simply into the private world of personal piety nor sat around and engaged in wishful thinking. They set forth on their respective pilgrimages with an inner compass. And each of these persons of faith helped change the course of human history.

Woven in and among these principles is love. The apostle Paul writes of faith, hope, and love in his first letter to the Christians at Corinth. He called love "the greatest" of these three (1 Corinthians 13:13). We have identified the centrality of love in the world's religions, symbolized by Jesus' call to love God and love your neighbor as yourself. Love of God and all of God's creation is the foundation for ethical behavior. For Jesus, this included the call to love even your enemies and those who persecute you (Matthew 5:43–44). Neither Jesus nor primary figures in other traditions promised an easy journey. On the contrary, life's sojourn is always demanding and at points life threatening. Jesus warned that the way of compassionate love might not be reciprocated; it might even lead to death, as it did for Gandhi and Martin Luther King Jr. But imagine for a moment how different the world would and could be if millions of people who identify themselves with a religious tradition constantly consulted their spiritual compass, found their bearings, and took the next step on their journey with the golden rule as their guiding principle.

Thinking in terms of a spiritual compass has two additional benefits. First, it alters the way one approaches diversity, including the bewildering array of problems and detours we all inevitably encounter in life. A compass provides a confidence that, despite the magnetic declination of our human limitations, we are oriented toward a meaningful goal. Security comes not from having or assuming we have all the answers; it comes from knowing which direction we are going and being able to respond to confusion, crisis, and even calamity on the basis of time-tested principles. The diversity we experience—in relation to those nearby as well as those who are far away—need not be seen as a threat; it can become part of the rich texture of life on the journey. When we travel to distant, sometimes exotic places, it is not because we want to experience exactly what we experience every week in our home settings. We seek diversity, from which we learn, grow, and enrich our lives. It is nice to get home from a long journey. But it wouldn't occur to us that returning home would be accompanied by a declaration that I'm the only one who really understands what home means or where it is located. A spiritual compass can help us see religious, ethnic, and national diversity—in our neighborhoods, country, and world—as enriching rather than threatening.

A second benefit of the image of the spiritual compass is that it leads to an emphasis on practice in daily life. Notice that the various points on the compass have much less to do with carefully constructed belief systems than with how one orients oneself in the world. For me, it is the difference between thinking of my Christian identity in terms of a noun or an adjective. The powerful distinction between the two hit me with some force many years ago when an Arabic-speaking Muslim I'd just met in the Middle East asked, "Are you Christian?" I assumed that he meant "a Christian" but simply left out the indefinite article. I answered, "Yes." But later that day his question haunted me. Am I "Christian" in my attitudes and behavior? It is easy enough to say I am *a* Christian; honesty and a healthy dose of humility prevent a casual or overly confident claim to Christlike behavior. Other people are better suited to comment on how *Christian* I am on a given day in a particular situation. Their assessment will be based on how they experience me relating to others. As we have noted at points throughout the book, behavior is critically important in the major religious traditions. The Day of Judgment in both Islam and Christianity is not portrayed as a final exam in which your answers to true-or-false questions about doctrines of God determine whether you pass.

All metaphors have limitations, and this one is no different. Thinking of God as a direction and enduring principles as points on a spiritual compass is helpful. But as the paragraphs above reveal, most human beings, including me, inevitably resort to more anthropomorphic images. The religious traditions provide these as well. God is like a parent, a loving and nurturing mother or father. Human beings are often described in familial terms: we are all God's children; we are brothers and sisters. The language of neighbors is also commonly used. Our neighbors are not simply the people living physically nearby, people who share the same community. The world today is our neighborhood. The phrase is overworked, but it reflects the reality of economics, ecology, communication, and politics in the new millennium: our world community is increasingly becoming a global village.

The Importance of Religious Traditions

With globalism a defining reality in our world today, it is urgent for us to assess the real and potential dangers posed by extremists within particular religious traditions. As we have noted, some people now argue that whatever value the religious traditions may have provided in the past, they have outlived their usefulness. They fear that deep loyalty to particular religious traditions inevitably feeds a kind of tribalism that is at odds with global cooperation; it is kindling that fuels an impending conflagration as civilizations clash. Our investigation lends credence to these concerns if the dangerous and violence-prone corruptions of religion remain unchecked.

Some religious seekers also wish to transcend the particularity of traditions. In individual religious exploration and in a range of New

Age religions, a growing number of people selectively draw from the wisdom and practices of major religions as well as smaller, indigenous traditions such as are found among Native Americans. Visit the religion section in any major bookstore, and you will find many books catering to people whose spiritual quest takes them easily across the boundaries presumed to define religions. For some, this is the natural outgrowth of the study and engagement with the sacred literature and practices found in the various wisdom traditions. We have seen that gaining access to texts of many religions and engaging in personal encounters with adherents of different traditions is a fairly recent development, one that offers many promising benefits and some possible pitfalls.

A strong case can and should be made, however, for the continuing importance of the major religious traditions. These traditions have served millions of people extremely well throughout much of recorded history. They contain time-tested wisdom and provide the frameworks for ethical and legal systems. For the vast majority of people worldwide, their religious tradition—like their family, tribe, or nation—anchors them in the world. Religious traditions provide structure, discipline, and social participation in a community. Returning to Thomas Friedman's striking image, one's religious tradition is like an olive tree that has deep and secure roots. Religious traditions, Wilfred Smith reminds us, engender and sustain human faith.

For most people through the millennia, their religious tradition has been a fact of birth. While many people in the West today approach religions with the idea of choosing one or none, the reality is more complex. Our ways of seeing and interpreting the world, of framing issues, and even of asking questions are strongly tied to the social, religious, geographical, and historical circumstances into which we were born and raised. When someone learns that I was born in 1950 in Tulsa, Oklahoma, in the midst of the post–World War II baby boom, that I attended public schools, and that I was raised in a Christian family, she or he already knows a good deal about my olive tree. I did not choose to be born in Tulsa and raised by Christian parents. Had I been born in Boston like the large majority of my extended family, I would have been raised—as were my many cousins—in a Jewish home. Had I been born in Cairo, there is a 90 percent chance that my parents would have been Muslims.

What if I had been born in Boston or Cairo or Calcutta? I've pondered that question many times as I've traveled and worked with people in various parts of the world. Extensive involvement with Christians in Lebanon, Israel/Palestine, and Egypt, for instance, has taught me that our shared religious tradition is a major factor in how I see and interact with the world; it is not, however, the only determining factor. Cultural context, family, national identity, and education also shape my worldview—often in ways that are distinctly different from those of my Christian friends in the Middle East. I am strongly persuaded that I would be writing this same book had I been born in Boston within the Jewish branch of my family. The approach and examples would be different in places, since I would be writing, no doubt, from a perspective of Jewish pluralism. But the thrust of the analysis would be very much the same. Religious traditions do not determine who we are, but they are a part of the givenness of most people.

Established religious traditions continue to be valuable in other ways as well. They provide institutional structures that are essential in many ways. Consider, for instance, all of the humanitarian relief and development work in response to disasters, wars, and rampant poverty. Countless human service agencies are connected to religious traditions. These institutions are often among the first to respond to crises, and they are present for the long haul in many developing countries. Having worked for seven years coordinating the relief and development work of the major U.S. Christian denominations through the ecumenical structure of Church World Service and Witness, I know well the importance of such institutional structures. The stories of cooperation—ecumenical and interfaith—in response to the conflicts in Lebanon, Israel/Palestine, and Iraq as well as of ongoing work among the poorest people in Egypt are powerful, inspiring, and often unknown.[9] Well-organized institutional structures, including those of established religious traditions, are essential. Personal spiritual growth and insight may occur as one moves in and among various traditions; systematic efforts to respond substantially to human beings in great need require functioning institutions.

Religious institutions, like similar structures in business, education, and government, are often developed to meet particular needs and facilitate work toward identifiable goals. As needs—and sometimes goals—change, institutions, too, must be modified. Many institutions, including religious ones, are notoriously slow to adapt to changing circumstances. While religious institutions are vital to communal life and work on many levels, these institutions are human constructs that can also be obstacles or even vehicles for destructive corruptions of the very religions they are there to serve. My experience working within the National Council of Churches (NCC) and among the major member communions—Methodists, Presbyterians, Lutherans, Episcopalians, various Orthodox and Baptist churches, and so on—illuminates this common problem.

The NCC was founded in the mid–twentieth century when many Christian communions were enthusiastic about new forms of ecumenical cooperation. For three decades the NCC flourished; thirty to forty denominational bodies worked together on a wide range of programs and projects, from mission and service ministries worldwide to biblical translation initiatives resulting in the Revised Standard Version and New Revised Standard Version of the Bible. When I was elected to the staff in 1983, support for the NCC was strong among the member churches. But resources for ecumenical programs were shrinking since many of the mainline churches were themselves experiencing decreased revenues. During my seven years at the NCC, I was involved directly in three major restructuring initiatives. The program staff and the representatives from the member communions were continually faced with difficult decisions on how best to pursue their ministries with dwindling resources. Each round of reorganization revealed how difficult it was for almost all people concerned to let go of previously successful institutional structures and programs, even though financial and other circumstances were clearly changing. Ecumenism was (and is) alive and well, but the established structures of the NCC were sometimes not flexible enough. In my experience, several of the most successful domestic and international ecumenical programs during the 1980s were inspired within the hallowed halls of 475 Riverside Drive in New York, but they needed new, more flexible institutional structures to flourish.

Ecumenical and interfaith cooperation is happening today on all levels and among people in all religious traditions. At the same time, people operating within religious traditions can and do foster the most destructive forms of tribalism. William Sloane Coffin, my former pastor at New York's Riverside Church, succinctly spelled out the challenge before us in his provocative book *A Passion for the Possible:*

> The challenge today is to seek a unity that celebrates diversity, to unite the particular with the universal, to recognize the need for roots while insisting that the point of roots is to put forth branches. What is intolerable is for difference to become idolatrous. When absolutized, nationalism, ethnicity, race, and gender are reactionary impulses. They become pseudoreligions, brittle and small, without the power to make people great. No human being's identity is exhausted by his or her gender, race, ethnic origin, or national loyalty. Human beings are fully human only when they find the universal in the particular, when the recognize that all people have more in common than they have in conflict, and that it is precisely when what they have in conflict seems overriding that what they have in common needs most to be affirmed. Human rights are more important than the politics of identity, and religious people should be notorious boundary crossers.[10]

Religious argumentation has defined and reinforced needless boundaries that many religious people—especially Christians and Muslims—have had difficulty crossing. Today, however, we can find strongly encouraging signs that more open, welcoming approaches to religious diversity are gaining ground.

EMBRACING RELIGIOUS DIVERSITY

Three of the major religions included in this study—the Hindu, Buddhist, and Jewish traditions—have long, well-established, non-exclusivist approaches to religious diversity. We have identified corruptions within these three traditions, but they are more obviously exceptions within the larger tradition than is the case with Christianity and Islam. The Hindu and Buddhist traditions are pluralist and inclusive by definition. Although there is an element of exclusivity in the notion of Israel as the chosen people, Jews have not traditionally understood their corporate role as being the only people in relation to God. Rather, their spiritual responsibility is to be "a priestly kingdom and a holy nation" (Exodus 19:6) and thereby a light unto the nations. Through the people of Israel, all the people of the earth are promised God's blessing (Genesis 12:3).[11]

Although many Muslims today articulate a narrow exclusivism, Islam as a religion has always articulated an inclusive message. We have described the Islamic understanding of God's revelation coming through various prophets and messengers. Many passages in the Qur'an focus on prominent biblical figures; Jews and Christians constitute legitimate communities of faith whose book—the Torah and the Gospel—comes from recognized prophetic figures. Muslims readily affirm the truth of the revelations guiding People of the Book. The problem arises in the presumed distortions these communities have introduced; the truth that should guide them has been obscured. Why Jews, Christians, and others cannot readily see what is obvious to Muslims—that God's same, true revelation is now available without distortion in the Qur'an—has always puzzled Muslims. The Qur'an includes many passages affirming the People of the Book, warning against dangerous distortions—most notably the divinity of Jesus and the Trinity—and urging unity within the parameters of Islam:

> O People of the Book, do not exceed beyond the bounds in your religion or say things about God save the truth. The Messiah, Jesus, son of Mary, is only a messenger of God, and His word that He conveyed to Mary, and a spirit from Him. So believe in God and His messengers and say not, "Three." Stop. It is better for you. God is only one God. It is far removed from His majesty that He should have a son. (Qur'an 4:171)

> O People of the Book, let us come to a common word between us and you, that we worship none but God, and that we associate nothing with Him, and that none of us take others for lords apart from God. (Qur'an 3:64)

As long as Jews and Christians do not embrace Islam, they should be treated as *dhimmis* ("protected people") under Islamic rule. The practical implications of *dhimmi* status have fluctuated from time to time and place to place in Islamic history, but the principle remains: however much Jews and Christians may have distorted their revelations, they are to be considered legitimate communities deserving "protection" under Islamic authority.

OPTIONS FOR CHRISTIAN THINKING

Religious diversity presents a challenge today that people may meet with rigid doctrinal positions or unstated intuitive or experiential perceptions. Significant shifts have been taking place during the past half century, particularly as people have come to hold more nuanced and appreciative understandings of other traditions and an arrogance often shown by Christians has been more clearly named.

Broadly, Christian responses to religious diversity can be grouped into three major paradigms or schools of thought: exclusivism, inclusivism, and pluralism. While these terms help clarify major contemporary emphases, considerable variety exists within and among the categories; the dividing lines, like the dividing lines between religious traditions, are often amorphous and hard to place.

Exclusivism

The exclusivist position has been dominant among Christians over the centuries. It rests on the conviction that Jesus Christ provides the only valid way to salvation. Today, however, considerable variation exists among those who would locate themselves within this theological framework. On one end of the exclusivist spectrum are those with sharply defined, literalist views. Whether we like it or not, these people argue that their narrow interpretation is the blunt reality taught by the Bible; the case is closed. It is difficult to detect much hard grappling with complex issues posed by religious diversity among those who draw the theological lines so sharply.

Many other exclusivists, however, take a more flexible and open position. I experienced this first in 1971 while working as a summer youth minister in a Southern Baptist church in Tulsa. During a conversation in the home of the pastor, who was an aggressively evangelical preacher, I indicated that I was interested in studying world religions in seminary and exploring biblical passages on religious diversity. His response surprised me and stunned his children. He immediately pointed out that God is far greater than our understanding of God. This man—who often led revival meetings and could not rest easy knowing that a particular Jewish friend (whom he had been proselytizing on the golf course for fifteen years) had not accepted Christ—began to cite biblical passages he believed pointed toward God's activity beyond the walls of the church.[12] Even though he said he was "95 percent sure" that explicit faith in Christ was not the only means to salvation, he indicated that he would continue to preach and teach the scriptures as he had for forty years. He explained his rationale in this way: I *know* what Christ has done for me; my responsibility is to share the good news with others; even though I'm 95 percent sure (based on biblical teachings alone) that all kinds of people are meaningfully related to God, the 5 percent of uncertainty remains; whether the Christian faith is the only way or a primary way to salvation, I am still responsible for proclaiming what God has done in Christ. This pastor went on to encourage my study and exploration in seminary without fear of discovering new truths. It was a wonderful, liberating moment.

Many Christians who would categorize themselves as exclusivists point to the Book of Job and Paul's Epistle to the Romans as they readily concede that no one knows the mind of God. They are committed to bearing witness to the revelation of God in Jesus Christ even as they openly advocate tolerance and respectful dialogue and practice cooperation across religious lines. Since public attention most often gravitates toward people with the most extreme views, it is important to recognize that one can embrace an exclusivist theology and also interact productively with people in other traditions.

Inclusivism

The inclusivist position is one that affirms *both* the saving presence and activity of God in all religious traditions *and* the full, definitive revelation of God in Jesus Christ. Many people—including many Catholics—are shocked to learn that the Roman Catholic Church officially embraces an inclusivist theology. Three of the sixteen official documents of Second Vatican Council, the global gathering convened in the mid-1960s, dealt explicitly with interfaith relations. The document addressing many issues most directly was "The Declaration on Relations of the Church to Non-Christian Religions" (*Nostra Aetate*). Promulgated by Pope Paul VI on October 28, 1965, the document announces a fresh approach to non-Christians with these words about Muslims:

The Church also has high regard for Muslims. They worship God, who is one, living and subsistent, merciful and almighty. . . . They strive to submit themselves without reserve to the hidden decrees of God, just as Abraham submitted himself to God's plan . . . ; they await the day of judgment and the reward of God following the resurrection from the dead. For this reason, they highly esteem an upright life and worship God, especially by way of prayer, alms-deeds and fasting.[13]

The text pleads poignantly with both Christians and Muslims to forget the "many quarrels and dissensions" of the past centuries, to make a "sincere effort to achieve mutual understanding" and jointly "to preserve, and promote peace, liberty, social justice and moral values." Another text adopted by the Second Vatican Council, "Light to the Gentiles" (*Lumen Gentium*), embraces the view that salvation is possible for people outside the church: "Those, who through no fault of their own, do not know Christ or his Church, but who nevertheless seek God with a sincere heart, and moved by grace, try in their actions to do his will as they know it through the dictates of their conscience—those too may achieve eternal salvation."[14]

This broad affirmation has great significance for both Christian mission and interfaith dialogue. The Roman Catholic Church's position since Vatican II has shifted its long-standing theological emphasis on "no salvation outside the Church." The implications of these changes are enormous—and hopeful in our religiously diverse, interdependent world community. This new orientation enables the world's largest Christian communion to avoid some of the damaging corruptions examined earlier. As with other theological positions, the boundaries of an inclusivist position are not fixed.

In the nearly four decades since Vatican II, the Catholic Church has pursued a wide range of programs—from mission and interreligious dialogue initiatives to publications—designed to implement the spirit of this affirmation. Although many people perceive Pope John Paul II as traditional and conservative because of his outspoken positions on birth control, celibacy for priests, and women in ministry, he has been progressive and actively involved in the inter-faith arena. The pontiff has met frequently with Muslims, Jews, Hindus, Buddhists, and others during their visits to Rome and on his many trips around the world; he has written and spoken on interfaith issues frequently for twenty-five years. In a highly visible event in October 1986, the pope invited many religious leaders to Assisi for a World Day of Prayer for Peace. The pope's inclusivist theology was clearly visible when he spoke to a gathering of the Roman curia following the event:

> The fact that we came together in Assisi to pray, to fast and to walk in silence—and this, in support of peace which is always so fragile and threatened, perhaps today more than ever—has been, as it were, a clear sign of the profound unity of those who seek in religion spiritual and transcendent values that respond to the great questions of the human heart, despite concrete divisions. . . . The Day of Assisi, showing the Catholic Church holding hands of brother Christians, and showing us all joining hands with the brothers of other religions, was a visible expression of these statements of the Second Vatican Council. With this day, and by means of it, we have succeeded, by the grace of God, in realizing this conviction of ours, incul-cated by the Council, about the unity of the origin and goal of the human family, and about the meaning and value of non-Christian religions—without the least shadow of confusion or syncretism.[15]

Pluralism

Advocates of a pluralist position see Christianity neither as the only means to salvation nor as the fulfillment of other religious tradi-tions. The pluralist position affirms the viability of various paths.

John Hick, perhaps the most prominent advocate of this approach, called for a "Copernican revolution" in theological thinking thirty years ago. Extending the analogy from astronomy, Hick argued for a theocentric approach, a "shift from the dogma that Christianity is at the centre to the realisation that it is God who is at the centre, and that all religions . . . serve and revolve around him." Hick develops his theocentric position in his book *God Has Many Names*. Hick argues that the world's religious traditions are best understood as "different response to the one divine Reality." The distinctions among religious communities, in his view, arise largely through perceptions conditioned by historical and cultural circumstances.[16]

Wilfred Cantwell Smith articulated a more radical approach to pluralism in his book *Towards a World Theology*. Smith was suspicious of any Christian theological framework that maintained a "we-they interpretation from within a boundaried and self-sufficient Christian position looking out over other communities of faith as objects or even people upon whom to make pronouncements, however generous." He attempted—and encouraged Christians, Muslims, Hindus, Jews, Buddhists, Sikhs, and others to attempt—something grander: "to interpret intellectually all human faith, one's own and others', comprehensively and justly."[17]

Harvey Cox's popular book *Many Mansions* facilitated a discussion of religious pluralism among local clergy and people in the pews.[18] The title of his book is taken from the King James translation of John 14:2: "In my Father's house there are many mansions; if it were not so I would have told you." Cox's pluralist approach invites people to gather for mutually enriching dialogue. Diana Eck, whose extraordinary leadership in documenting the religious landscape in the United States at the turn of the millennium led President Clinton to award her with a National Humanities Medal in 1998, identifies herself as a "Christian pluralist":

Through the years I have found my own faith not threatened, but broadened and deepened by the study of Hindu, Buddhist, Muslim, and Sikh traditions of faith. And I have found that only as a Christian pluralist could I be faithful to the mystery and the presence of the one I call God. Being a Christian pluralist means daring to encounter people of different faith traditions and defining my faith not by its borders but by its roots.[19]

Eck's theological outlook has been shaped both by the study of other religious traditions and by her personal encounter with Hindus, Muslims, Buddhists, Jews, Sikhs, and others.[20] Her first in-depth experience of another major religious tradition came in college during an extended visit to India. For Eck, the personal encounter with pious, practicing Hindus challenged many presuppositions related to her upbringing as a Methodist in Montana. Personal encounter is often the catalyst for an inner dialogue that prompts theological reflection on religious diversity. For me, the process began with a Jewish grandfather and extended family. Personal experience and dialogue with those of other faiths are common denominators for many Western Christians who study world religions and try to articulate a coherent theology of pluralism. For people in many parts of the world, of course, self-conscious awareness of religious diversity is not new; dialogical encounter has been a way of life for centuries.

John Hick, Wilfred Smith, Huston Smith, Harvey Cox, Diana Eck, and a host of other scholars have stimulated widespread reflection on issues of particularity and pluralism. For two decades Christian self-understanding in the midst of religious diversity has been at the center of serious theological debate.[21] The discussion has been lively also among lay Christians. During the past quarter century, I have traveled throughout the United States speaking on college campuses, in churches, and at conferences on issues related to the Middle East, Islam, and Jewish-Christian-Muslim relations. Almost without exception, people want to talk about how they view Christianity amid the multiplicity of religions. I have often found that nonspecialists are well ahead of Christian leaders in being willing to explore with an open mind the ideas and practices in other religions. These people are often developing their reflection in the context of a religiously mixed marriage or through friendship with a Jewish neighbor or a Hindu co-worker.

Nothing approaching consensus is taking shape as various forms of exclusivist, inclusivist, and pluralist paradigms are presented, dissected, and critiqued. In my view, each position has value. When I am asked about my own views on these matters, I sometimes respond like my former college professor: "What I think is not what is important for you. What do *you* think? And, more importantly, what do you feel *you* should *do* as a responsible Christian (or Muslim or Jew) in your religiously diverse neighborhood and interdependent world community?" I respond this way at times because some people want an authority figure to provide simple answers for them. We all have to think and be responsible for ourselves. Sometimes it is clear that a questioner wants to put me (or whomever) into a category he or she deems heretical in order to justify dismissing all that has been said. I've always been puzzled and saddened by people who make clear that they couldn't be very happy in heaven unless hell was full to overflowing with people who disagree with their particular theology.

I am a Christian and a member of the clergy. My study, teaching, writing, and ecumenical ministry in the Middle East are all connected to a strong sense of vocation. I have learned a great deal from and been immeasurably enriched by people whose religious traditions—or deep skepticism about religion—provide a distinctly different worldview. But in my study and experience, I have yet to discover truths that compel me to embrace another religious tradition as my own. My olive tree has deep roots. Like Diana Eck, I have found that the powerful truths and spiritual discipline I've seen among Jews, Muslims, Hindus, and others has often opened my eyes to dimensions of the Christian tradition that previously had been obscured or unknown to me. At the same time, I know many Muslims, Hindus, Jews, Buddhists, and others who not only say the same thing about their religious tradition with sincerity and conviction but visibly live out their faith in compassionate service for others. Experience makes plain that my experience of God, my human view of truth, does not begin to exhaust the possibilities.

What I find most encouraging in the serious, ongoing debates and personal investigations is that none of the options necessarily precludes positive, cooperative engagement with people of other traditions on common problems facing our communities, our nations, and our world. Working together for the common good must be a major focus of interfaith dialogue in the years ahead. Christians and Muslims, for example, do not need to come to theological agreement before they can work hand in hand to meet the needs of the poor in their community or address such issues as equitable public education or the proliferation of drugs in society. When people from different faith traditions get to know one another, they often discover quickly that they have a great deal in common, particularly in terms of what their faith requires in relation to their neighbors. Whatever one's theology, it should be shaped both by the wisdom of time-tested sources such as scripture and tradition and in the context of new information as well as contemporary life experiences.

At the conclusion of *Many Mansions*, Harvey Cox issues a call to action, arguing that the future is now in our hands because God has placed it there.

> Thus, the possibility of self-annihilation requires us to put all our questions not in the form, What will happen? but rather in the form, What must we do? . . . As time-bound creatures, we must work with the stubborn stuff of past and present. Among the "givens" are our existing religious traditions, which, far from dying out, appear to be leaping into a period of resurgence. But neither can we wait for kismet to deliver us

into a new era in which we no longer need to project our inmost terrors onto the heavens or onto other peoples and nations. We must now take the initiative, not just to predict the future—including the future of religion—but to shape it.[22]

Cox's call to action, to take the initiative to shape the future, resonates with the approach I have advocated throughout this book. Nowhere is the call to action more needed today than in the Middle East.

THE MIDDLE EAST AS A MICROCOSM

When Abraham packed up his family and belongings, the Genesis story tells us, he looked toward a promised land with the assurance that God's blessing would extend through him to all the people on earth. Today, nearly half the world's population traces its spiritual heritage back to Abraham. While Jews, Christians, and Muslims share a claim in God's blessing, the everyday reality has often been disturbingly different. Time and again we have seen violent and destructive behavior by Christians, Muslims, and Jews. Many of the most volatile and dangerous religious corruptions today are directly connected to the Middle East—most visibly, though not exclusively, to the Arab-Israeli-Palestinian conflict. The dynamics in Israel/ Palestine represent a kind of microcosm for the world community. If we are not able to find nonviolent ways to move forward toward justice, peace, and security in these lands, it does not bode well for the rest of us inhabiting the religiously diverse, interdependent world community.

As I said in the previous chapter, people in the United States bear a particular responsibility. We are citizens in the democratic nation that is also the world's superpower, and we are responsible for what is said and done in our name. Unlike the government of Sri Lanka or Sweden, the U.S. government has a profound and daily impact on the lives of people in the Middle East and elsewhere. "We the people" are represented by this government. Those who declare the Middle East conflict is too complicated or who justify noninvolvement by saying "those people have always fought and always will" are being irresponsible as citizens and, if they claim a religious identity, as people of faith. Christians are called to a pastoral, prophetic, and reconciling ministry in the world. As William Sloane Coffin reminds us, Jesus' teachings and the writings of Paul are to be applied precisely where the challenges are greatest. There are no easy answers or simple solutions. But, like Martin Luther King Jr. or Bishop Desmond Tutu in South Africa, we have a spiritual compass to provide an orientation and the principles on which to base our action.

Jews and Muslims also have a major stake as citizens and as people of faith. Jews are rightly concerned with security and stability for Israel. If the conflicts during much of the past century have taught anything it is that security cannot ultimately be achieved by force. Israel's overwhelming military superiority has not secured the peace. Israel's long-term self-interest is inextricably linked to peace, political stability, and economic prosperity. None of these is possible apart from peace, security, political stability, and economic opportunity for Palestinians. Most Jews I know have a deep attachment to Israel *and* a deep concern for the well-being of others. Both require active pursuit of policies that will facilitate peaceful coexistence in the Middle East.

For Muslims, the Middle East conflict presents an enormous challenge and opportunity. We have identified a number of serious problems contributing to frustration and fostering extremism in certain predominantly Islamic lands. Muslims living in the West must lead the way in calling for a halt to human rights abuses and for new forms of participatory governments, religious freedom, and economic opportunities. While there is no fast track to a healthy future in many countries, violent extremism is clearly not the answer. It is both contradictory to the spirit of Islam and highly counterproductive. Muslims committed to peaceful coexistence and constructive change through nonviolent means must step forward and provide leadership that truly reflects their affirmation that Islam is a religion of peace.

Wishful thinking? Perhaps, but I don't think so. While no one can predict the future, we can learn from the horrific mistakes and corruptions of the past. This is what we must do, in fact, if we hope to enjoy a future together on this planet. Having spent a great deal of my professional life in the midst of Middle East issues, I remain optimistic. Behind the headlines and sinister behavior of people on the extremes can be found the large majority of people in the Middle East—Jews, Muslims, and Christians—who deeply desire peace. People there, like people everywhere, long for a better future for their children and grandchildren. And many individuals and organizations are working actively for political reconciliation and a shared future in the land God promised to Abraham's descendants.[23]

Can we achieve justice and peace in the Middle East? Perfect justice and total peace are beyond our reach, particularly since people define these goals in different terms and through different understandings of truth. But proximate justice and peaceful coexistence are realistic goals for those who avoid the pitfalls of absolute truth claims and who are committed to working toward a better future using means that are consistent with the desired ends. People in various faith traditions must be clear among themselves and with one another: holy war is not an option.

Far from exhausting all the paths toward peace, we have only begun to marshal the positive energies of religious people. Marc Gopin's book, *Holy War, Holy Peace: How Religion Can Bring Peace to the Middle East,* is full of thoughtful and practical ways people can move away from the model of cosmic conflict and toward the model of reconciliation among estranged family members. Scott Appleby's recent work also provides extremely helpful guidance on how religious communities and nongovernmental organizations can lead the way in transforming conflict and helping to bring about reconciliation. There are many options for those who take seriously the call to be peacemakers.[24]

As people of faith look toward the future—in the Middle East and in their own communities—we would all do well to focus on the twofold mandate to love God and to love our neighbor. The Qur'an provides a wise word that celebrates our diversity even as it guides us on the journey of faith, in which our vision and understanding of ultimate truth remain limited: "If God had so willed, He would have created you one community, but [He has not done so] that He may test you in what He has given you; so compete with one another in good works. To God you shall all return and He will tell you the truth about that which you have been disputing" (Qur'an 5:48).

NOTES

INTRODUCTION

1. The entire English translation of the document was published in *The Washington Post*, September 28, 2001.

2. George W. Bush, quoted in *New York Times*, September 21, 2001.

3. I prefer to use *Qur'an* as the English name for the sacred scripture in Islam. It not only is the correct transliteration from the Arabic but also encourages a pronunciation that is closer to the Arabic than the more anglicized version, *Koran*. The same holds true for the name of the prophet of Islam: *Muhammad* (rather than *Mohammed*).

4. Precise demographic information is difficult to acquire, particularly for populations in parts of Asia, Africa, and Latin America. These numbers do not reflect any degree of active participation. A substantial number of people in the United States, for instance, would identify themselves as Christian (as opposed to Jewish, Muslim, Buddhist, and so forth) but are not particularly active in the organized structures of the church.

5. See Diana L. Eck, *A New Religious America: How a "Christian Country" Has Become the World's Most Religiously Diverse Nation* (San Francisco: HarperSanFrancisco, 2001).

6. Wilfred Cantwell Smith, "Comparative Religion—Whither and Why?" in *The History of Religions: Essays in Methodology,* ed. M. Eliade and J. M. Kitagawa (Chicago: University of Chicago Press, 1959), 34. Smith was the pivotal figure in founding the Islamic Studies Center at McGill University and developing the Center for the Study of World Religions at Harvard University. He served as president of both the American Academy of Religion and the Middle East Studies Association. Although he was a profoundly influential figure in Islamic studies and the comparative study of religion, his many books and articles have

remained largely unknown outside scholarly circles. He updated and republished one of his most accessible works, *The Faith of Other Men* (New York: Harper & Row, 1962), under the title *Patterns of Faith Around the World* (Oxford: Oneworld Publications, 1998). His last major work, *What Is Scripture?* includes a good bibliography of his other major publications.

CHAPTER ONE

1. The *Christian Science Monitor* reported in its October 2, 2001, issue that numerous universities added courses on Islam, the Middle East, and South Asia for the spring semester of 2002. While the interest level on campuses was clearly high, only a small percentage of people are college students who can incorporate a semester-long course into their curriculum.

2. The Five Pillars of Islam are *shahadah* ("confession of faith"), *salat* (five daily prayers facing Mecca at prescribed times), *zakat* ("charitable giving"), *sawm* ("fasting" during the daylight hours of the month of Ramadan), and *hajj* (the annual "pilgrimage" to Mecca).

3. There are several ways to discern the religious meaning of something for an individual or group. You can read and analyze relevant writings and behavior, but another method of researching contemporary people is more feasible today than ever before: ask them personally. I have done this systematically with a wide variety of Jews, Christians, Muslims, and overtly nonreligious people over several decades. When people know that you've done your homework and are genuinely interested in understanding them, most will openly discuss the religious meaning close to their heart.

4. Manichaeism was a syncretistic religion inspired by the teachings of Mani, a prophet who lived in Babylonia from 216 to 277 C.E. The religion combined elements of Zoroastrianism, Christianity, Gnosticism, and Buddhism. Mani taught that Zoroaster, Jesus, the Buddha, and he were agents of liberation from darkness by the Father of Light. The religion enjoyed a following in various places between the Mediterranean and China for well over one thousand years.

5. The most sacred city is Mecca, whose central feature is the Kaaba, the black stone building Muslims believe was built by Abraham and Ishmael (some say Adam built it originally) as a house of worship to the one God. Muslims all over the world orient themselves in the direction of this sacred space, this *axis mundi*, five times each day for prayers. The Kaaba is the focal point of the annual pilgrimage, the *hajj*. Medina, the second most sacred city, is the site of the first Muslim community, established in the year 622 C.E. Muhammad and many of the early leaders of Islam are buried in Medina.

6. Few miracle stories are associated with Muhammad. The most famous story is perhaps that of the *mi'raj* ("night journey" to Jerusalem) and the *isra'* ("ascent to heaven" on a white horse). This story not only connects Muhammad with Jerusalem and the prophets in the biblical tradition; it also accounts for the origin of the five daily prayers in Islam. While in the seventh heaven, Muhammad

pledged that the Muslims would pray fifty times a day. Before departing from the heavenly realm, Moses suggested Muhammad remember how forgetful and selfish people can be. Moses reminded him of what he found when he came down from Mt. Sinai with the Ten Commandments. The "pious" people had fashioned a golden calf in his absence! Moses encouraged Muhammad to renegotiate the number of daily prayers. Then, in a sequence similar to the negotiation with God before the destruction of Sodom and Gomorrah (Genesis 18:16–33), Muhammad's pledge for the number of daily prayers is reduced to five.

7. Abraham Joshua Heschel, "No Religion Is an Island," in *No Religion Is an Island*, ed. Harold Kasimow and Byron Sherwin (Maryknoll, NY: Orbis Books, 1991), 6.

8. See Robert Ellsberg, ed., *Gandhi on Christianity* (Maryknoll, NY: Orbis Books, 1991).

9. The "apology" came in October 1992 when Pope John Paul II received the report on the findings of the Galileo Commission. The report noted, "It often happens that, beyond two partial points of view which are in contrast, there exists a wider view of things which embraces them both and integrates them." (The addresses of the pope and Cardinal Poupard are published in *L'osservatore Romano*, November 1, 1992.)

10. The power, beauty, and rich texture of the biblical creation stories was the subject of two episodes of the celebrated ten-part PBS series hosted by journalist Bill Moyers in 1997, *Genesis: A Living Conversation*. The video series is available in many libraries. The discussions among Jews, Christians, and Muslims, clergy, laity, writers, skeptics, and others bring these ancient stories to life in sometimes startling new ways. Viewers readily discover that the power of these sacred stories does not depend on embracing these ancient accounts as literally, historically, and scientifically true at every point.

11. Huston Smith, *The World's Religions*, rev. ed. (San Francisco: HarperSanFrancisco, 1991). The original text, *The Religions of Man*, was first published in 1958. Huston Smith, *Why Religion Matters: The Fate of the Human Spirit in an Age of Disbelief* (San Francisco: HarperSanFrancisco, 2001).

12. The John Templeton Foundation, founded and endowed by Sir John Templeton, is one of the more intriguing ventures bringing together science and religion. The foundation publishes books and supports a variety of initiatives of spiritual exploration, particularly through scientific discovery.

13. Smith, *Why Religion Matters*, 274–75.

14. Bill Moyers, *The Power of Myth*. Produced for the Public Broadcast System in the 1980s, this series remains readily accessible in videotape. The series continues as a provocative, visual resource in college and university religion courses.

15. Thomas L. Friedman, *The Lexus and the Olive Tree* (New York: Farrar, Straus & Giroux, 1999), 20, 32–33, 31.

16. I have heard versions of this hundreds of times in public presentations such as media reports, speeches, sermons, and so on. Three times in the past

year, I've heard "expert" analysts declare, "Christians and Muslims have been fighting for two thousand years!" The absolute certainty with which people make such pronouncements is staggering. Not only is it patently untrue that Christians and Muslims are always fighting, but the Islamic religious tradition (as we know it) began only fourteen hundred years ago!

17. Stephen L. Carter, *The Culture of Disbelief: How American Law and Politics Trivialize Religious Devotion* (New York: Basic Books, 1993).

18. The source of evil and injustice is central in the ancient epic poem the Book of Job. Why do the righteous or innocent people suffer? What is God's relationship with evil and suffering? These questions run so deep that Job was included in the Hebrew Bible even though Job's story is located outside Israel. The questions continue to be central today because evil and injustice are persistent realities. Rabbi Harold Kushner's insightful book, *When Bad Things to Good People* (New York: Schocken Books, 1981), explores the problem of "natural" evil. Many fundamentalist Christians simply place everything considered evil at the feet of Satan and his minions. At the other end of the spectrum, Hindus in the classical tradition see a unity beyond the illusion of good and evil in this phenomenal world. As long as one is caught in the cycle of existence, the law of *karma* maintains justice in the midst of evil and suffering over many lifetimes.

CHAPTER TWO

1. Wilfred Cantwell Smith, *Patterns of Faith Around the World* (Oxford: Oneworld, 1998), 71–72. Smith's lectures were first published in 1962 under the title *The Faith of Other Men*.

2. The number of denominations is mind-boggling. Baptists alone, in the United States today, have more than eighty officially recognized groups. These range in size from the Southern Baptist Convention, the largest Protestant denomination in the country, numbering more than sixteen million, to the National Baptist and Progressive National Baptist Conventions to small communions like the Primitive, Free Will, and Seventh-day Baptists. My colleague at Wake Forest, Bill Leonard, an American church historian and a Baptist, says this of the multitude and diversity of Baptist subdenominations and the controversies that spawned them: "Baptists are a people who multiply by dividing!"

3. Although stopping abortion is the raison d'être of the Army of God, its Web site includes uncompromising positions on other issues, including a major section on Islam as a "Satan-inspired religion." The Reverend Don Spitz, director of Pro-Life Virginia and keeper of the Web site, declares his view with these chilling words: "Moslems should not be allowed to live in the United States. They should be forced to live in one of their satanic countries if they refuse to give up their satanic religion" (www.armyofgod.com).

4. Deidre Sullivan, *What Do We Mean When We Say God?* (New York: Doubleday, 1990). See Robert Fulghum, *Uh-Oh: Some Observations from Both Sides of the Refrigerator Door* (New York: Ballantine Books, 1991), for several provocative,

insightful, and humorous essays on human understandings of the divine. Like thousands of baby boomers in college in the 1960s and '70s, I found my conceptual framework challenged by J. B. Phillips's popular little book, *Your God Is Too Small.*

5. "Two TV Evangelists Lay Blame," *Dallas Morning News,* September 14, 2001. Reverend Falwell's remarks in full read as follows: "We make God mad. I really believe that the pagans, and the abortionists, and the feminists, and the gays and lesbians who are actively trying to make that an alternative lifestyle, the ACLU, People for the American Way—all of them who have tried to secularize America—I point my finger in their face and say, 'You helped this happen.'"

6. Muslims often quietly recite or meditate on the ninety-nine names of God with the aid of prayer beads. Islamic prayer beads are readily distinguished by the number of beads—eleven, thirty-three, or ninety-nine—which facilitate the meditation on the ninety-nine names. Handling prayer beads during mundane activities like drinking coffee at a sidewalk café is a way of remembering God at all times.

7. Karen Armstrong, *A History of God: The 4,000-Year Quest of Judaism, Christianity, and Islam* (New York: Alfred A. Knopf, 1993); Jack Miles, *God: A Biography* (New York: Alfred A. Knopf, 1995).

8. At the 2002 Annual Meeting of the Southern Zgotist Convention, Jerry Vines, a former president of the SBC, took his place in this sordid history when he denounced Muhammad as "a demon-possessed pedophile." And declared that Allah was not the God of the Bible. Vines, who is the pastor of a 25,000-member church in Jacksonville, Florida, went on to condemn "religious pluralism" as a major problem in America. The *New York Times* (June 15, 2002) reported strong and widespread criticism of Vines's remarks among Jewish, Christian, and Muslim leaders.

9. See "Rissho Ankoku Ron" (Establishment of the Legitimate Teaching for the Protection of the Country), *Selected Writings of Nichiren,* trans. Burton Watson et al. (New York: Columbia University Press, 1989), 24–34.

10. Zen Buddhism stands at the opposite end of the spectrum among more than a dozen Japanese Buddhist groups. Practitioners of Zen typically don't rely on sacred texts. Some Zen Buddhists have even used texts as fuel for warming fires in lean times or to make a point.

11. The devastating impact on the perception of U.S. military might was deflected, in part, by the almost immediate invasion of the tiny island nation of Grenada. Media attention turned rapidly away from failure in Lebanon and focused instead on the predictable military success against a nation of 100,000 people that was said to pose a communist threat to the world's leading power.

12. *The Sword of Islam* (British Broadcasting Company, 1987). Sad ironies abound in this situation. When HAMAS first organized, the Israeli government actually supported its visibility. This group opposed Yasser Arafat's moderation and peace initiatives, opting instead for harsh rhetoric against the continued

existence of Israel. As the group became more militant and gained power, particularly in Gaza, many of its leaders were imprisoned. In the middle of the night in 1994, hundreds of HAMAS leaders were taken from their cells and transported into southern Lebanon, where they were unceremoniously released. These militants were supported and trained by Hizbollah leaders during the subsequent twelve months. Most HAMAS members were later allowed back into the occupied territories. See *The Mind of a Suicide Bomber* (MSNBC, 2001) for a startling account of the direct connections between Hizbollah and HAMAS.

13. For an excellent study of Islamic eschatology, see Jane I. Smith and Yvonne Y. Haddad, *The Islamic Understanding of Death and Resurrection* (New York: State University of New York Press, 1981).

14. See 2:62 and 5:69 in the Qur'an. The fundamental teaching within the Qur'an affirms Jews and Christians as *ahl al-kitab* ("People of the Book"). Judaism and Christianity are based on the same true revelation that came through the prophet Muhammad. Although the Qur'an and *hadith* make clear that those who came after Moses and Jesus have distorted the revelation, Jews and Christians are still to be embraced as legitimate communities that deserve "protection" under Islamic rule.

15. *The Mind of a Suicide Bomber* includes interviews with three Lebanese Shi'ite men currently imprisoned in Israel. These men were captured when the explosives strapped to their bodies failed to detonate as planned. The profile of suicide bombers began to change in 2001 and 2002. Some of the September 11 terrorists were well educated and from the middle class. In the spring of 2002, for the first time, several Palestinian women joined the ranks of suicide bombers.

16. See Jim Hill and Rand Cheadle, *The Bible Tells Me So: Uses and Abuses of Holy Scripture* (New York: Doubleday, 1996), for a critical look at the many ways people in control have used the Bible to support their views.

17. Some of the "original" materials are even translations. Jesus, for instance, spoke Aramaic and possibly some Greek. By the time Jesus' teachings were recorded in the Gospel accounts, they had been translated, sometimes awkwardly, into Greek, the literary language of the day. Another major obstacle related to claims of verbal inspiration of the original text is that no "original" texts of the Bible are extant. We have thousands of manuscripts and fragments of texts, but no originals. And all the copies vary in different ways. Through the painstaking work of textual criticism, scholars are confident that we can reconstruct the original texts of the New Testament. The *HarperCollins Study Bible* and the Oxford Annotated edition of the New Revised Standard Version both include extensive notes to help guide readers though the textual and many other areas of scholarly research on the Bible. The intriguing passage about picking up poisonous serpents in Mark 16, for instance, is found in later versions of that Gospel, which have a longer ending.

18. Peter J. Gomes, *The Good Book: Reading the Bible with Mind and Heart* (New York: William Morrow, 1996; HarperSanFrancisco reprint edition, 2002), 45.

19. The Gospel of John is distinctly different from the synoptic Gospels (Matthew, Mark, and Luke). The chronological sequence of events is not the same (for example, Jesus' cleansing of the Temple occurs at the beginning of the last week of his life in the synoptics as opposed to the second chapter of John). The synoptic Gospels portray Jesus as speaking primarily about the Kingdom of God or Kingdom of Heaven. In the synoptics, Jesus frequently engages in a traditional rabbinical style of dialogue; in John, Jesus proclaims his unique relationship with God. A number of passages in which Jesus tells people to keep silent about his identity—a theme called the messianic secret—are conspicuously absent in John. The opening verses of each Gospel account provide a clear indication of the primary intent of the author. John's approach puts Jesus in a cosmic context: Jesus is the Word of God through whom all creation came into being.

20. Robert Alter, *The Art of Biblical Narrative* (New York: Basic Books, 1981), 12.

21. In addition to Gomes, *The Good Book,* see also Marcus J. Borg, *Reading the Bible Again for the First Time: Taking the Bible Seriously but Not Literally* (New York: HarperSanFrancisco, 2001), for a wise and accessible guided tour of the most influential texts in human history. An enlightening introduction to classical Jewish approaches to meaningful reading of the Bible is found in Burton L. Visotzky, *Reading the Book: Making the Bible a Timeless Text* (New York: Doubleday, 1991).

22. See John Berthrong, *The Divine Deli: Religious Identity in the North American Culture Mosaic* (Maryknoll, NY: Orbis Books, 1999), for a creative approach to contemporary experiments with pluralism.

23. Wilfred Cantwell Smith, *What Is Scripture? A Comparative Approach* (Minneapolis: Fortress Press, 1993), x.

24. George E. Tinker, *Missionary Conquest: The Gospel and Native American Cultural Genocide* (Minneapolis: Fortress Press, 1993), 44–45.

25. Tinker, *Missionary Conquest,* 47, 4. For a compelling study of major economic, social, political, military, and religious factors shaping Catholic missions in the eighteenth and nineteenth centuries, see Robert H. Jackson, *From Savages to Subjects: Missions in the History of the American Southwest* (Armonk, NY: M. E. Sharpe, 2000).

26. See Charles A. Kimball, *Angle of Vision: Christians and the Middle East* (New York: Friendship Press, 1992), for an overview of major mission and service ministries pursued by Christians working ecumenically in the Middle East today.

27. Wesley Ariarajah, *The Bible and People of Other Faiths* (Geneva: World Council of Churches, 1985; Maryknoll, NY: Orbis Books, 1989), 23.

28. Ariarajah, *Bible,* 25–26.

CHAPTER THREE

1. Mark R. Mullins, "Aum Shinrikyo as an Apocalyptic Movement," in *Millennium, Messiahs, and Mayhem: Contemporary Apocalyptic Movements,* ed. Thomas Robbins and Susan Palmer (New York: Routledge, 1997), 319.

2. See D. Bromley and J. Hadden, eds., *The Handbook on Sects and Cults in America* (Greenwich, CT: JAI Press, 1993). See also "The Religious Movements Homepage" (religiousmovements.lib.virginia.edu) for up-to-date information and many helpful links at a Web site managed by the Religious Studies Department at the University of Virginia.

3. Christianity's intimate connection with the Jewish tradition is obvious in the various ways Jesus is portrayed as a rabbi whose interpretation of the tradition challenges and upsets the established religious leaders. The Book of Acts records a major debate about the degree to which this new movement is bound up with the Jewish religion. The question turns on the issue of circumcision. Must non-Jewish believers be circumcised? In effect, is it possible to become a follower of Christ without becoming Jewish? The answer ultimately is yes. The vigorous debate and the misgivings over Paul's missionary outreach to the gentile world reflect the degree to which many early Christians viewed themselves as organically tied to Judaism. With regard to Hinduism and Buddhism, Siddhartha's distinctive teachings were understood within the broader context of religious life in India. Many Hindus still do not think of Buddhism as a separate religion; rather, it offers helpful paths toward the ultimate goal. Although Siddhartha appears to have been atheistic, teaching that there is no ultimate deity "out there" or in our soul essence to help us, throughout Indian history many have considered the Buddha to be one of the *avatars,* or incarnations of the Lord Vishnu. Where and how one draws the lines between religions is far less clear than traditional Western books on world religions often suggest.

4. Mark Lane, *The Strongest Poison* (New York: Hawthorn Books, 1980), presents a detailed and controversial account of the final weeks at Jonestown and subsequent reporting on the multilayered events. Lane was closely connected to the people and events as a lawyer retained by Jones to seek government files through the Freedom of Information Act and as a confidant of one of Jones's top aides, a woman who left the group three weeks before the tragic end. Lane was in Guyana along with Congressman Leo Ryan's delegation on November 17 and 18, 1978. He was one of the few who escaped into the jungle, where he hid overnight and lived to tell his version of the story.

5. John R. Hall, *Gone from the Promised Land: Jonestown in American Cultural History* (New Brunswick, NJ: Transaction Books, 1987), 42–52.

6. Hall, *Promised Land,* 62.

7. Quoted in Marshall Kilduff, *The Suicide Cult: The Inside Story of the Peoples Temple Sect and the Massacre in Guyana* (New York: Bantam Books, 1978).

8. Quoted in Kilduff, *Suicide Cult.*

9. Ken Levi, *Violence and Religious Commitment: Implications of Jim Jones's*

Peoples Temple Movement (University Park: Pennsylvania State University Press, 1982), 78.

10. Many television ministries in the United States today take a decidedly different approach to stewardship. They advocate a so-called prosperity gospel. In brief, this approach teaches that God wants to bless God's people with material goods. In order to tap into the bountiful storehouse, faithful believers must plant a "seed," that is, contribute a designated amount of money to the particular ministry in question. This approach appeals both to the fear that one will "miss out on the blessing God has in store" for him or her and to base human desire for material wealth.

11. Shimazono Susumu, "The Evolution of Aum Shinrikyo as a Religious Movement," in *Religion and Social Crisis in Japan,* ed. R. Kisala and M. Mullins (New York: Palgrave, 2001), 23–25.

12. Susumu, "Evolution of Aum Shinrikyo," 33.

13. Susumu, "Evolution of Aum Shinrikyo," 35.

14. Susumu, "Evolution of Aum Shinrikyo," 40.

15. Maekawa Michiko, "When Prophecy Fails: The Response of Aum Members to the Crisis," in *Religion and Social Crisis in Japan,* ed. Kisala and Mullins, 192.

16. The term *ayatollah* is a combination of two words: an *ayah* is a verse in the Qur'an; *Allah* is the Arabic word for God. Each *ayah* is considered a miracle or sign. Thus *Ayatollah* is an honorific title meaning "sign from God." The title is given to the most learned Shi'ite *mujtahid* (jurist).

17. I observed a curious version of this phenomenon during the intense weeks after September 11 and before the start of the war in Afghanistan. While channel surfing, I came across Hal Lindsay, a popular author and "expert" on Bible prophecy (whose views will be noted in chapter 4), who was a guest on a Trinity Broadcast Network program. He was urgently connecting various contemporary events with passages in the Old and New Testaments. At one point he announced with clear regret, "I'm sorry to say that I don't find the United States in Bible prophecy. It is just not there." The clear implication was that cataclysmic events were on the horizon and the United States was not going to be a major factor. He then went on to say that Christians could change this if they joined together in prayer and hard work to set this nation on the right course. I was struck by the incongruity of his position. On the one hand, Lindsay had made a career—and a fortune—piecing together current events with biblical passages so believers could see the puzzle coming together. On the other hand, he seemed to be saying Christians (in the United States in particular) could alter God's meticulous master plan with prayer and action at the eleventh hour. In a manner similar to that of Asahara Shoko and Jim Jones, Lindsay was offering a measure of hope in the face of the impending apocalypse.

18. A number of Christian leaders, most notably in Protestant fundamentalist groups during the nineteenth and twentieth centuries, became persuaded that they knew the precise time and place of Jesus' return to earth. Notwithstanding

Jesus' words in the Gospels that "no one knows the day and the hour" but God, these discerners of biblical prophecy led small groups to their designated spot at the appointed time. When the time passed and Jesus was a no-show, they often went back to the drawing board to look for the slight miscalculation they obviously had made. Unless followers had sold everything or cut all ties, little harm was done. In cases like this it is usually less a matter of religion being evil and more an example of religion being embarrassingly silly.

19. See Norman Cohn, *The Pursuit of the Millennium,* rev. ed. (Oxford: Oxford University Press, 1970).

20. See Gershom Scholem, *Sabbatai Sevi: The Mystical Messiah, 1626–1676* (Princeton: Princeton University Press, 1973), for a comprehensive study of this phenomenal movement within Judaism.

21. The entire report is accessible on several Internet sites, including www. cesnur.org (Center for Studies on New Religions).

22. See Cyril Glasse, *The Concise Encyclopedia of Islam* (San Francisco: Harper & Row, 1989), for a thorough summary of the religious and political history of the Assassins.

23. Some early Christian groups did begin to baptize people on their deathbed, since the danger of sinful behavior in this fallen world was quite high, and they viewed baptism as literally washing away sins.

24. Dean M. Kelly, "Waco: A Massacre and Its Aftermath," *First Things* 53 (May 1995): 22–23. See Isaiah 45 for the reference to Cyrus as messiah.

25. See J. D. Tabor and E. V. Gallagher, *Why Waco? Cults and the Battle for Religious Freedom in America* (Berkeley and Los Angeles: University of California Press, 1995), for a thorough study of David Koresh and the Branch Davidians.

26. Congregations in the "free church tradition" elect their own ministers and establish their membership criteria free from government or other external authoritative structures. In addition to Baptists and Pentacostals, Congregationalists, Disciples of Christ, Mennonites, and Quakers are among the "free" Protestant churches.

27. Speaking at the fall convocation at Wake Forest University in November 1997, Bill Moyers humorously underscored this point by noting that Jesse Jackson, Jesse Helms, Bill Clinton, Al Gore, Pat Robertson, and Jerry Falwell were all Baptists. He went on to make the following observation about Baptists (the tradition from which Moyers also comes): "Baptists are a lot like jalapeño peppers. One or two make for a tasty dish. But when you get a bunch of them together in one place, it is sure to bring tears to your eyes!"

28. Quoted in E. A. Burtt, ed., *Teachings of the Compassionate Buddha* (New York: Mentor Books, 1955), 49–50.

CHAPTER FOUR

1. Ilan Ziv, producer, *Shrine Under Siege* (Tamouz Productions, 1985).

2. The most widely publicized of these assaults include a 1969 attack on al-Aqsa Mosque by an Australian arsonist, the 1981controversy over Jewish students excavating tunnels and establishing synagogues underneath the Temple Mount, and the 1982 incident in which an Israeli soldier, Alan Goldman, opened fire on Muslims during Friday prayers. The rash of events in the early 1980s led Israeli filmmaker Ilan Ziv to produce his startling documentary *Shrine Under Siege*. The program, shown in Israel, Great Britain, and Canada, exposes ways various groups—Jewish and Christian—are actively engaged in efforts to facilitate the rebuilding of the Jewish Temple on this sacred place.

3. The great Temple was erected during the reigns of Kings David and Solomon. It was destroyed when the Babylonians captured Jerusalem in 587 B.C.E. Half a century later the people of Israel began a long process of rebuilding and renovation. The Romans in 70 C.E. destroyed the Temple a second time.

4. Armageddon, the "hill" at Megiddo, is located in the Galilee region of northern Israel. The book of Revelation identifies Armageddon as the gathering place for the final, decisive battle between the forces of good and evil.

5. Hal Lindsay, *The Late Great Planet Earth* (Grand Rapids, MI: Zondervan, 1970). As a senior in college, I purchased and read Lindsay's book in February 1972. Twenty months after its publication, the book was in its eighteenth printing and had sold over one million copies. The front cover of the edition in print today boasts "Over 15 million copies in print"; the back cover quotes the *New York Times* calling Lindsay's book "the most widely read nonfiction book of the decade [1970s]." Many other evangelical and fundamentalist Christian authors have written similar books. See, for example, John Walvoord's *Armageddon, Oil, and the Middle East Crisis: What the Bible Says About the Future of the Middle East and the End of Western Civilization*, rev. ed. (Grand Rapids, MI: Zondervan, 1990). The 1990 edition of this book also claims "over one million copies in print."

6. *Shrine Under Siege.*

7. *The Omen, The Rapture,* and *Rosemary's Baby* are among the most popular films in this genre. Jack van Impe Ministries presents a weekly program wholeheartedly devoted to this approach. Nicknamed "the Walking Bible," van Impe recites verses and half-verses from the Hebrew Bible and the New Testament as his spouse, Rexella, reads accounts of political and military developments from major papers and weekly news magazines. The viewer is shown each week how very close we are to the impending cataclysmic events. The observant viewer might well wonder why he or she should bother ordering one of the special video or cassette tape series offered at the end of most programs, particularly when they are invited to make convenient payments over several months.

8. *Shrine Under Siege.* See also Gershon Gorenberg, *The End of Days: Fundamentalism and the Struggle for the Temple Mount* (Oxford: Oxford University Press, 2000).

9. The Shi'ites today constitute roughly 15 percent of the Muslim community. They are present in various parts of the Islamic world and constitute a majority in Iran (over 90 percent) and Iraq (over 50 percent). They are also the largest Muslim group in Lebanon. The commemoration of Hussayn's martyrdom is arguably the most important day in the religious calendar for Shi'ites today.

10. See Benard Lewis, *What Went Wrong? Western Impact and Middle Eastern Response* (Oxford: Oxford University Press, 2002), for the most recent exploration of various factors that contributed to the decline of Islamic civilization.

11. The problem of human rights is not limited to Muslim countries, of course. The picture worldwide is grim. The data for any country are easily available through Amnesty International, Human Rights Watch, and the annual reports published by the U.S. Department of State.

12. Benjamin Barber, *Jihad vs. McWorld: How Globalism and Tribalism Are Reshaping the World* (New York: Ballantine, 1996).

13. See Milton Viorst, *In the Shadow of the Prophet: The Struggle for the Soul of Islam* (Boulder, CO: Westview Press, 2001), for an accessible overview of contemporary developments in the Sudan, Algeria, Iran, Saudi Arabia, and Jordan.

14. Saddam Hussein's charge referred to Mecca and Medina, places where non-Muslims are prohibited. There is no prohibition against non-Muslims being in other parts of Arabia. There were Jews and Christians living there during the time of Muhammad.

15. See Charles Kurzman, ed., *Liberal Islam: A Sourcebook* (New York: Oxford University Press, 1998). See also John L. Esposito, *The Islamic Threat: Myth or Reality?* 3rd ed. (Oxford: Oxford University Press, 1998), for a helpful overview of revivalist movements and various political debates within and about Islamic countries. Professor Muhammad Talbi, a historian at the University of Tunis, introduced me to these debates among Muslims. Talbi was as an active Muslim participant in the interfaith dialogue programs sponsored by the World Council of Churches and the Vatican from the 1960s through the 1990s, and his work was one of the main subjects of my doctoral dissertation. His writings and personal views draw deeply on Islamic history and tradition, which lead him to support strongly the kind of secular state visible in Tunisia and to advocate a similar approach elsewhere. Although Tunisia's population is over 90 percent Muslim, it stands at the opposite end of the spectrum from Saudi Arabia and the Gulf States. Women in Tunisia, for instance, have equal rights and legal protection under the law. Women drive cars and vote; polygamy is illegal; birth control and abortion are legal. Talbi represents a progressive tradition within Islam, arguing that Islam must continually adjust and adapt to the realities of the day. Today, he believes, secular states protecting religious freedom hold the key to developing a community of communities in our interdependent, pluralist world.

16. *Six Days Plus Twenty Years: A Dream Is Dying,* NBC News, June 2, 1987. For a detailed study of the Gush Emonim and related groups, see Ian S. Lustick,

For the Land and the Lord: Jewish Fundamentalism in Israel (New York: Council on Foreign Relations Press, 1988).

17. David Grossman, *The Yellow Wind,* trans. Haim Watzman (New York: Farrar, Straus & Giroux, 1988). Many books and articles written before and after Grossman's account articulate different perspectives. See Raja Shehadeh, *Samed: Journal of a West Bank Palestinian* (New York: Adama Books, 1984), for deeply moving reflections from a Palestinian lawyer committed to both justice and nonviolence. Several leading American journalists have produced superb studies based on years of active involvement in the midst of this long-standing conflict, including Milton Viorst, *Sands of Sorrow: Israel's Journey from Independence* (New York: Harper & Row, 1987); David K. Shipler, *Arab and Jew: Wounded Spirits in a Promised Land* (New York: Times Books, 1986); and Thomas L. Friedman, *From Beirut to Jerusalem* (New York: Farrar, Straus & Giroux, 1989).

18. The Foundation for Middle East Peace, based in Washington, D.C., publishes an eight-page, bimonthly report on Israeli settlements. These reports include an assortment of statements from U.S., Israeli, and Palestinian leaders as well as excerpts from the Hebrew press in Israel.

19. Many within Israel connected the open hostility of settlers toward Menachem Begin with the timing of the 1982 Israeli invasion of Lebanon. The invasion to the north came on the heels of violent protests related to the dismantling of the Jewish settlement at Yamit, part of the land returned to Egypt. I was in the Middle East at the time. People across the Israeli political spectrum were shocked by the vehement response of the settlers, even though the process had been clearly planned and the settlers had been paid excessively high prices for their housing. Part of their defiance included bulldozing all the structures before returning the land to Egypt. A constant refrain for many years thereafter harked back to this event. Many Israelis and Palestinians have suggested that internal divisions within Israel presented a bigger challenge for Israel than making peace with the Palestinians. Pointing to the hostility aimed at the right-wing government of Begin, many wondered how Israel could ever afford—politically or economically—to dismantle settlements in the West Bank or Gaza.

20. In addition to following Kahane in the media, I heard him speak and met him personally once near the Western Wall in the Old City of Jerusalem. His demeanor was similar to that of some unsavory Christian and Muslim leaders I will introduce later. He was absolutely unshakable in his certainty that he was God's man for the time. His confidence, clarity of purpose, and charisma were unmistakable. To say he was a frightening person would be an understatement. In the 1987 NBC documentary, Kahane was reminded that Palestinians living in the occupied territories did not want to move to Jordan. His reply: "I'm not asking them." For a detailed study see Robert I. Friedman, *The False Prophet: Rabbi Meir Kahane* (New York: Lawrence Hill Books, 1990).

21. See J. Wallis and C. Kimball, "The Clock Is Ticking: A Fading Opportunity for Peace in Palestine," *Sojourners* (November 1989).

22. I have written extensively and spoken frequently over many years in strong support of a negotiated settlement that guarantees security and territorial integrity for Israel and the Palestinians. Palestinian self-determination includes the right to an independent state based on the pre-1967 borders. The parameters and particular process needed to address major issues like precise borders, the status of Jerusalem, the rights of displaced refugees, and equitable sharing of limited resources (most notably water) will require the best efforts of adversaries and the collective support of others in the community of nations. See Charles A. Kimball, *Religion, Politics, and Oil: The Volatile Mix in the Middle East* (Nashville: Abingdon, 1992), and Charles A. Kimball, *Angle of Vision: Christians and the Middle East* (New York: Friendship Press, 1993).

23. Beverly Milton-Edwards, *Islamic Politics in Palestine* (London: I. B. Tauris, 1996), 163. The book places the Islamist movements within the historical context of the past fifty years. See also Ziad Abu-Amr, *Islamic Fundamentalism in the West Bank and Gaza* (Bloomington: Indiana University Press, 1994).

24. Several books detail the various ways Israeli Arab Muslims, Christians, and Druze experience discrimination within Israel proper. See, for example, Ian S. Lustick, *Arabs in the Jewish State: Israel's Control of a National Minority* (Austin: University of Texas Press, 1980); Elias Chacour, *We Belong to the Land: The Story of a Palestinian Israeli Who Lives for Peace and Reconciliation* (San Francisco: HarperSanFrancisco, 1990); and Rosemary Radford Ruether and Herman J. Ruether, *The Wrath of Jonah: The Crisis of Religious Nationalism in the Israeli-Palestinian Conflict* (San Francisco: Harper & Row, 1989).

25. See Nancy Ammerman, "North American Protestant Fundamentalism," in *Fundamentalisms Observed,* ed. Martin E. Marty and R. Scott Appleby (Chicago: University of Chicago Press, 1991), 1–65, for an excellent overview of the major developments in the twentieth century. See also Bill Moyers's three-part series *God and Politics* (Public Broadcasting System, December 1987).

26. See Charles A. Kimball, "'No Pray, No Play' Trivializes Piety," *Los Angeles Times,* September 7, 2000.

27. Ammerman, "Fundamentalism," in *Fundamentalisms Observed,* ed. Marty and Appleby, 51, 53.

28. Gary North, *The Theology of Christian Resistance* (Tyler, TX: Geneva Divinity School Press, 1983), 63.

29. Pat Robertson, *The Turning Tide* (Dallas: Word, 1993), 62–63.

30. On November 12, 1993, I attended a "God and Country Rally" sponsored by the Christian Coalition. Some four thousand people came to the civic center in Greenville, South Carolina, to sing gospel and patriotic songs and hear keynote addresses from Pat Robertson and Ralph Reed, the executive director of the Christian Coalition. The next day, 150 people from the area attended a day-long seminar to learn about effective political activism. A news item in the *Christian Century,* March 10, 1993, 262, reported on plans to train over five thousand evangelicals in some seventy "leadership schools" across the country that year.

31. Pat Robertson on *The 700 Club,* November 17, 1993.

32. A number of well-known organizations openly challenged the ideology and tactics of the Christian Coalition and related groups during their rise to power. See, for instance, "Unmasking Religious Right Extremism," *American Association of University Women* (February 1994), and the "National PTA's Guide to Extremism," published by the National PTA, based in Chicago.

33. "Taped Speech Discloses Robertson's Goals," *New York Times,* September 18, 1997.

34. "Taped Speech."

35. See Karen Armstrong, *The Battle for God* (New York: Random House, 2000), for a superb, wide-ranging, comparative study of Jewish, Christian, and Muslim fundamentalists' responses to modernity.

36. Timothy D. Sisk, *Islam and Democracy: Religion, Politics, and Power in the Middle East* (Washington, DC: United States Institute of Peace, 1992), for a thoughtful examination of this issue as viewed through the lens of case studies in Iran, Algeria, Egypt, Jordan, Palestine, and the Gulf States; Barber, *Jihad vs. McWorld,* 276ff. Thomas Friedman argued in the *New York Times,* November 23, 2001, that Muslims—including women—can thrive in the pluralist democratic societies.

37. Thomas Friedman echoed this view when he wrote about his visit to Iran in the *New York Times,* June 16, 2002. Friedman writes about the "third wave" of Iranians, the new generation that wants the good life, good job, more individual freedom, and more connections with the outside world.

CHAPTER FIVE

1. "12 Million Could Die at Once in an India-Pakistan Nuclear War," *New York Times,* May 27, 2002. U.S. military officials estimated that Pakistan had "a couple dozen" and India had "several dozen" nuclear warheads. Both countries have multiple means for delivering these weapons of mass destruction.

2. "Graveside Party Celebrates Hebron Massacre," BBC News, March 21, 2000.

3. Babylonian Talmud, Shabbat 31a.

4. Advani's Hindu nationalist party is the Bharatiya Janata Party.

5. See Carroll, *Constantine's Sword: The Church and the Jews,* 135–43, for a treatment of the Jewish-Christian dynamic in the writings of Paul. On 89–99 Carroll offers an analysis of various scholarly treatments of the distinct shifts of emphasis between Mark, the first Gospel, written in about 68 C.E., and John, the final Gospel, written some thirty years later.

6. For the cross of Jesus as a sword, see Carroll, *Constantine's Sword,* 152. On the virulent rhetoric of the church, see C. M. Leighton and D. Lehmann, "Jewish-Christian Relations in Historical Perspective," in *Irreconcilable Differences? A Learning Resource for Jews and Christians,* ed. D. F. Sandmel, R. M. Catalano, and C. M. Leighton (Boulder, CO: Westview Press, 2001), 23.

7. John Chrysostom, quoted in Rosemary Radford Ruether, *Faith and Fratricide: The Theological Roots of Anti-Semitism* (New York: Seabury Press, 1974), 178.

8. Ambrose, quoted in Ruether, *Faith and Fratricide*, 193.

9. Rodney Stark, *One True God: Historical Consequences of Monotheism* (Princeton: Princeton University Press, 2001), 129–33. See also Edward J. Flannery, *The Anguish of the Jews* (New York: Paulist Press, rev. ed. 1985).

10. Many Christians, of course, actively opposed the efforts to exterminate Jews, gypsies, and others deemed subhuman by the Nazi regime. At Yad Vashem, the Holocaust memorial in Jerusalem, righteous Gentiles, including Oskar Schindler, are honored. See David P. Gushee, *The Righteous Gentiles of the Holocaust: A Christian Interpretation* (Minneapolis: Fortress Press, 1994).

11. Quoted in the *New York Times*, March 3, 2002.

12. A number of excellent studies have been done by and about women and gender issues in Islam today. See, for example, Yvonne Y. Haddad and John L. Esposito, eds., *Islam, Gender, and Social Change* (Oxford: Oxford University Press, 1998), for a series of articles on developments in particular countries and an extensive bibliography.

13. Female genital mutilation is one of the human rights issues monitored by Amnesty International. Information is available by writing or visiting their Web site at www.amnesty.org. Statistics on clitoridectomy are from Geraldine Brooks, *Nine Parts of Desire: The Hidden World of Islamic Women* (New York: Doubleday, 1995), 54.

14. Seth Adams, "In Pakistan, Rape Victims Are the Criminals," *New York Times*, May 17, 2002, reports at length on a story of a young Pakistani woman who was raped by her husband's brother. Her story was "not uncommon." She admitted that she was raped. Her punishment was death by stoning. The judge ruled that Islamic law forbids any sexual intercourse outside of marriage. The law "bans all forms of adultery, whether the offense is committed with or without the consent of the parties."

15. The State Department's report is *Erasing History: Ethnic Cleansing in Kosovo* (Washington, DC: Department of State, 1999). In 1993 an American Muslim woman, Zainab Salbi, and her husband organized an effort to assist women victimized by rape in the former Yugoslavia. Within a decade, the organization, Women for Women International, had helped thousands of women in Bosnia-Herzegovina, Rwanda, Kosovo, Bangladesh, Nigeria, and Pakistan. For information on their efforts and links with other organizations seeking to help victimized women, see www.womenforwomen.org.

16. Harvey Cox, *Many Mansions: A Christian's Encounter with Other Faiths* (Boston: Beacon Press, 1988), 53–57.

17. S. Pfeiffer, M. Rezendes, and M. Carroll, "The Cardinal's Apology: A 'Grieving' Law Apologizes for Assignment of Geoghan," *Boston Globe*, January 10, 2002.

18. The full text of "The Bishop's Charter to Protect Children" and details

about the highly visible national meeting were published in the *New York Times,* June 15, 2002.

19. See Anne Llewellyn Barstow, *Witchcraze: A New History of the European Witch Hunts* (San Francisco: HarperSanFrancisco, 1994), for an analysis of this phenomenon, in particular the ways in which witch hunts reflected patterns of violence and dehumanization of women.

20. For a helpful introduction to the preliminary conclusions resulting from this new access to documents and information, see *The Inquisition,* a two-hour program that MPH Entertainment prepared for The History Channel.

21. This famous story about Jesus does not appear in the earliest versions of the Gospel of John. Most scholars consider it an authentic incident since it is consistent with other teachings and actions.

22. M. K. Gandhi, *Non-Violent Resistance* (New York: Schocken Books, 1961), 250–52.

CHAPTER SIX

1. See C. John Cadoux, *The Early Christian Attitude to War,* 2nd ed. (New York: Seabury Press, 1982), for a classic overview of Christian writers and documents from the first three centuries of Christianity.

2. John Ferguson, *War and Peace in the World's Religions* (New York: Oxford University Press, 1978), 103.

3. See James Carroll, *Constantine's Sword: The Church and the Jews* (Boston: Houghton Mifflin, 2001), 165–207, for an extensive treatment of the fascinating and complex religious and political dynamics during this pivotal time in the history of Christianity and the history of the Roman Empire.

4. Roland H. Bainton, *Christian Attitudes Toward War and Peace* (Nashville: Abingdon, 1960), 88–91. Thirty years in the making, Bainton's classic study remains an invaluable resource four decades after it first appeared.

5. Bainton, *Christian Attitudes,* 95–98.

6. Bainton, *Christian Attitudes,* 110, records the converging influences and expectations in an oath taken by Robert the Pious (996–1031). The "rules" are being refined, but many loopholes allow for exceptions: "I will not infringe on the Church in any way. I will not hurt a cleric or a monk if unarmed. I will not steal an ox, cow, pig, sheep, goat, ass, or a mare with a colt. I will not attack a vilain or vilainesse or servants or merchants for ransom. I will not take a mule or a horse male or female or a colt in pasture from any man from the calends of March to the feast of All Saints unless to recover a debt. I will not burn houses or destroy them unless there is a knight inside. I will not root up vines. I will not attack noble ladies traveling without husband, nor their maids, nor widows or nuns unless it is their fault. From the beginning of Lent to the end of Easter I will not attack an unarmed knight."

7. On Charlemagne and the "infidels," see Ferguson, *War and Peace,* 106–7. Bainton, *Christian Attitudes,* 104, reports that ten German bishops fell in battle

between 886 and 908; around 1000 Bishop Bernward "fought with a spear containing some of the nails from the cross of Christ"; and the archbishop of Mainz indicated that he had personally dispatched nine men in battle using a mace rather than a sword "because the Church abhors the shedding of blood." The archbishop was apparently sensitive to the letter if not the spirit of New Testament and early church teachings.

8. Ferguson, *War and Peace,* 111.

9. Ferguson, *War and Peace,* 111.

10. Quoted in Bainton, *Christian Attitudes,* 111–12.

11. Paul Johnson, *A History of Christianity* (New York: Atheneum, 1980), 245, reports, "Twelve Jews were murdered at Speier, 500 at Worms, 1,000 at Mainz, 22 at Metz."

12. *Jerusalem,* vol. 2 in *The Crusades* (London: British Broadcasting Corporation, 1995). Crusaders carrying the heads of Muslims was reported by Cambridge University professor Jonathan Riley-Smith.

13. Raymond of Agiles, quoted in Bainton, *Christian Attitudes,* 112–13.

14. An indulgence offered forgiveness for the temporal penalties of sin for a penitent person who performed some arduous or virtuous task designated by the church. The abuse of indulgences was one of the major factors sparking the Protestant Reformation led by Martin Luther and others.

15. Many resources cover the Crusades and the multiple dynamics at work over several centuries. For an excellent collection of essays and contemporary bibliography, see Jonathan Riley-Smith, ed., *The Oxford History of the Crusades* (New York: Oxford University Press, 1999). For a helpful summary of Christian-Muslim interaction during these tumultuous centuries, see Rollin Armour, *Islam, Christianity, and the West: A Troubled History* (Maryknoll, NY: Orbis Books, 2002), 61–79.

16. The Eastern Orthodox churches are more familiar to many in the West. They include the Greek, Russian, and Serbian Orthodox churches. The Coptic, Syrian, and Armenian Orthodox churches are the primary Oriental Orthodox churches. They are located mostly in the Middle East, where they have lived side by side with Islam since its advent in the seventh century.

17. See Charles A. Kimball, *Religion, Politics, and Oil: The Volatile Mix in the Middle East* (Nashville: Abingdon, 1992), for an extended analysis of the interplay between religious, political, and economic factors during and after the Gulf War.

18. President George H. W. Bush, quoted in the *New York Times,* August 9, 1990.

19. This phenomenon was reenacted daily for several months following the attacks on September 11, 2001.

20. Examples of misinformation include the following: the percentage of "smart" bombs that hit their intended targets was much lower than had been reported; several Iraqi claims about civilian targets being bombed that were dis-

missed during the war proved to be correct; widely reported horrific stories about Iraqi soldiers looting Kuwaiti hospitals, disconnecting infants from incubators in the process, turned out to be without foundation. Pete Wilson was quoted in the *New York Times,* September 21, 1991.

21. In 1990–91, the Middle East Council of Churches, a body made up of all major Orthodox, Protestant, and Catholic communions in the region, issued a number of statements and documents reflecting strong unanimity among Middle Eastern Christians.

22. Bishop Browning was a member of an ecumenical delegation whose visit to Iraq included a meeting with Saddam Hussein. The Christian leaders issued a statement entitled "War Is Not the Answer: A Message to the American People," on December 22, 1990. See *Sojourners* (February-March 1991), 5, for the full text of the statement.

23. Public statement released on February 13, 1991.

24. The *s* and the *sh* are distinctive letters in Arabic and Hebrew; they are often transposed in parallel words in the two languages. Satan, for instance, is the Hebrew name for the Devil; in Arabic his name is Shaytan.

25. Jesus is mentioned by name ninety-three times in fifteen different chapters of the Qur'an. He is called a prophet, a messenger, a servant of God, a Word from God, the Messiah, and one inspired or aided by the Spirit of God.

26. S. H. Nasr, *The Heart of Islam* (San Francisco: HarperSanFrancisco, 2002), 220–221.

27. Patrick Healy, "At Harvard, a Word Sparks a Battle," *Boston Globe,* May 29, 2002. Under pressure, Yasin later changed the title of his speech to "Of Faith and Citizenship: My American Jihad." The subtitle was not printed in the Commencement program.

28. *The Long Search* is an award-winning, thirteen-part series on world religions. Produced twenty years ago for the BBC and PBS, the video series is still available in many libraries and for purchase through Time Life Video.

29. John L. Esposito, *Unholy War: Terror in the Name of Islam* (New York: Oxford University Press, 2002), 31ff.

30. John Kelsay, *Islam and War: A Study in Comparative Ethics* (Louisville, KY: Westminster/John Knox Press, 1993), 36.

31. Esposito, *Unholy War,* 41–43, 71ff.

32. It is vital to understand various groups and movements in their respective contexts. Some common themes and perceptions run through the Muslim world, but individual leaders and groups take shape in specific places with distinctive histories and contemporary circumstances. Islam is not monolithic. Sweeping generalizations will lead inevitably to erroneous conclusions. Egypt is not Algeria; Algeria is not Afghanistan; Afghanistan is not Iran; and so on, just as we cannot speak about Greece, England, Sweden, and France as though they were interchangeable. Although these countries are all Western European with Christian majorities, we know enough about the religious and political history of

each to know that accurate analysis must be contextual. The same is true for Muslim countries.

Consider Egypt. While my experiences in Egypt—living in Cairo as a student and working for years with the Coptic Orthodox Church and Muslim leaders— have been extremely positive, long-standing frustrations run deep in this poor, overpopulated country. For many centuries Egypt, and al-Azhar University in particular, has been at the intellectual center of the Muslim world. Early in the twentieth century Egypt gave birth to the Muslim Brotherhood. Various reform movements have come and gone; some have been crushed; some have been radicalized over the decades.

Anwar Sadat was popular in the West, but not all Egyptians felt the same way about their leader; Islamic Jihad extremists assassinated him in 1981. Fringe religious groups convinced that the regime of Hosni Mubarak is beyond redemption have surfaced in Egypt on a number of occasions over the past twenty years. They have attacked tourist groups from Japan and Germany as a ploy to dry up an indispensable source of revenue for Egypt: tourism. Their goal was to destabilize the Mubarak government. A group of twelve Egyptian nationals, led by the blind cleric Umar abd al-Rahman, were convicted of the first attempt to blow up the World Trade Center in 1993. They also had plans to kill Mubarak and Butros Butros Ghali, the Egyptian who was serving as general secretary of the United Nations. The ringleader for the September 11 hijackings and attacks was Muhammad Atta, an Egyptian. Another Egyptian, Dr. Ayman al-Zawahiri, was Osama bin Laden's closest adviser leading up to September 11. His transition from medical doctor to violent revolutionary occurred over a twenty-year span, primarily in Egypt.

To understand the religious, political, and social dynamics informing Hizbollah, one must look closely at the convoluted history of Lebanon. Similarly, the Islamic Salvation Front is inseparable from the French colonial and more recent history of Algeria. HAMAS—which includes educational, social, political, and military institutional structures primarily in Gaza—cannot be understood apart from the tortured history of the Israeli-Palestinian conflict.

A number of helpful studies focus on particular countries and groups. In addition to Esposito's *Unholy War,* see, for example, John L. Esposito, *The Islamic Threat: Myth or Reality?* 3rd ed. (New York: Oxford University Press, 1999), and Milton Viorst, *In the Shadow of the Prophet: The Struggle for the Soul of Islam* (Boulder, CO: Westview Press, 2001).

33. Esposito, *Unholy War,* 11–12.

34. Glen Stassen, ed., *Just Peacemaking: Ten Practices for Abolishing War* (New York: Pilgrim Press, 1998).

35. Numerous remarkable, religiously based organizations are educating and modeling cooperation and coexistence in Israel/Palestine today. The same is true within the United States. One of the more hopeful initiatives in America is the U.S. Interreligious Committee for Peace in the Middle East. This organization,

which began in 1986, is made up of more than a thousand Jewish, Christian, and Muslim religious leaders with a common vision for the Middle East. Many avenues are open for peacemaking in one of the most intractable conflicts on Earth. See Marc Gopin, *Holy War, Holy Peace: How Religion Can Bring Peace to the Middle East* (New York: Oxford University Press, 2002), for a thorough and thoughtful series of options that draw upon the resources of the religions.

CHAPTER SEVEN

1. Martin E. Marty and R. Scott Appleby, eds., *The Fundamentalism Project*, 5 vols. (Chicago: University of Chicago Press, 1991–1995).

2. R. Scott Appleby, *The Ambivalence of the Sacred: Religion, Violence, and Reconciliation* (Lanham, MD: Rowman & Littlefield, 2000), 16–17.

3. Several variations of this sentiment are widely attributed to Albert Einstein. See www.giga-usa.com/gigaweb1/quotes2/quateinsteinalbertx005.htm.

4. Stephen R. Covey, *The Seven Habits of Highly Effective People* (New York: Simon & Schuster, 1989), 101.

5. Covey, *Seven Habits*, 34–35.

6. Smith, *Why Religion Matters*, 3.

7. I am indebted to Jeff Rogers at many points, as he has challenged and refined my thinking frequently for more than a decade. His reflections on the image of a theological compass were included in a sermon for graduating seniors on May 26, 2002, entitled "The Cross Your Compass, Christ Your Guide" (www.fbcgvlsc.com).

8. Wilfred Cantwell Smith, *Faith and Belief* (Princeton, NJ: Princeton University Press, 1979), 12, 169–70. For more information on Smith, see note 6 in the Introduction.

9. See Charles A. Kimball, *Angle of Vision: Christians and the Middle East* (New York: Friendship Press, 1992), for an extended treatment of various types of ecumenical and interfaith cooperation in the Middle East.

10. William Sloane Coffin, *A Passion for the Possible: A Message to U.S. Churches* (Louisville, KY: Westminster/John Knox Press, 1993), 7–8.

11. The Bible is not a book about comparative religion. The clear focus of the Hebrew Scriptures is on the people of Israel. Even so, these sacred texts include many examples of God's active engagement with people outside of Israel. The first eleven chapters of Genesis record God's activity among the nations. Following the account of the great flood, Genesis 9:8–17 tells of God's universal and unconditional covenant with all human beings and living creatures. In the stories about Abraham, there are intriguing references: in Genesis 14:18–19 the strange figure of Melchizedek, "a priest of the Most High," blesses Abraham; in Genesis 20 we read of God's intervention with Abimelech, the king of Gerar. Other biblical figures, such as Moses' father-in-law, Jethro, and Pharaoh's daughter are described as non-Israelite people motivated by God. The entire Book of Job takes place outside the nation of Israel. The sailors in the Jonah story are described as

"calling upon the name of the Lord." All of these strands seem to connect to the declaration found in the final book of the Hebrew Bible: "For from the rising of the sun to its setting my name is great among the nations, and in every place incense is offered to my name, and a pure offering; for my name is great among the nations, says the Lord of Hosts" (Malachi 1:11).

12. See Ariarajah, *The Bible and People of Other Faiths*, for a thoughtful and accessible introduction to key biblical passages related to religious diversity.

13. Austin P. Flannery, ed., *Documents of Vatican II*, 2nd ed. (Grand Rapids, MI: Eerdmans, 1980), 739–40.

14. Flannery, ed., *Vatican II*, 739–40, 367.

15. See "Pope's Address to the Roman Curia," *Bulletin—Secretariatus pro non-Christianis* 22, no. 1 (1987): 54–62.

16. John Hick, *God Has Many Names* (London: Macmillan, 1980), 6; Hick, *God and the Universe of Faiths* (New York: St. Martin's Press, 1973), 131.

17. Wilfred Cantwell Smith, *Towards a World Theology: Faith and the Comparative History of Religion* (Philadelphia: Westminster Press, 1981), 152.

18. See chapter 5, note 16.

19. Eck, *A New Religious America*, 23.

20. See Diana L. Eck, *Encountering God: A Spiritual Journey from Bozeman to Banares* (Boston: Beacon Press, 1993), for a compelling story of her personal pilgrimage—from an active involvement in Methodist youth groups to the scholarly study of world religions and a decade of leadership as the moderator of the World Council of Churches' Subunit on Dialogue with People of Living Faiths.

21. Many thoughtful works could be cited. The most comprehensive collection of publications and useful bibliographical information is found in the *Faith Meets Faith* series published by Orbis Books. More than forty books have already been published in this collection. Although it is rooted in a Christian theological perspective, the series endorses no single school of thought. Rather, it seeks "to promote interreligious dialogue by providing an open forum for exchanges among followers of different religious paths."

22. Cox, *Many Mansions*, 212.

23. There are literally dozens of groups and organizations working for reconciliation across political and religious lines. Their respective focus and program activities vary from political policies in groups like Peace Now to human rights with *al-haqq* ("the truth," formerly called Law in the Service of Man). Some organizations foster cooperative sports and educational programs. I have worked personally with many different groups, in particular indigenous religious organizations and groups like the American Friends Service Committee and the Mennonite Central Committee. The reconciling ministries of Jews, Muslims, and Christians are often challenged by mistrust arising from violence and extremism, but most people in the region know that their future is interconnected. *New York Times* columnist Tom Friedman captured this sentiment eloquently in an opinion piece on November 21, 2001. He identified Rabbi David Hartman as the kind

of "general" needed to fight the "real war," the one taking place in the schools, mosques, churches, and synagogues. Hartman combats religious totalitarianism in Israel by teaching that "God speaks multiple languages and is not exhausted by one faith."

24. In *Holy War, Holy Peace* Gopin includes over one hundred pages of "practical applications" for people who are serious in their desire to facilitate peace in the Middle East. See also Scott Appleby's chapters "Religion and Conflict Resolution," "The Promise of Internal Pluralism: Human Rights and Religious Mission," and "Ambivalence as Opportunity: Strategies for Promoting Religious Peacebuilding" in *Ambivalence of the Sacred*.

SELECTED BIBLIOGRAPHY

Appleby, R. Scott. *The Ambivalence of the Sacred: Religion, Violence, and Reconciliation.* Lanham, MD: Rowman & Littlefield Publishers, Inc., 2000.

Ariarajah, S. Wesley. *The Bible and People of Other Faiths.* Maryknoll, NY: Orbis Books, 1989.

Armour, Rollin. *Islam, Christianity and the West: A Troubled History.* Maryknoll, NY: Orbis Books, 2002.

Armstrong, Karen. *The Battle for God.* New York: Ballantine Books, 2000.

Carroll, James. *Constantine's Sword: The Church and the Jews.* New York: Houghton Mifflin Co., 2001.

Carter, Stephen L. *The Culture of Disbelief: How American Law and Politics Trivialize Religious Devotion.* New York: Basic Books, 1993.

Coffin, William Sloane. *A Passion for the Possible: Message to the Churches.* Louisville, KY: Westminster/John Knox Press, 1993.

Cox, Harvey. *Many Mansions: A Christian's Encounter with Other Faiths.* Boston: Beacon Press, 1988.

Eck, Diana L. *Encountering God: A Spiritual Journey from Bozeman to Banaras.* Boston: Beacon Press, 1993.

———. *A New Religious America: How a "Christian Country" Has Become the World's Most Religiously Diverse Nation.* San Francisco: HarperSanFrancisco, 2001.

Esposito, John L. *The Islamic Threat: Myth or Reality?* New York: Oxford University Press, 3rd ed. 1999.

———. *Unholy War: Terror in the Name of Islam.* New York: Oxford University Press, 2002.

Friedman, Thomas L. *From Beirut to Jerusalem.* New York: Farrar, Straus & Giroux, 1989.

————. *The Lexus and the Olive Tree: Understanding Globalization.* New York: Farrar, Straus & Giroux, 1999.

Gomes, Peter J. *The Good Book: Reading the Bible with Mind and Heart.* New York: William Morrow and Company, Inc., 1996; HarperSanFrancisco reprint edition, 2002.

Gopin, Marc. *Holy War, Holy Peace: How Religion Can Bring Peace to the Middle East.* New York: Oxford University Press, 2002.

Juergensmeyer, Mark. *Terror in the Mind of God: The Global Rise of Religious Violence.* Berkeley, CA: University of California Press, 2000.

Kimball, Charles A. *Religion, Politics and Oil: The Volatile Mix in the Middle East.* Nashville, TN: Abingdon Press, 1992.

————. *Striving Together: A Way Forward in Christian-Muslim Relations.* Maryknoll, NY: Orbis Books, 1991.

Kurzman, Charles, ed. *Liberal Islam: A Soucebook.* New York: Oxford University Press, 1998.

Lustick, Ian S. *For the Land and the Lord: Jewish Fundamentalism in Israel.* New York: Council on Foreign Relations Press, 1988.

Marty, Martin E., and R. Scott Appleby, eds. *The Fundamentalism Project,* 5 vols. Chicago: University of Chicago Press, 1991–1995.

Miles, Jack. *God: A Biography.* New York: Alfred Knopf, Inc., 1995.

Nasr, Seyyed Hossein. *The Heart of Islam.* San Francisco: HarperSanFrancisco, 2002.

Smith, Huston. *Why Religion Matters: The Fate of the Human Spirit in an Age of Unbelief.* San Francisco: HarperSanFrancisco, 2001.

————. *The World's Religions.* San Francisco: HarperSanFrancisco, rev. ed. 1998.

Smith, Wilfred Cantwell. *Faith and Belief.* Princeton: Princeton University Press, 1979.

————. *Patterns of Faith Around the World.* Oxford: Oneworld Publications, 1998.

Stassen, Glen, ed. *Just Peacemaking: Ten Practices for Abolishing War.* New York: Pilgrim Press, 1998.

Viorst, Milton. *In the Shadow of the Prophet: The Struggle for the Soul of Islam.* Boulder, CO: Westview Press, 2001.